Signs of Change

New Directions in Theatre Education

Revised and Amplified Edition

By Joan Lazarus

intellect Bristol, UK / Chicago, USA

First published in the UK in 2012 by
Intellect, The Mill, Parnall Road, Fishponds, Bristol, BS16 3JG, UK

First published in the USA in 2012 by
Intellect, The University of Chicago Press, 1427 E. 60th Street,
Chicago, IL 60637, USA

Series: Theatre in Education
Series ISSN: 2049-3878
Cover designer: Holly Rose
Copy-editor: Emma Rhys
Production manager: Jessica Mitchell
Typesetting: Mac Style, Beverley, E. Yorkshire

ISBN 978-1-84150-629-6

Signs of Change

To Michael – the light of my life.

I have such a yearning for the future. It is boundless!
Eric Overmyer, *On the Verge*

Credits

The author and publisher wish to thank those who have generously given permission to reprint borrowed material:

Figure 5–2: Graphic courtesy of William P. Ward.

Figure 6–1: Photograph courtesy of Grace Park.

Contents

Contents

Foreword to the Revised and Amplified Edition

With *Signs of Change: New Directions in Theatre Education* Joan Lazarus has written (and now revised) a courageous, intelligent, compassionate book. Unlike the typical "how to" text for theatre teachers, Joan is challenging all of us, novice and experienced teachers alike, to accept change in our teaching as the norm. The goal for each of us is to grow as we continue our journey to discover and implement best practices in the field – keeping abreast of the times, engaging students from all backgrounds as decision makers in the process of making theatre, creating socially significant theatre, as well as developing our skills as artists and teachers. In other words, we are challenged to meet the great potential of theatre education as a means to artistically – physically, mentally, socially – affect the lives of our students. The book gives us challenges to review our work, to make personal checklists, to journal. It supports us as we work to seek and cherish growth in our teaching.

This is an intelligent book based on solid research in the literature of education, theatre education, and theatre. In addition, the many ideas are backed with original field research. Joan has observed teachers across the country in their classrooms and followed with in-depth interviews. Descriptions of these exchanges are included throughout the text to give authenticity to the concepts presented. The descriptions of the teachers in action and the quotes about their practices and philosophies make the work tangible and manageable.

This is also a compassionate book. Today, the pressure for excellence in the classroom coupled with the monetary constraints that threaten programs can be, I'm certain, stifling. Who better than Joan Lazarus to accompany us on the journey to excellence? She is a master teacher with a background of high school teaching followed by years of working with community drama teachers and teaching undergraduates and graduates – future and current theatre teachers. She has completed this mission of commitment to the field with years of involvement in state and national associations devoted to supporting theatre teacher-artists and artists working with and for young people. She has a vision of the field tempered with a deep knowledge of the perks and foibles of the workplace and the community.

Besides, *Signs of Change: New Directions in Theatre Education* is a good read. Enjoy the journey and the challenge. It can be exhilarating and the rewards enormous.

Lin Wright

Lin Wright, Ph.D. and former high school theatre teacher, joined the faculty of the Arizona State University Department of Theatre to help build the Theatre for Youth program. She later chaired the department for twelve years. Her organizational work includes state and national presidencies for theatre for youth associations as well as chairmanships for numerous committees dealing with theatre education research and curriculum development. She chaired the task force that wrote the first national K-12 theatre standards and served on the National Governance Committee for the Kennedy Center Arts Education Network.

Foreword to the First Edition

Even educational institutions, often slow or resistant to change – holding steadfast to tradition – undergo transformation. In *Signs of Change: New Directions in Theatre Education*, Joan Lazarus gives us a glimpse of some change makers in secondary school theatre education. For them, change is sometimes an exhilarating adventure, sometimes an intimidating trial. They are teachers who create and promote different and dynamic theatre programs, often within institutions that perceive theatre as mainstream, conventional, and structured by decades-old pedagogies.

Programs that nurture fresh perspectives require teachers to experiment with the shape, form, and content of their pedagogy. If change requires experimentation, how do we build a bridge long and stable enough for both experienced and new teachers to cross from tradition to experimentation? *Signs of Change* is a part of that bridge.

Joan Lazarus compiles and synthesizes the voices of teachers across the United States whose teaching and directing displaces common perceptions of theatre education. She captures with sensitive clarity the struggles inherent to teachers whose risks are changing the face of theatre education. From them we learn that interrogating our own practice is necessary to sustaining the vitality of our programs. Much of what we discover about ourselves and about theatre occurs when we are confident enough to say to students, "I don't know. Let's find out together." *Signs of Change* offers suggestions for encouraging students to contemplate critical issues, involving students as co-artists, and including students who represent marginalized components of a school. Joan's emphasis on socially responsible theatre teaching and student-centered learning points to the kind of change in theatre teaching that can make significant shifts in the way we practice the art of teaching theatre.

This book fills a great void in theatre education literature because it is comprised of our colleagues' voices. In this unique and substantial resource, Joan organizes and connects discussions of theatre education philosophies, descriptions of detailed activities, and stories of cautious risk taking, all of which define innovative approaches to teaching theatre. Joan introduces companions who will encourage you to forge ahead with your instincts, even though your instincts may contradict the traditions of your training or your institution's expectations to maintain the norm.

Signs of Change represents a journey for Joan of which I have had the privilege to be a part. With Joan's crucial leadership, and support from professional organizations and many colleagues, Joan and I have launched think tanks on theatre education reform at conferences from New York to San Diego. Over late-night, long-distance telephone conversations, in hotel rooms and lobbies, and in the think tanks themselves, I have observed the questions emerge that are central to this book: What is "best practice," and what does best practice look like in theatre classrooms and rehearsals? How do classrooms and rehearsals operate when the student is at the center of the learning process? What does it mean to be a "socially responsible" teacher or student? *Signs of Change* reflects Joan's long-term commitment to theatre teachers whose innovative strategies transfigure theatre education.

The fundamental shift into this transfigured practice requires teacher-directors and students to negotiate new and contingent relationships. The traditional secondary school theatre director is the decision maker who is driven by deadlines, maintains the through-line of the play, and orchestrates teams of young artists and technicians. When teachers relinquish the expected role of authority in favor of a student-centered methodology, the risks increase: we may send cross-signals to our students, fear administrative condemnation, and lose confidence. Nevertheless, the rewards of a student-centered and socially responsible theatre program are immense.

Signs of Change: New Directions in Theatre Education is both stimulating and validating. If you are soon to enter the field, the models presented here may inspire you to experiment with an idea that "goes against the grain." If you are a veteran teacher, you may see your own practice resonate with those of your colleagues whose work Joan documents in this book, and you will gain fresh insight. Change happens one teacher, one classroom, and one production at a time. Together, we will change secondary school theatre education to render students as responsible agents who will practice the art and craft of theatre in ways that will prepare them for life.

Jo Beth Gonzalez

Jo Beth Gonzalez, MFA, Ph.D., is an award-winning teacher, scholar, director, and published author. She currently teaches theatre and English at Bowling Green High School in Ohio.

Acknowledgements

Without the steadfast support and encouragement of colleagues at The University of Texas at Austin (UT) – Megan Alrutz, Katie Dawson, Sharon Grady, Coleman Jennings, Roxanne Schroeder-Arce, and Suzan Zeder – neither the first nor second edition of this book would have been completed. My research for the book was generously supported by the UT Vice President for Research, the College of Fine Arts, the Department of Theatre and Dance, and the Children's Theatre Foundation of America.

Many thanks are due to colleagues around the country who recommended teachers and artists to interview and who read drafts of the book. Great gratitude is also due to Cheryl Green, research assistant, proofreader, and transcription wizard, and to Lara Greene and Scott Tatum for their help with the first edition. I am indebted to Austin Beasley-Rodgers who served as my research assistant for the 2009–2011 study on best practice, which informs portions of this edition. Heartfelt praise also goes to Cynthia Sampson for her keen eye, practiced editorial skill, and many kindnesses while preparing this second manuscript for publication.

I am grateful to the many mentors and friends who afforded me inspiration for this project through their example: Jenny Akridge, Sue Bishop-Gill, Wayne Brabender, Susan diRende, Don Doyle, Anne Elgood, Kris Fiuty, Jodie Flint, Jo Beth Gonzalez, Debbie Kyle Green, Jean Stark Hebenstreit, Lynn Hoare, Bruce Jordan, Rhoda Kittelson, Linda Kustka, Michelle Pullen, Chuck Quittner, Trey Schmidt, Laurel Serleth, Nancy Shivers, Kim Wheetley, Sue Wood, Lin Wright, and the Women of Velocity. I am also grateful to family and friends who have taught me, encouraged me, and supported me over the years.

I have been best equipped for this journey by the students I have had the privilege of working with at Newcastle High School, Nickerson High School, Lincoln High School, various youth theatre programs around the country, The University of Wisconsin–Madison, and The University of Texas at Austin. Each has enriched me by their ideas, questions, and especially by the challenges they presented.

Sincere thanks go to those who granted me an interview, shared their materials, or otherwise offered their generous assistance with this project.* These people give me hope for the future of this field.

Abigail Adams, People's Light and Theatre Company, Malvern, Pennsylvania
Tara Affolter, East High School, Madison, Wisconsin
Deb Alexander, Bailey Middle School, Austin, Texas
Dave Barnes, Oswego High School, Oswego, Illinois
Donna, Barnes, Oswego High School, Oswego, Illinois
Ann Batten-Bishop, Garland McMeans Junior High School, Katy, Texas
Gretta Berghammer, University of Northern Iowa, Cedar Rapids, Iowa
Steve Bogart, Lexington High School, Lexington, Massachusetts
Amy Burtaine, Austin Waldorf School, Austin, Texas
Carol Cain, West Side Magnet School, LaGrange, Georgia
Ben Cameron, Theatre Communications Group, New York, New York
Autumn Samsula Casey, Plano Senior High School, Plano, Texas
Jennifer Chapman, University of Wisconsin–Madison, Madison, Wisconsin
Frank Chuter, Kingwood High School, Kingwood, Texas
Gloria Bond Clunie, Chute Middle School, District 65, Evanston, Illinois & Victory Gardens
    Theatre, Chicago, Illinois
Bob Colby, Emerson College, Boston, Massachusetts
C. Gary Cooper, Klein Forest High School, Klein, Texas
Joanna Cortright, Perpich Center for Arts Education, St. Paul, Minnesota
Bryar Cougle, Department of Public Instruction, North Carolina
Barbara Cox, Perpich Center for Arts Education, St. Paul, Minnesota
Eleshia Crotwell, Guyer High School, Denton, Texas
Russell Davis, People's Light and Theatre Company, Malvern, Pennsylvania
Brandi de los Santos, McCallum High School, Austin, Texas
Sandra DiMartino, Lexington High School, Lexington, Massachusetts
Susan diRende, Teaching Artist, Los Angeles, California
Dave Dynak, Department of Theatre, University of Utah, Salt Lake City, Utah
Gillian Eaton, Teaching Artist, Detroit, Michigan
Lindsey Ervi, Pleasant Hill Elementary School, Leander, Texas
Jason Ewing, Kingsley School, Evanston, Illinois
Rick Garcia, Johnston High School, Austin, Texas
Carlin Gilseth, Woodlands High School, The Woodlands, Texas
Jo Beth Gonzalez, Bowling Green High School, Bowling Green, Ohio
Fursey Gotuaco, Richland Hills High School, North Richland Hills, Texas
Jennifer Gotuaco, Smithfield Middle School, North Richland Hills, Texas
Benjamin Gooding, The University of Texas at Austin
Maxine Greene, Emeritus Professor, Columbia University, New York
Tal Gribbons, Grady Middle School, Houston, Texas
Chris Griffith, Galumph Theatre, Minneapolis, Minnesota
Brian Hall, Mountainside Middle School/Saguaro High School, Scottsdale, Arizona
Bill Hansen, Lincoln High School, Manitowoc, Wisconsin
Rebecca Harding, Small Middle School (retired), Austin, Texas
Andrew Harris, Stage One, Louisville, Kentucky

Acknowledgements

Billie Harvey, Breckenridge High School, Breckenridge, Texas
John Heinemann, Lincoln High School, Lincoln, Nebraska
J. Daniel Herring, Stage One, Louisville, Kentucky
Karen Kay Husted, Education Consultant, Douglas, Arizona
Jeanne Jackson, Consultant, Conroe, Texas
Rebecca Jallings, West High School, Madison, Wisconsin
Justine, Johnston, Parent, Crete, Nebraska
Steven Jones, Stage One, Louisville, Kentucky
Daniel Kelin, Honolulu Theatre for Youth, Honolulu, Hawaii
Brendan Kelley, Wylie High School, Wylie, Texas
Sarah Kent, Manor High School, Manor, Texas
Aline Knighton, Crockett High School, Austin, Texas
Patsy Koch Johns, Lincoln High School, Lincoln, Nebraska
Candace Koern, Cy-Fair High School, Cypress, Texas
Kris Kissel, Sabino High School, Tucson, Arizona
Kati Koerner, Lincoln Center, New York
Valerie Roberts Labonski, Morton West High School, Berwyn, Illinois & College
Park High School, The Woodlands, Texas
Linda Leedberg, Consultant, Des Moines, Iowa
Jeffrey Leptak-Moreau, Educational Theatre Association, Cincinnati, Ohio
Angie Lindbloom, Trinity Meadows Intermediate School, Keller, Texas
Brianna Lindahl, Thunder Ridge Middle School, Centennial, Colorado
Jenny Lutringer, Richland Hills High School, North Richland Hills, Texas & Lake
Travis Middle School, Lake Travis, Texas
Bobby Malone, Anderson High School, Austin, Texas
Jan Mandell, St. Paul Central High School, St. Paul, Minnesota
Laura McCammon, University of Arizona, Tucson, Arizona
Jean McCullough, Bowling Green High School, Bowling Green, Ohio
Gillian McNally, People's Light and Theatre Company, Malvern, Pennsylvania
Marissa Meek, Lehman High School, Kyle, Texas
Susan Morrell, Cactus High School, Glendale Arizona
Bethany Nelson, Emerson College, Boston, Massachusetts
Renee Norris, Haltom High School, Haltom City, Texas
David O'Fallon, McPhail Center for the Arts, Minneapolis, Minnesota
Lena Paulauskas, Fossil Hill Middle School, Keller, Texas
Julia Perlowski, Pompano Beach High School, Pompano Beach, Florida
Tory Peterson, Perpich High School for the Arts, St. Paul, Minnesota
Abi Pierce, Carpenter Middle School, Plano, Texas
Rebecca Podsednik, The University of Texas at Austin, Austin, Texas
Nancy Prince, Thomas J. Rusk Middle School, Nacogdoches, Texas
Betsy Quinn, Haven Middle School, District 65, Evanston, Illinois
Sue Scarborough, Enloe High School, Raleigh, North Carolina
Rebecca Schlomann, The University of Texas at Austin, Texas

Roxanne Schroeder-Arce, McCallum High School, Austin, Texas & The University of Texas at Austin

Dan Seaman, Weaver High School, Greensboro, North Carolina

Kent Seidel, University of Cincinnati, Cincinnati, Ohio

Laurel Serleth, District 65, Evanston, Illinois

Nancy Shaw, People's Light and Theatre Company, Malvern, Pennsylvania

Richard Silberg, Martin Luther King Middle School, Berkley, California

Kent Sorensen, Marana High School, Marana, Arizona

Jerry Smith, Salem High School, Conyers, Georgia

Debbie Spink, Washougal High School, Washougal, Washington

Holly Stanfield, Bradford High School, Kenosha, Wisconsin

Diane Stewart, Cypress High School, Fort Myers, Florida

Wendy Jo Strom, Winterhaven School, Portland, Oregon

Dan Sullivan, Parkside Elementary School, Leander, Texas

April Gentry Sutterfield, Teaching Artist, Little Rock, Arkansas

Spencer Sutterfield, Parkview Arts/Science Magnet High School, Little Rock, Arkansas

Kathleen Tate, South Keller Intermediate School, Keller, Texas

M. Scott Tatum, McCallum High School, Texas

Theatre students, Bowling Green High School, Bowling Green, Ohio

Misty Valenta, The University of Texas at Austin, Austin, Texas

Eric Vera, West Mesquite High School, Mesquite, Texas

Chris Vine, Creative Arts Team, New York, New York

Bill Ward, Flint Youth Theatre, Flint, Michigan

Kim Wheetley, Southeast Center for Education in the Arts, Chattanooga, Tennessee

Helen White, Creative Arts Team, New York, New York

Mandy Whitlock, Brandeis High School, San Antonio, Texas

Nancy Wilkinson, Peninsula High School, Gig Harbor, Washington

Sue Wood, Consultant, Flint, Michigan

Youth cast members and staff, ... *My Soul To Take,* Flint Youth Theatre, Flint, Michigan

Youth Members, Creative Arts Team Youth Theatre, New York, New York

Youth participants and staff, People's Light and Theatre Company, Malvern, Pennsylvania

Sandi Zielinski, Illinois State University, Bloomington, Illinois

Lynda Zimmerman, Creative Arts Team, New York, New York

And the more than one hundred Texas teachers who participated in the 2010 survey on best practice.

*Affiliations are current as of the time of the interview or observation.

The author wishes to thank Lisa Barnett, Lynne Reed Costa, and the staff at Heinemann for their encouragement and faith in the first edition and Jessica Mitchell, Melanie Marshall, May Yao, and the wonderful staff at Intellect for their enthusiastic and invigorating support of the second edition.

Introduction: A Yearning for Change

I have been wondering a lot about change: how it happens, why it happens, and how I can contribute to the positive change I desire for my field. I am inspired and intrigued in my quest for change by the more than two hundred and twenty-five theatre teachers, teaching artists, arts administrators, college professors, and students who contributed to the revised and amplified edition of this book. All were recommended to me by colleagues, students, co-teachers, or professional organizations. Some of the interviewees I knew well or had heard of; some were fresh acquaintances whose work was new to me. I met many of them as strangers and parted from them feeling a bond, a shared passion, as people moving together with eyes fixed on a common goal.

As author of this book, I am like the child on a summer evening who tries to capture all the fireflies she can in an attempt to illumine the whole backyard. I am the gatherer, the one trying to capture the ephemeral nature of others' work. I hope that the teachers, future teachers, teacher educators, and artists who read *Signs of Change* find some light in these pages, some inspiration and practical ideas to help them embrace change and ensure a promising future for our field.

This revised and amplified edition remains an invitation to eavesdrop on conversations with a group of successful educator-artists who work with young people in dynamic and compelling ways. More than 50 percent of this edition is new material, including new and fuller interviews with teachers, invited essays by some of the best thinkers in theatre teacher education, in-depth profiles of teachers and their practice, references throughout to current research, trends, and initiatives in education and arts education, and more than one hundred and forty additional works cited. Fresh and revised examples of best practice have been added and selected resources have been expanded at the end of each chapter. Major portions of the original text have been revised for greater clarity and to create meaningful intersections with the newly added material.

It has been both a joy and a challenge to write a book like this. The joy comes from the opportunity to observe and talk at length with dedicated professionals who are passionate about theatre with secondary school students. My research into best practice for over a decade has been a blissful opportunity to talk to, dream with, and learn from remarkable people. The challenge comes from trying to capture in so few words a collection of insights and experiences that are broad, rich, diverse, and are redefining theatre with adolescents. As is also the case with gifted teacher-artists, this work, which is often intuitive and organic, rarely exists in detailed notes, plans, or other documented forms. To capture the passion and potency of their various approaches, I include interview excerpts and written responses from the teacher-artists themselves as illustrations of the characteristics and elements of best practice in the field. I highlight recurring themes and share individual and composite stories and lessons related to some of the most effective aspects of their practice. Field notes from observations of classes and rehearsals and quotes from teachers and other published writers appear within and around the text as a backdrop, counterpoint, and partner in the conversations. Altogether, the book is both a celebration of advances in the field and a call for change and action. It is a record of multiple versions of the best of what is possible in secondary school theatre education today.

It is important here to note what this book is not. It is not a comprehensive and definitive look at secondary school theatre education in the twenty-first century, nor is it a step-by-step roadmap to best practice. Critical and theoretical works – as well as textbooks and anthologies on so vast a subject – remain for others to do. *Signs of Change* presents the best of secondary school theatre in an era of change and against a backdrop of the end of the Industrial Age.

I have been privileged to be, in essence, a conduit between these theatre education professionals and their present and future counterparts. Some readers will find that the ideas and practices in this book resonate with their current practice. I hope these people find affirmation and encouragement in this book. Others will find inspiration and practical strategies to bring to life their long-held convictions about the power of theatre to change the lives of our children. Still others will find territory unfamiliar and uncomfortable as they compare their current practice to that explored in these pages. May all of us glean from the voices in this book the wisdom, courage, and good humor that make true change possible.

Chapter 1

Signs of Change and the Need for Change

The engaged voice must never be fixed and absolute but always changing, always evolving in dialogue with a world beyond itself.

bell hooks

The world we have made as a result of the level of thinking we have done thus far creates problems we cannot solve at the same level of thinking at which we created them.

Albert Einstein

I think I have been writing this book my whole life. From as early as I can remember, I wanted to be a teacher. I wanted to change the world, to make the world better. I also was enthralled by theatre and its power to capture and convey feelings and ideas as big and powerful as my feelings and ideas seemed to be. Now, years after I began teaching, I am still yearning for change in theatre and education.

This book explores the convergence of a passion for teaching and a love of theatre as it bears upon the education of young people in middle school and high school. It is a collection of effective practices used by a small but growing number of veteran and novice educator-artists who are deeply committed to their work. Though the perspectives of professional theatre artists, administrators, students, scholars, and university theatre education professors are included, the voices in this book are primarily those of middle school and high school theatre teachers.

Each of these professionals works at the intersection of artmaking and education, of process and product, of knowing and doing, of teaching and learning. They are in the business of bringing about change in the lives of individual students as well as in their schools and communities. They are pioneers evolving their practice of theatre education in their own frontiers of change, their classrooms.

This book is but a glimpse at the imaginative, forward-looking work being undertaken by dynamic theatre teachers in urban, rural, and suburban settings throughout the country. I welcome you as another pioneer moving toward a new, or perhaps, recycled, practice of theatre education.

CHANGE

Change of any kind – moving, switching jobs, financial loss, or losing a family member – is fraught with a wide range of emotions. There are many reasons I continue to be catapulted into change as a theatre educator. Sometimes I change to accommodate new mandates or initiatives, shifts in programmatic thrust, changes in administration or facilities, or reduction in funding. Often, I change because of some restlessness or dissatisfaction I feel in my work or just from the desire for something new, something better. One thing I am learning is that whatever the catalyst for change, I have three choices:

1. I can hang on to my old views and behaviors, determined that if I just stay the course or work harder and better surely all will be well or change will not come.
2. I can go into denial that there even is a problem or that change is needed or imminent.
3. I can reflect on my views and practices and actively recycle them into something new.

Just talking and thinking about change makes me take stock of what really is my present situation, a thing rarely easy or comfortable to do. Inspired by the work of David Cooperrider, I know that a look at *what is* brings with it the realization of *what is not*, that my vision is not yet my reality. If I try to envision *what could be* and *what ought to be*, I get wildly enthusiastic, but then I face fears of what may never be (Cooperrider et al. 2000; Cooperrider 1999).[1] I sometimes get myself stuck in a cycle of denial, ambivalence, hope, and fear. Whether I initiate change or it is imposed, if positive change is to occur, I must take action that may be at once hard, thrilling, risky, hopeful, and daunting.

I recall the many changes I encountered during my years teaching high school theatre. In one school, I had over one hundred students involved in the thriving program, which included theatre classes, productions, touring plays for young audiences, a group doing drama in the pre-schools, a Thespian troupe, and various other performing entities and enterprises. Although I was insanely busy at school every day from before sunup until well after sundown, I felt restless, like there was more, or something different, I could or should be doing to reach students more effectively.

I attended conferences and learned what I could, believing the problem was in what I did not know and that the elusive solutions were "out there" for me to discover. I found my way to a graduate program that helped me expand and investigate a new range of approaches and techniques. It was when I implemented that learning with students that I saw fundamental and enduring change begin

It was really good to contemplate the positives of our practice! It got me thinking about adjusting how I'm thinking about everything in our field. Focusing on the negative – because it will always be there – is not very productive. And focusing on the positive does not mean that you have to be naive about what is not working in our field. Jennifer Chapman

26

to take place in my teaching and directing practice. I began adapting, exploring, experimenting, and making these new approaches my own. I allowed myself to make mistakes, to not know, to learn *with* my students. Thus began my present journey, one in which I am learning how to embrace change. My long-held passion for teaching and theatre is now being grounded in my day-to-day practice.

CHANGE AND EDUCATION

In the pages that follow, I consider the state of theatre education, the need for change to ensure a future for the field, and the emergence of best practice. Before looking at these aspects of our work, it is helpful to examine the broader context for the challenges and opportunities we in theatre education face. This requires an honest look at the present state of our schools and a backward glance at what shaped our current educational system.

The changes in my personal teaching practices began amidst the rush of reform movements in the late twentieth century. I have heard that change accelerates at the close of each century and this was certainly true over one hundred years ago as the world moved from the nineteenth to the twentieth century. It is difficult to imagine how rapid those changes really were and how significant an impact they had. Farm families lost children to big city factories. People from around the world moved to the United States. More women began working outside of the home and in jobs previously reserved for men. With the advent of child labor laws and mandatory education, a space between childhood and adulthood was created and adolescence emerged. Where and how people lived, worked, communicated, and traveled changed dramatically in a relatively short span of time.

These changes rolled and rippled into the twenty-first century. They led to the revolutions in technology and information that today have increasing impact on the way we live, work, and interact in our homes, with family, and in our local and global communities. In addition to the enormous benefits we have received from twenty-first century advances and conveniences, we have been left with some "hazardous debris" from the twentieth century. Poverty, discrimination, disenfranchised youth, dysfunctional families, failing communities, faltering public institutions, corrupt private enterprises, and threats to the environment – while not entirely new to this century – are also part of the legacy of change.

I find it ironic that while we move ever faster in search of better and more efficient material goods and services, much of our thinking remains stuck in early twentieth-century models. This is most apparent in public schools where, despite the trappings of reform, thinking is fixed in a schools-as-factories or "schooling machine" model of education. Kirsten Olson, writing about schools that actually wound with their outdated policies, describes this "Old School culture" as a set of old-fashioned ideas and attitudes [...] that construct teaching as hierarchical, learning as passive, and the bureaucratic structures of school as about serving adults, not kids. Old School culture also says: "We can't change school, that's just the way it is," or "It's too hard to change school, it's too complicated, this isn't the right moment. Just wait." (Olsen 2009, 203)

Entrenched, Old School thinking about education has a direct impact on how theatre is typically taught in our schools.

This view of education took hold at the beginning of the twentieth century when public schools were literally re-formed to prepare factory workers for the emerging Industrial Revolution. Teachers were being "trained" in record numbers. Students were being taught to follow directions, repeat tasks, and be responsible citizens. Now, in the twenty-first century, many schools still use that same model of factory worker education when in fact the world has need of creative thinkers and independent, innovative problem-solvers. While our schools have embraced technology and various educational reform strategies, these "advances" have not procured the hoped-for panacea, but rather short-term and spotty relief from the systemic problems embedded over one hundred years ago. Many reform efforts continue to treat schools like machines with various broken parts. Each has tried to fix what is "broken," be it the teachers, students, curriculum, standards, buildings, equipment, or the textbooks. Truly effective change has only come about when there has been a fundamental change in the way we think about teaching and learning.

David O'Fallon[2] (2002) has been a theatre teacher, scholar, arts education advocate, and arts activist for decades. Reflecting on the state of education, he calls for major shifts in our thinking and practices and voices concern that the old educational models place little emphasis on learning that requires imagination. He alerts us to the dangers of schools structured in much the same way they were in the 1920s when his mother was a young teacher.

She taught a school year of about one hundred seventy or so instructional days, with a six or seven period day. [...] That is still just about the length of the school year and the school day. [...] It's the same size box that we had [nearly a hundred] years ago, and we're [...] trying to stuff more and more [...] into that box. And it's exploding.

In these extremely crowded, Industrial-model schools, there's hardly any room left for the imagination. [...] We need some profound transformation of how we think. [...] We are at the end of the Industrial Age of education. (O'Fallon 2002)

Kim Wheetley (2009) describes the twenty-first century education needed for our "increasingly complex, diverse, globalized, and media-saturated society."

> Education must be reinvented to meet the needs of our ever-changing twenty-first century world. Students have to be able to function, create, and communicate personally, socially, economically, and politically in local, national, and global venues. Schools must develop an interdisciplinary culture of inquiry where students work independently and collaboratively, employing critical thinking and multiple intelligences for imaginative problem solving. (Wheetley 2009)

Zemelman, Daniels, and Hyde (2005) agree. They highlight the futility of repeatedly using methodologies proven to be ineffective.

> Unfortunately, we are coming to understand that the basic things we do in American schools – what we teach and how – *don't* work; we don't empower kids, don't nurture literacy, don't produce efficient workers, don't raise responsible citizens, don't create a functional democracy. If we really want to change student achievement in American schools, we must act directly on teaching and learning. More of the same is not the answer. (Zemelman, Daniels, and Hyde 2005, 5, original emphasis)

Clearly the time has come, as O'Fallon says, for "some profound transformation of how we think" about learning and education (O'Fallon 2002).

A DIFFERENT FUTURE FOR THEATRE EDUCATION?

It is the artist who must midwife the new reality that we [...] eagerly await. Viola Spolin

Can this view of the current state of general education be a rallying call to theatre educators? I have seen theatre teachers who *do* empower students, nurture literacy, and teach responsible work ethics and characteristics of healthy citizenry. What is happening in these theatre classrooms that has eluded many other teachers? What makes some theatre programs grow and thrive while others die, stall, or are marginalized? Might theatre teachers bring another view of education to the table?

Dee Hock, in his forward-thinking work, *Birth of the Chaordic Age* (1999), gives reasons for hope as we pursue answers to these questions.

In truth, there are no problems "out there." And there are no experts "out there" who could solve them if there were. The problem is "in here," in the depth of the collective consciousness of the species. When that consciousness begins to understand and grapple with the false Industrial Age concepts of organizations to which it clings; when it is willing to risk loosening the hold of those concepts and embrace new possibilities; when those possibilities engage enough minds, new patterns will emerge and we will find ourselves on the frontier of institutional alternatives ripe with hope and rich with possibilities. (Hock 1999, 78)

Theatre teachers who grapple with Industrial Age thinking and practices are pioneers on "the frontier of institutional alternatives ripe with hope and rich with possibilities." If, as Hock asserts, the problems and solutions we are encountering at all levels of our society, including our schools, are not "out there" but "in here," we must confront in our own "consciousness" the threats to effective education in general and to effective theatre education in particular. It means changing the way we *think* about theatre education and letting that thinking shape our actions. It means looking anew at why we teach, whom we teach, what we teach, and how we teach. This self-reflective practice examines fundamental assumptions, values, policies, and objectives and side-steps resistance or merely reworking the same strategies that have failed repeatedly. This reflection results in positive action and change and is what Argyris and Schon (1992) refer to as double-loop versus single-loop learning. Only double-loop thinking embraces shifts in understanding and brings about change.

Most theatre teachers already feel overwhelmed with work responsibilities. Some may see educational reform as change of such magnitude that, given their schedules, they do not even enter the conversation. Others may wonder, "Can thinking about and embracing change in this way really evolve more effective practice and make a lasting difference?"

As so many in this book testify, when even a few teachers reconsider their practice and make manageable changes in their classrooms or production work, it *does* make a difference – a difference in students' lives, the theatre program, and the school. Each step of change made by a teacher or teaching artist has an impact and is essential to the survival of theatre in our schools. This is practical and effective change we can hope for right now. Work at the national, state, and district levels create a foundation and sow seeds for a shift in thought, but real change must be seen in what happens in a classroom each day between teacher and students. Without these changes, I question if theatre education will still be in the schools by the end of the twenty-first century.

WHY CHANGE NOW?

Secondary school theatre education is at a crossroads in America. Down one road there are programs still in the box of Industrial Age thinking, removed from contemporary practice in theatre and emerging theories and methodologies in education. In these settings, theatre work with students is often hierarchical, teacher-centered, and is an attenuated or dated version of college or conservatory study. Focus in some schools is almost exclusively on production of plays and musicals from the Broadway and regional theatre repertoire, more often than not unrelated to the lives of the majority of students in the school community. In many schools, theatre work is undervalued, fragmented, and accessible only after school and mostly to white, middle-class, able-bodied students (Lazarus 2000, 38). In a time of budget cuts coupled with the ever-shifting sea of education reforms, theatre education programs around the country are eroding. In many areas, as personnel move or retire and funding shifts to other priorities, theatre education is losing ground. Some states are not offering or are discontinuing certification of theatre teachers. Despite national and state standards in the arts, theatre as an academic subject is not mandated to be taught, and, in fact, is a classroom subject rarely offered in many states (National Center for Education Statistics 2011).

Researchers and educators from all vantage points are raising voices of concern about the state of education in the arts. Nearly two decades ago, Zemelman, Daniels, and Hyde (1998) spoke to problems that still characterize access to arts education across the country.

> [T]he role of the arts in public education has weakened even further. [...] Since 1990, forty-five states have slashed arts funding. [...] Arts teachers have been let go, programs dropped, and time allocations distorted, while class loads for the surviving arts specialists swell to ludicrous numbers.

In its report, *Creative America*, the President's Committee on the Arts and the Humanities (1997, 17) bluntly describes the arts programming of the average American school as "impoverished or nonexistent" (158–59). More recently, in the Project Zero report *Qualities of Quality*, (2009), the authors state,

> Many children in the United States have little or no opportunity for formal arts instruction, and access to arts learning experiences remains a critical national challenge. Additionally, the *quality* of arts learning opportunities that are available to young people is a serious concern. (Seidel et al. 2009, original emphasis)

The College Board National Task Force on the Arts in Education (2009) reports,

> Arts education in K–12 schools, colleges, and universities is facing an escalating crisis, which, if not dealt with soon, will deepen in both intensity and gravity. It will continue to directly, and adversely, affect the quality of education available to our students and, most importantly, the well-being of the nation. (2009)

As the 2011 President's Committee on the Arts and the Humanities report, *Reinvesting in Arts Education*, makes clear,

> due to budget constraints and emphasis on the subjects of high stakes testing, arts instruction in schools is on a downward trend. Just when they need it most, the classroom tasks and tools that could best reach and inspire these students – art, music, movement, and performing – are less available to them. Sadly, this is especially true for students from lower-income schools, where analyses show that access to the arts in schools is disproportionately absent. (2011, vi)

From this vantage point, one can see a theatre education legacy of gross inequities in both access to and quality of programs, personnel, and facilities across communities and the nation. As more and more parents are those who have never taken a theatre class or attended a live theatre performance, we will likely see a drop in attendance and support for professional, community, and educational theatre across the population (Lazarus 2000, 37).

This is a pretty bleak view of the present state of theatre education in the United States, but it is a snapshot of a good deal of current practice in our schools and communities. If change is to occur, we, as pioneers of change, must have the courage to look unabashedly at all versions of *what is*.

Fortunately there are other views of theatre education. From the crossroads where we now stand, I see other, more hopeful, directions in which the field is headed. This is the frontier of "alternatives ripe with hope and rich with possibilities" as Hock says (1999, 78). When I take in this view, I hear teachers and students speaking with a very different passion and vision. This practice involves the design and implementation of comprehensive, integrated curricula. It includes programs in which students are engaged in the exploration of social, historical, and educational issues through the study and production of theatre (Lazarus 2000, 38). This theatre education is learner-centered, socially responsible, provocative, and connected to the world in which students live. This is theatre education facilitated by teachers who understand the power of theatre to give voice to young people's concerns and ideas while connecting them to real and fictional figures throughout time. Embraced successfully by novice and veteran teachers, this approach is what I am calling best practice in theatre education.

Quality high school theatre and speech experiences can not only significantly influence but even accelerate adolescent development and provide residual, positive, lifelong impacts throughout adulthood. Laura McCammon and Johnny Saldaña

BEST PRACTICE

Growing out of the frenzy surrounding the educational reform movements of recent decades and grounded in a desire to effect lasting change in "actual, day-to-day teaching and learning," the notion of best practice in education emerged. The term was borrowed from the legal and medical professions to describe "solid, reputable, state-of-the-art work in a field" and was birthed by veteran teachers Steven Zemelman, Harvey Daniels, and Arthur Hyde. (2005, vi). They describe a practitioner following best practice standards.

> [H]e or she is aware of current research and consistently offers clients the full benefits of the latest knowledge, technology, and procedures. [...] Until recently, we haven't had an everyday term for state-of-the-art work in education. In fact, some veteran teachers will even *deny* the need for a current, research-based standard of instruction. [...] One wonders how long such self-satisfied teachers would continue to go to a doctor who says: "I practice medicine exactly the same way today that I did thirty years ago. I haven't changed a thing. I don't pay attention to all that newfangled stuff." (Zemelman, Daniels, and Hyde 2005, vi, original emphasis)

Zemelman's team was impelled by their experiences in the classroom and as specialists in curriculum and staff development. They drew from professional associations in each discipline, from research centers, and from individual researchers and teachers in all fields as they gathered "the current, national consensus recommendations about 'best educational practice'" in various curricular areas (2005, 5–6). What they discovered was a high level of agreement across dissimilar fields about "how kids learn best." They culled their findings into thirteen "interlocking principles, assumptions, or theories" (2005, 9–10). Then, working with teachers in the Chicago public schools, they observed these principles in practice, documenting "teachers who were bringing them to life, practicing state-of-the-art instruction in their classrooms every day" (Zemelman, Daniels, and Hyde 1998, vii).

Zemelman, Daniels, and Hyde discovered that across most disciplines, authorities agreed about the principles of instruction that were best for student learning. Fundamentally, these principles were not new, just merely "misplaced" in the moves through Industrial Age and Information Age thinking. While somewhat reminiscent of the progressive educational reform movements of the 1930s and 1960s, best practice principles of learning build on the strengths of that work and link it to current research about cognition to create a lasting impact on learning. (See Figure 1.1.)

The first five elements address various aspects of student-centered teaching and learning.

- **STUDENT-CENTERED.** The best starting point for schooling is young people's real interests; all across the curriculum, investigating students' own questions should always take precedence over studying arbitrarily and distantly selected "content."
- **Experiential.** Active, hands-on, concrete experience is the most powerful and natural form of learning. Students should be immersed in the most direct possible experience of the content of every subject.
- **Holistic.** Children learn best when they encounter whole ideas, events, and materials in purposeful contexts, not by studying subparts isolated from actual use.
- **Authentic.** Real, rich complex ideas and materials are at the heart of the curriculum. Lessons or textbooks that water-down, control, or oversimplify content ultimately disempower students.
- **Challenging.** Students learn best when faced with genuine challenges, choices, and responsibility in their own learning.

The next five principles draw our attention to cognitive and developmental aspects of teaching and learning.

- **COGNITIVE.** The most powerful learning comes when children develop true understanding of concepts through higher-order thinking associated with various fields of inquiry and through self-monitoring of their thinking.
- **Developmental.** Children grow through a series of definable but not rigid stages, and schooling should fit its activities to the developmental level of students.
- **Constructivist.** Children do not just receive content; in a very real sense, they re-create and reinvent every cognitive system they encounter, including language, literacy, and mathematics.
- **Expressive.** To fully engage ideas, construct meaning, and remember information, students must regularly employ the whole range of communicative media—speech, writing, drawing, poetry, dance, drama, music, movement, and visual arts.
- **Reflective.** Balancing the immersion in experience and expression must be opportunities for learners to reflect, debrief, abstract from their experiences what they have felt and thought and learned.

The final three principles remind us to attend to the social and interpersonal aspects of teaching and learning in schools.

- **SOCIAL.** Learning is always socially constructed and often interactional; teachers need to create classroom interactions that "scaffold" learning.
- **Collaborative.** Cooperative learning activities tap the social power of learning better than competitive and individualistic approaches.
- **Democratic.** The classroom is a model community; students learn what they live as citizens of the school.

(Zemelman, Daniels, and Hyde 2005, 10–11)

Figure 1.1: Principles of Best Practice Learning.

BEST PRACTICE IN THEATRE EDUCATION

Before I learned of Zemelman, Daniels, and Hyde's work, I had been gathering ideas about effective secondary school theatre education based on my experiences as a high school theatre teacher, theatre artist, professional development coordinator, and university theatre teacher-educator. As I observed and interviewed teachers and teaching artists around the country, my ideas evolved into the "Characteristics of Best Practice in Theatre Education." (See Figure 1.2.)

These three characteristics overlap and intersect in many unique ways within an effective theatre program. Based on recurring themes culled from more than two hundred and twenty-five surveys, interviews, and observations conducted with teachers, artists, and others involved with theatre education, I also compiled "Common Elements of Best Practice in Theatre Education." (See Figure 1.3.) Teacher-artists whose work is characterized in these ways effectively and responsibly engage young people in learning. These characteristics and elements

---

- *Learner-centered classroom and production work*
  The students' place at the center of the learning process is acknowledged, valued and nurtured. Learning together, students and teacher-artists pose questions, investigate and consider ideas from multiple perspectives, and reflect on discoveries. Content is correlated with familiar ideas, lived experiences, and relevant social issues. There is shared decision making and individual and collective action. Dialogue, collaboration, risk-taking, and experimentation are hallmarks of this practice.

- *Socially responsible practice*
  Students learn in, through, and about theatre as members of society and citizens of the school and the world. Material studied and produced is relevant to students and their communities and is developmentally appropriate. Students and adults show respect for each other, the program, and the art form in all formal and informal communications and interactions. The program is physically, academically, and socially accessible to all students in the school regardless of age, race, gender, religion, socioeconomic status, sexual orientation, physical ability, or disability.

- *Comprehensive theatre education*
  Instruction is holistic, authentic, and allows students to learn and practice collaboratively in the roles of actor, director, playwright, designer, technician, critic, researcher, and audience. Curricular and co-curricular work intertwines production, history, criticism, and aesthetics. Integration of theatre study and practice takes place across arts disciplines, in other subjects, and in the school and community.

Figure 1.2: Characteristics of Best Practice in Theatre Education.

- The teacher-artist's primary focus is on teaching *students* versus teaching *theatre*. Study and practice of theatre - learning in, through, and about theatre - is the means and method for effectively teaching students.
- The program encourages students to value theatre as an art form, profession, and lifelong interest.
- Students are actively engaged in high quality theatre-making in classroom work and productions.
- A process versus product construct is seen as a false dichotomy. Theatre classes and co-curricular productions are equally valued as learning opportunities. Productions are often viewed as laboratories for applying class instruction. Instruction and artmaking are imbedded in both classes and productions.
- Community and ensemble building is intentional and fundamental to the success of the program. The program encourages students to value themselves and others and there is healthy and heartfelt caring for the welfare of all involved.
- There is a component of the program that focuses on creation of new works with and/or by students.
- The implicit political nature of theatre provides a forum for exploration, reflection, and expression of self and society.
- Theatre is seen as a catalyst for civic dialogue. Social issues are considered and explored through the art form in the classroom, production work, and activities in the school and community.
- Theatre is seen as potentially about any topic and therefore is fertile ground for cross-curricular study.
- Classroom and production work is used to connect the past, present, and future to the lives of students and vice versa.
- Classroom management strategies are clear, fair and enforced. Students and teachers are self-disciplined, accountable, have self-efficacy, and freedom to create and collaborate.
- Strong organizational and managerial skills allow for the successful accomplishment of many tasks and responsibilities.
- The teacher asks for help and actively involves students, teachers, administrators, parents, and community members in appropriate roles in the program.
- The teacher assumes a leadership role and is an active citizen in the school.
- Outside funding through grants or artist-in-residence programs is actively pursued to enhance or extend the school program.
- Partnerships with or employment at local colleges, universities, and theatres is common and seen as of mutual benefit to the teacher and their partner organization or institution.
- Supportive administrators are seen as a critical factor to the program's success.
- The National Standards movement is seen as an important catalyst for precipitating change in theatre education at the national, state, and local level.
- Risk taking and change, while scary, is embraced.

Figure 1.3: Common Elements of Best Practice in Theatre Education.

embody the principles of best practice learning identified by Zemelman, Daniels, and Hyde and are central to an effective twenty-first century theatre education program.

These characteristics and elements represent the qualities of teaching and learning that speak most to why I chose to become a theatre teacher in the first place. I am encouraged by the fact that they also speak to the heart of so many theatre teachers and resonate with the work of other researchers and large numbers of teachers from other disciplines.

SO WHAT'S NEW?

Reading Zemelman's list of the principles of best practice in learning, (Figure 1.1) many of us will see we already draw on a number of the principles in our theatre classrooms or rehearsals every day. With, and often without, conscious planning, our students work collaboratively and experientially. Theatre education by its very nature can be student-centered, reflective, democratic, social, holistic, and developmentally appropriate. Auditions, productions, and classroom work can be as complex and authentic as in professional practice. Active learning, reflection, and cognitive experiences can be central to a theatre lesson or rehearsal. They *can* be. Countless articles, research projects, and conference sessions have indeed promoted theatre education as a sort of cure-all for what ails our students and schools today. The *potential* of theatre education as best practice seems boundless.

But the operative word in best practice is *practice*. It implies intentional *action* as illustrated in the Characteristics and Elements of Best Practice in Theatre Education. (See Figures 1:2 and 1:3.) Until my thinking changes and I take action on my knowledge of best practice, unless I *practice* these principles in deliberate ways day to day, the potential of theatre education is just that, unrealized potential, an unfulfilled promise. *Nothing changes*. It is like learning that there is a marvelous gift for me in a place just beyond my vantage point, but then not taking the time – or being too afraid, complacent, or arrogant – to move to it, open it, and use it.

The new literacy is learning, unlearning, and relearning. Julia Perlowski, Teacher

No one claims perfect adherence to this level of practice, however, and it can be scary to work in a new way or from an unfamiliar perspective. We are each on an individual journey toward best practice. It is as much a direction in which we are moving in our careers as it is a destination. No one is starting at the same point or having to travel the same distance or across the same terrain. The journeys taken by each teacher-artist in this book are the result of a broad range of professional and educational backgrounds, student populations served, budgets, and facilities, as well as the size, condition, and support for their programs. These and other factors influence their work day to day with students. Their practice is grounded in a willingness to be pioneers, to make change, to grow their practice as artists and teachers. They each, in their own way, embody the spirit, if not the full letter, of best practice in theatre education. Candace Koern (2011), a high school teacher near Houston, captures this pioneer spirit.

> A [...] big thing for me is "the more you do the better you get." I see no weakness in trying and not hitting a slam dunk. In fact, I think that getting things right on the first go at it is an anomaly. [...] Artists must expand their comfort zones, and this includes me. I try to reach beyond what I think I have mastered and am not afraid to bomb here and there because I know I will learn from the pitfalls and make it better next time. Teachers should allow themselves to be fallible. (Koern 2011)

In the best of all situations, and for a few of the teacher-artists I interviewed, all of the elements and characteristics of best practice are fully present throughout their programs. Changes in practice evolve differently for each teacher, however, and change unfolds over an entire career. A teacher with gifts in learner-centered practice may not yet use discipline-based methodologies or explore curriculum in an integrated or socially engaged manner. Directors who stage socially responsible plays tied to the school curriculum or world events may still direct in a traditional, director-centered style. Change is a journey we take as individuals and the rate and characteristics of our journey will be unique to our individual circumstances. It is movement toward – or away from – best practice that most characterizes our work.

NEW DIRECTIONS

The next chapters raise provocative questions while focusing on teachers and artists' work with students. Discussion and examples of each of the characteristics and elements of best practice are woven throughout since they are not mutually exclusive and serve to highlight the cohesive nature of programs that embody best practices principles. Chapter 2 considers what is learner-centered practice and presents a range of practices from teachers' classroom and production experiences. Chapter 3 explores the nature of socially engaged and socially responsible work and offers program descriptions and teacher profiles to illustrate the multiple ways in which programs using best practice principles are established and operate. Chapter 4 puts forward varied approaches to comprehensive theatre education and integrated arts education, giving examples from teacher-artists' practice. Chapter 5 looks to the roles community-based theatre education plays in the lives of students seeking experiences beyond traditional school-based programs. Ideas from teaching artists appropriate to all those working with secondary school students are included. Chapter 6 highlights the need to examine theatre teacher education and professional development programs as a central part of bringing best practice to our schools. In Chapter 7, dynamic teachers, writers, and arts activists share their visions, hopes, and desires for change in theatre education.

This book shares multiple and authentic views of this journey toward best practice. To this end, excerpts from interviews, anecdotes, composite stories, lesson and curriculum ideas, projects, and rehearsal strategies are incorporated throughout the book. Each chapter concludes with ideas for further reflection, selected resources, and extended examples of practice discussed in that chapter.

CLARIFYING TERMS

Some terms I use in the remainder of the book when discussing production work in secondary schools may need clarification. I use the term "learner-centered" versus "performer-centered" because I want to highlight practices appropriate to those still learning about theatre. I also want to acknowledge that everyone involved in producing theatre – performers and non-performers – is essential to the production. I wish to celebrate best practice in devising and production work with performers *and* student directors, designers, dramaturgs, playwrights, crew members, and stage managers, and to align production activity with artmaking, classroom work, and lifelong learning. I also want to disrupt the hierarchy that can dog a program when those onstage appropriate or are given a more important and powerful role in a theatre program than "the techies" and those, literally, behind the scenes. To this end, I use the word "company" to refer to all engaged in work on a given production. I use specific terminology where appropriate, for clarity, or emphasis.

I use the term "theatre" to denote any performative event. Theatre as an art form continues to evolve. The lines between theatre, dance, music, art, electronic media, and film continue to blend and blur. Using "theatre" is more efficient in this context than calling up plays, musicals, movement pieces, performance, site specific, digitalized, mixed-media, interactive, or improvisational work each time I refer to performance with students. I use the words "play" or "production" for similar reasons. I mean to refer to whatever performance piece students are producing.

I continue to employ the terms teacher, artist, and director interchangeably or use them in combination, as in "teacher-director," "teacher-artist" to emphasize the multiple roles professional theatre educators assume when working with students and young artists.

A student-actor must learn that "how to act" [...] is inextricably bound up with every other person in the complexity of the art form. Viola Spolin

THE PIONEER'S JOURNEY

In his play, *On the Verge (or The Geography of Yearning)*, Eric Overmyer depicts the trek of three "lady adventurers" as they travel through Terra Incognita from the end of the nineteenth century forward into the future of the late twentieth century (Overmyer 1993). In the closing pages of the play, two of the travelers elect to remain in the comfort of the mid-twentieth century. They ask the third what she can see of her trek forward. Mary, the third traveler, describes a future beyond their present state whose meaning she does not fully understand.

Somewhat like Mary, I feel I have just glimpsed the possibilities of a theatre education that respects students as co-learners and collaborators, one that engages a wide cross section of students in respectful practice and study of the art form. This is theatre education that is relevant, integrated, challenging, and comprehensive. It is not a destination but a journey through the Terra Incognita of secondary school theatre where young people are engaged in active learning, inquiry, and artmaking, and where the potential of theatre can be realized. But this is a journey for which there are no tried and true maps, waymarks, or well-traveled highways. You can see just the merest glimmers of this practice as you embark. But remember, it is a journey that is self-paced and self-defined, one charted by reshaping, recycling, and reinventing theatre education anew in your own classroom and school. And there are sturdy pioneers on the path with you. You are not alone (Lazarus 2000).

Overmyer closes his play with Mary's words as she glimpses the journey awaiting her. "Billions of new worlds, waiting to be discovered. Explored and illuminated. [...] I am on the verge" (1993). The remainder of this book is for those who also are "on the verge." It is my hope that reading and referencing this book will encourage a shift in thinking, an embracing of new possibilities, and a practice that will effect lasting change. This is a call to all of us to shift our vision of what secondary school theatre education can be. More than that, it is a call to "make it so," to fully inhabit the vision that called us to this work in the first place.

Voices from the field

WHAT DOES BEST PRACTICE LOOK LIKE?

When I am at my best "students are making something happen and they don't even really notice me or acknowledge my "fingers in the pie." The learning has become truly authentic. It is theirs and will be a part of them forever."

Marissa Meek

When I am at my best "I am relaxed, confident, patient, and enthusiastic. I have a specific plan for the lesson or rehearsal that I am not afraid to abandon if necessary. I am attuned to [...] my students and [...] what they need in that moment. I'm continually taking the temperature of the room to gauge where the students are [...] educationally, emotionally and socially. I'm questioning, circulating, encouraging [...] listening to what they are saying and not saying."

Valerie Labonski

When I am at my best "[...] [students are] working out something in a heated, involved way [...] and even taking a long time to do it. [...] I asked a group of kids to make me a tableau of 'disconnected' before we started rehearsals for One Flew Over the Cuckoo's Nest. *[...] [O]ne particular group argued for thirty minutes and then decided to 'give up' and all stand in a circle with their backs to the center [...] not touching. Give up? I don't think so!"*

When I am at my best "what is NOT happening is [...] two kids are talking about the people they have crushes on while three in their group are talking about the project [...] between texting."

Julia Perlowski

When I am at my best "students [...] are using all their capacity to solve problems so that everyone succeeds."

When I am at my best "what is NOT happening is [t]hey are not giving up, working on something else [...] lying, fighting."

Brendan Kelley

41

A Closer Look

BEST PRACTICES IN ACTION – MANDY WHITLOCK

Mandy Whitlock teaches at Brandeis High School in San Antonio. In 2009, she received both a district-wide Educator of the Year award and an ExCEL award that honors outstanding teachers in the greater San Antonio area (Whitlock 2011d). Mandy's is a school with a mixed population of students from all economic levels and a number of different racial and ethnic groups. Fine Arts and Junior ROTC share the same wing, which, Mandy notes, brings order and respect for the shared spaces and the different occupants' perspectives (2010).

Being in Mandy's program is fun as well as challenging. Students walk by her door between classes as she plays music they enjoy listening to. Mandy stands in the hallway greeting them as they pass or enter her room. Immediately after the bell rings, students in class are given a "Bell Assignment" to develop writing skills and to stimulate thinking about the topic of the day.

Mandy teaches in a black box theatre that is spacious, organized, and allows flexibility for these adolescents to move about as required. Each class has a designated area of the room with adjacent wall space and fabric boards on which student work, assignments, and colorful, enlarged instructions about the day's lessons are posted. There are tables near one wall with resource materials as well as a clearly marked area for completed work.

In her Theatre II class, they are working on a directing unit that requires students to apply skills and knowledge from different areas of theatre practice. Most of the students are sophomores, yet Mandy is differentiating instruction for each student. She has a cart with art supplies, CDs, markers, and other materials to encourage creativity and exploration with assignments. She has grouped students based on her assessment of their skills and work style and designed a "Meal Plan" for this unit. She hands out small "menus" with project assignments and grade percentages and they talk through the "menu items" together. Some menu assignments are due the next day, while others are due at the end of the week or are part of an ongoing class directing project. Mandy explains the quality

I want students to be in control of their learning. Mandy Whitlock

of work and critical analysis required and that students can work on the menu projects in any order. Most assignments require students to work in groups or with a partner. For an "Ad Appetizer," students are to write a detailed critique of posters students created for an earlier project. For their "Directing Dish," groups of students are to read a chapter from Francis Hodge's *Play Directing* (1994), design a poster presenting key ideas from the chapter, and prepare a group presentation of the chapter for the following day. They are to prepare a critical analysis of the chapter as well as discuss applications of the key ideas to their study and practice of directing. The "Scene Side Dish" is part of their ongoing directing project and requires pairs of students to take a scene from their play and divide it into units. The "Dessert Drawing" is a poster of sets for every scene in their play in "bird's eye view." In the "Training Treat" assignment, students are to create a teaching pamphlet for others to help them as directors. Mandy reminds them that, like being ready for an audience on opening night, "Deadlines are hard and fast." During and after going over the menu, there is not a single complaint or concern about the work load or level of excellence expected and students quickly start working (Whitlock 2011b).

Clearly garnering their respect, Mandy interacts easily with students. They remain focused much of the time as she moves around the room sharing her quick laugh and watching groups work on the day's projects. She quietly observes students and then moves to another group where she poses questions that deepen thinking and reflection. She offers words of encouragement or correction and shares additional ideas for students to consider. This is a program with a high level of challenge coupled with a high level of support, something Mandy offers through assignments and online resources as well as through her one on one mentoring.

Mandy describes how she structures differentiated instruction into a "meal plan."

I might create three appetizer activities for research on a topic […] each activity […] [focusing] on a different strength like creative, practical, or analytical [skills]. […] I do the same with three activities for a main course [which is] […] usually a group assignment involving a production of some kind […] and then three activities for extension with dessert activities. The students are told how many points each activity is worth and the expectations for each activity. Students choose the activities based on interest and how many points they wish to earn. Sometimes I will choose their groups or require them to choose at least one activity that focuses on analytical, practical, or creative [applications]. All activities encourage the students to apply the lesson to their lives, college readiness, real world applications. […] When individuals or groups present their work or perform, the room is transformed with curtains and lighting to create a performance environment and we offer written and verbal critiques.

Performances or presentations are opportunities where students are encouraged to incorporate all the senses to engage their audiences. They are encouraged to use [...] live or recorded [...] music, technology [...] lighting, power point, costumes, handouts, audience participation activities [...] visual or performance art, statistics, history, etc., to engage their audience. (Whitlock 2010)

Watching the Directing Dish presentations the following day, I am struck by how much of the information the students read they have truly grasped. For each presentation, group members introduce themselves in a professional manner and reference their posters to support key ideas. They make connections to prior learning and future applications. After each group presents, Mandy poses questions to the presenters. "What was the most eye opening or surprising [thing you read]?" "[What's one thing more you learned] than you knew before?" She asks questions to the class members who have been taking notes throughout. "What did you learn that was most surprising or...?" "How can we use this if we never did theatre again?" The students all seem very interested in thinking about applications of the readings to directing and also recognize the importance of the information in relation to their own lives and the larger world of the theatre. They have genuine ownership of the learning process and ideas discussed. Their level of preparation, thought, and investment is greater than that which I have observed in many college students (Whitlock 2011a).

Change is not scary me. Mandy Whitloc

Before the Theatre II class ends, Mandy talks with them about directing as a profession. In response to a student's question, she engages them in a discussion of some of the controversial aspects of casting. As they talk, she points out that Hollywood would "mostly go for the stereotype" and references how "Disney just presented their first black princess in 2010!" She tells the students that growing up they have been exposed to and therefore "trained with the stereotypes. [...]" She encourages them to open their thought and "as you go forward [...] [know that] people [are] playing with gender and race [in casting]." She explains that in professional theatre "you have to hone your skills and [be sure] that you are a good business person so you can create your own opportunities." She gives examples of how to become indispensible by being willing to work hard and to do the hard work. She shares her own professional theatre experiences and becoming indispensible through willingness to work really hard and be reliable. As the bell rings, she holds them to make her final point about whatever profession they pursue: "Make yourself indispensible" (Whitlock 2011a).

Mandy maintains a website with extensive resources she eagerly shares with both students and theatre teachers far and wide. She posts podcasts from various classes and students listen to them on their MP3 players before tests. As a result she has seen test scores "go way up." So that there is ongoing communication between students, families, and faculty, she maintains an extensive online handbook for her program that even includes a section on whining (not allowed) (2011c).

This is a program with high academic standards, rigorous attention to instructional design and implementation, and tremendous ownership by students and faculty. This sense of ownership extends beyond the theatre area or fine arts wing. Mandy is a citizen of the school and theatre education advocate in the state. She works actively for the state theatre education association, serving on their board and presenting sessions at their conferences. At the high school, she heads the fine arts area, offers professional development presentations for other teachers, participates on committees, partners with colleagues, and works with administrators for the good of the whole school.

In Chapter 4, Mandy talks about her interdisciplinary projects and below she discusses her evolution as a theatre teacher (2011a; 2011b; 2011c; 2010).

> What originally called me to be a teacher of theatre was my passion for the subject matter and my desire to spark that passion in my students. However, over the years, I have realized that I think what makes me a strong educator is not the subject matter I teach, but my constant desire to find ways to reach every student in my classroom and beyond.
>
> [...] I believe education should not be a secret or mystery. I want students to be in control of their learning so, as they move forward in their education, they are empowered to find answers and master concepts of interest on their own. [...] I want each student to leave my classroom or production understanding the power of their voice and how to work with others to positively express themselves and offer their thoughts.
>
> [...] I believe strongly in cross-curricular connections so that students understand that subjects are not independent but are connected. [...] I work with other teachers on campus to create activities that tie subjects together so students can make broader connections. [...] I have the ability to see where a student struggles and I am flexible enough with my curriculum and instruction to shape and individualize activities to reach them.
>
> [...] Change is not scary to me. [...] Teaching is never static or boring and that makes it something that keeps me interested. [...] I evolve. I research, learn, go to conferences, share ideas with others, listen to others, embrace technology, and use it daily. I acknowledge that I learn things through creativity, but not all of my students learn best that way. I develop lessons that reach students who are strong in other ways than my own and I challenge myself to see things from others' points of view. I am active in my school community so I know what happens outside of my room or auditorium and I understand the politics of schools and what needs to be done to make my subject relevant to the school, the community, and my students. I make myself valuable to my school, students,

art of what cripples ur profession is a eacher's inability o see that change is eality and you must onstantly evaluate nd improve. Mandy Vhitlock

and parents by doing my job to the best of my abilities and going above and beyond expectations in everything I do.

[...] I also keep in touch with students as they leave my class, [...] from the students who now work professionally in theatre to the soldier who came by to apologize for his refusal to use make-up in [high school] saying, "I will never put make-up on in real life," only to be in a foxhole having his commander tell him to put [...] some camo make-up on his face. He came by to tell me that he thought of me when he read the tube and it said "Ben Nye."

[...] I believe every student can learn and [...] I do not think I ever stop teaching and learning. [...] That part of me never shuts off and never gets tired. I think my students feed on that energy and make discoveries that they can apply to their life. (Whitlock 2010)

IDEAS FOR FURTHER REFLECTION

Reflective practice, the habit of considering and reconsidering what transpires in your interactions with students and others, is an important element of best practice. The practice of thinking deeply about your own work, asking tough questions, honestly looking at *what is* and pondering *what could be* brings about change in us and our work. Steve Seidel and his colleagues at Project Zero investigated the nature of quality arts education and they determined reflection and dialogue about excellence to be key components.

[C]ontinuous reflection and discussion about what constitutes quality and how to achieve it is not only a catalyst *for* quality, but also a sign *of* quality. In other words, thinking deeply about quality – talking about it, worrying about it, continually revisiting ideas about its characteristics and its indicators – is essential both to the pursuit of excellence in arts education and to its achievement. (Seidel et al. 2009, original emphasis)

To the end of supporting your pursuit of excellence, questions and opportunities for reflection, as well as additional resources, are presented throughout this book and at the end of each chapter.

Change in Your Life and Practice

- What in my world has changed in the last year? What has stayed the same?
- How has change and stasis affected my life? My school? My teaching? My program?

- Which of my students has been affected by change and how?
- How does my program reflect a responsiveness to change?
- Who might be traveling or willing to travel on this journey toward best practice with me?
- Who are the advocates for change and the mentors in my school?
- Are there others in my life outside of school who can serve as a support network, a nutritious community of change-seekers and change-makers?

In my own life, I don't experience equilibrium as an always desirable state. And I don't believe it is a desirable state for an organization. I've observed the search for organizational equilibrium as a sure path to institutional death, a road to zero trafficked by fearful people. Having noticed the negative effects of equilibrium so often, I've been puzzled why it has earned such high status. Margaret Wheatley

Reflecting Change

As busy professionals, we often do not take time for reflection or dismiss it as reminiscent of homework assignments. But there are all kinds of wondering and worries swirling about us each day that beg reflection. As you consider the ideas in this chapter in relation to your practice, what anecdotes, incidents, or questions come to mind? Begin a journal in which you free write about what you are thinking about related to changes and events that happen or have happened in your life and work. End each entry with "It Made Me Think…" Do not include what it made you think about; just describe the idea or incident. Like Professor Dumbledore's pensive introduced in *Harry Potter and The Goblet of Fire* (Rowling 2000), this metacognition allows you to take your thoughts out and look at them periodically over time and in relation to each other. You might find patterns or recurring themes to help you in your journey toward best practice.

Mapping Your Journey

Not all who wander are lost. J. R. R. Tolkien

When facing change, it is very helpful to think from a new perspective or find a new medium of expression. To this end, take out a sheet of paper and a pen, pencil, or marker. (You might feel resistant, but do it anyway.) Free draw a "map" of your journey to this point in your career. Draw a straight, curved, zigzag, or combination of lines that capture the path you have traveled thus far as a theatre teacher-artist. Be thoughtful as you map your journey and include key life events that have impacted that journey. Identify by symbols, icons, or words the events, people, interactions, and opportunities that were high points, low points, obstacles, and incentives along the way. When did you feel you were moving in a direction you wanted to head? When were you lost or wandering? Discuss your map with a trusted colleague, family member, or friend, or do some free writing about patterns you notice, things to celebrate, and thoughts that emerged as you drew. What can you learn about where you have been in your journey that can help in your next steps?

Where Do You Want to Go? Appreciative Inquiry and Best Practice

Whether you are a preservice theatre teacher or a veteran of many years, cultivation of a vision of where you can go in your practice is liberating and allows for change that often does not seem possible. Inspired by David Cooperrider, an "Appreciative Inquiry" approach celebrates the best of *what is*, as you journey towards *what could be, what ought to be*, and *what will be*. (See notes, page 51.)

The Best of *What Is*

Draft a shorthand description of *what is* – a brief account of the best in your present practice and/or program. Look over the characteristics and elements of best practice in theatre education. (See Figures 1.2 and 1.3 on pages 35–36.) Quickly list ways in which you actively engage in best practice now.

The Best Of *What Could Be*

- What are some of the heartfelt hopes stirring in you about theatre education and your practice? Jot down your thoughts.
- What is one powerful moment or experience that stands out as a time when you felt particularly effective, challenged, or alive as a teacher? When did you feel you were using your full capacities and were able to draw out the most positive and the best in the students you were working with? Add this information to your notes.
- If some people who know the very best about you were asked to name the three best qualities or capabilities you bring to teaching, what would they say? Add these to your notes.
- Who has stood out in your life as an example of a great teacher? What was it or is it like to be around this person? How has this person inspired you? How did this person work and live? Write these down and notice that often the qualities we admire in others are the qualities we too possess!

The Best of *What Ought To Be*

Imagine for a minute that you have fallen into a sound sleep. You awaken five years later. While you were sleeping, many changes happened, small and large. Theatre education, and your work in particular, was reconstituted in ways you would most like to see for yourself, your students, your school, community, and the field. You wake up and go into the world to take a full view of these changes. You are happy with what you see. It is a view of the kind of work you most want to be part of.

Figure 1.4: Journey on!

- What are some highlights you see? What is happening that is new, better, healthy, and good? Create a new list with these ideas.
- If you had been awake during this time, picture how *you* might have brought about these changes? Add this to your list.
- Visualize the projects, practices, and partnerships that were developed, created, and used. See them in detail. What do they look like? How were you involved? Jot these ideas down.

We must form per models in thought and look at them continually, or we shall never carve them out in gran and noble lives. M Baker Eddy

The Best of *What Will Be*

Now, if anything is possible…

- How can you use the ideas you have gathered to be an agent for positive change in your work?
- What steps can you begin in this direction?
- What advocates might you have to help you, listen to you, or be your partner in effecting these changes?
- What resources – intellectual, creative, financial – can you garner?

Save these ideas. Continue to revise and expand them as you read this book and envision more and more of your journey of best practice. Journey On!

SELECTED RESOURCES

In addition to the works cited in this chapter, the following offer ideas for further reading and reflection.

Arts Education Partnership. 2002. *Critical Links: Learning in the Arts and Student Academic and Social Development*. Washington, DC: Arts Education Partnership.

Bellanca, James, and Ron Brandt, eds. 2010. *21st Century Skills: Rethinking How Students Learn*. Bloomington, IN: Solution Tree Press.

Common Core State Standards Initiative. 2011. *Preparing America's Students for College and Career*. Accessed 8 February, 2011. http://www.corestandards.org/

Davidson, Cathy N. 2011. "How the Brain Science of Attention Will Transform the Way We Live, Work, and Learn." *Now You See It*. New York: Penguin Group USA.

Gallagher, Kathleen. 2007. *The Theatre of Urban: Youth and Schooling in Dangerous Times*. Toronto: University of Toronto Press.

Gardner, Howard. 1991. *The Unschooled Mind: How Children Think and How Schools Should Teach*. New York: Basic Books.

Gardner, Howard, Mihaly Csikszentmihalyi, and William Damon. 2001. *Good Works: When Excellence and Ethics Meet*. New York: Basic Books.

Glasser, William. 1993. *The Quality School Teacher*. New York: HarperPerennial.

Green, Elizabeth. 2010. "Building a Better Teacher." Accessed 12 December, 2011. http://www.nytimes.com/2010/03/07Teachers.

Pink, Daniel H. 2010. *Drive: The Surprising Truth About What Motivates Us*. Edinburgh: Cannongate Books.

Sergiovanni, Thomas. J. 1992. *Moral Leadership: Getting to the Heart of School Improvement*. San Francisco: Jossey-Bass.

Sizer, Theodore R., and Nancy Faust Sizer. 1999. *The Students Are Watching: Schools and the Moral Contract*. Boston: Beacon Press.

Zander, Rosamund Stone, and Benjamin Zander. 2000. *The Art of Possibility*. Boston: Harvard Business School Press.

NOTES

1. Appreciative Inquiry (AI) was developed by David Cooperider, a specialist in organizational development at Case Western Reserve University. AI contrasts with other problem-solving methods that present organizations, large or small, as "problems-to-be-solved." Instead, AI invites change by looking at the best of "What Is," the best of "What Should Be," and ultimately, "What Will Be." This is a view of an organization as a solution-to-be–embraced (Cooperider et al. 2000; Cooperrider 2009).

2. David O'Fallon was director of education at the National Endowment for the Arts. He later served at the Kennedy Center and became executive director of the Perpich Center for Arts Education, a state agency in Minnesota that houses a high school of the arts, a research centre, and a professional development institute. David went on to become the president of the McPhail Center for the Arts, a community-based arts organization in Minneapolis, and the president of the Minnesota Humanities Commission.

Chapter 2

Learner-Centered Practice

The teacher cannot be the only expert in the classroom. To deny students their own expert knowledge is to disempower them.

Lisa Delpit

Theatre is a language through which human beings can engage in active dialogue on what is important to them. It allows individuals to create a safe space that they may inhabit in groups and use to explore the interactions which make up their lives. It is a lab for problem solving, for seeking options, and for practicing solutions.

Augusto Boal

What is the nature of learner-centered practice? What does it look like in classroom and production settings? Margaret Wheatley (1994),[1] a specialist in organizational communication, has thought a lot about ownership and the role it plays in a meaningful connection to groups and organizations. Her ideas have special relevance to our students' investment in their own education.

> Ownership describes the personal links to the organization [school, class, program], the charged, emotion-driven *feeling* that can inspire people. [...] We know that the best way to build ownership is to give over the creation process to those who will be charged with its implementation. We are never successful if we merely present a plan in finished form to employees [students]. It doesn't work to just ask people to sign on when they haven't been involved in the design process, when they haven't experienced the plan as a living, breathing thing. (Wheatley 1994, 66, original emphasis)

Can we really, without chaos ensuing, "give over" our classrooms to students and allow access so they "sign on"? How do we fairly accommodate everyone's voice and incorporate everyone's ideas in a democratic classroom? What about teacher accountability and classroom management? What about student achievement and performance?

WorldBlu was formed by Traci Fenton to change the "command and control" model in workplaces to a democratic model. Her purpose is "to unleash human potential and inspire freedom by championing the growth of democratic organizations worldwide" (WorldBlu 2011). By shifting thought to worker-centered business practices, WorldBlu has seen small, large, nonprofit, for-profit, and nearly bankrupt businesses worldwide create engaged, humane working environments and become wildly successful (Fenton 2011). Can we learn from this model and "unleash human potential and inspire freedom" in learner-centered theatre programs so our children are wildly successful? Liberating approaches to education reminiscent of WorldBlu's Ten Principles of Organizational Democracy[2] are embodied by teachers engaged in best practice (WorldBlu 2011). When a theatre program has systems and processes in place that support purpose and vision, transparency, dialogue and listening, fairness and dignity, accountability, value for individual and collective contributions, choice, integrity, decentralization of power, reflection and evaluation – core values of democratic organizations (WorldBlu 2011) – there is learner-centered practice.

LEARNER-CENTERED PRACTICE IN A THEATRE PROGRAM

The child shall have the right to freedom of expression: this right shall include freedom to seek, receive, and impart information and ideas of all kinds . . . either orally, in writing or in print, in the form of art, or through any other media of the child's choice. (UN Convention on the Rights of the Child, Article 13)

It has been said that effective teachers don't think about teaching all of their students, they think about teaching each of their students. What is the subtle difference between these two ways of thinking? It seems to reside in whether the class is seen as a single entity or as being composed of individuals. The word "each" reminds us that our students differ from each other in many ways and that our teaching should be responsive to those differences. (The Knowledge Loom, Brown University)

Just as with workers in a democratic workplace, learner-centered teaching is not an entirely student-led or child-driven approach to teaching in which the learners make all decisions regardless of their emotional, social, or academic maturity. In learner-centered instruction, the teacher assesses the skills and interests of students and then structures meaningful learning experiences that engage everyone in a democratic classroom environment. Learning together, students and teacher pose questions, consider ideas from multiple perspectives, investigate topics, and reflect on discoveries.

Learner-centered practice is the opposite of what Freire refers to as "the banking concept of education." In this approach "the scope of action allowed to students extends only as far as receiving, filing, and storing the deposits." Freire contrasts this with education that liberates, claiming "[e]ducation must begin with the solution of the teacher-student contradiction [...] so that both are simultaneously teachers *and* students" (Freire 1998, 53, original emphasis). Discussing learning that is student-centered, Zemelman, Daniels, and Hyde (1998, 8) state "The best starting point for school is young people's real interests; all across the curriculum, investigating students' own questions should always take precedence over studying arbitrarily and distantly selected 'content.'"

In learner-centered practice, both teacher and students raise questions and shape learning opportunities. All discover answers while information and skills in the curriculum are learned. For example, while reading *The Diary of Anne Frank* (Goodrich, Hackett, and Kesselman, 1958)[3] in an Introduction to Theatre class, students may pose questions about the interpretation of a particular role, depiction of a setting, or the various political and social issues in the play. In this instance, students also may be concerned about an attack or war in their own country. The teacher might encourage them to shape their concerns about war into questions. Students can then investigate how theatre artists and others have explored similar questions or faced and endured war. Students could then develop and share various design, dramaturgical, playwriting, or performance projects that further investigate their questions. Learning then can be related back to the play and the students' lives. Additional questions may be framed for further study during the semester.

Middle school teacher Deb Alexander did just this. She designed a theatre curriculum using *The Diary of Anne Frank* as a springboard into exploration of themes and topics of interest to her students. This curriculum is described in Chapter 4 on page 240.

Billie Harvey, who teaches in a small community of around fifty-six hundred people, says,

> I try to make everything student-centered. I'm more of a guide [...] in the sense that [...] if I do a lecture, it's for just a little bit and then I give them the tools to continue where I left off. [...] I do a lot of praising to help them [...] and build them up [so they are] comfortable in making their own decisions. (Harvey 2010)

In her theatre production class, students break into groups and act as production teams. Each team works with the same script and develops a concept that they write about in a "concept essay." Teams design costumes and make-up for two characters, create sound cues and a CD, light cues, a ground plan, a 3D model,

Figure 2.1: A student-designed poster for a high school production of *The Diary of Anne Frank.*

and a computer generated poster. For productions, she spends time with students discussing themes and gathering ideas about design aspects based on their research for the show. They share their views and discuss them; then she shares her views. The best ideas are blended together. She comments that a lot of ideas that students come up with she likes and that they end up solving a lot of problems. "If they know that their decisions are useful, then they are more apt to keep [offering] [...] those decisions" (Harvey 2010).

When Eric Vera taught in a Title I school near Dallas, he began each class with

> normal, everyday conversation. [...] We start off with "hot topics" [...] [and] discuss current issues that they find interesting or [...] relevant to their lives. [...] I segue from that to the current subject matter. And we talk. What do they know about this? What do they want to know about this? [...] How do they know about this? [...] With YouTube, Movies, and TV, [...] theatre is something the students find very hard to relate to at times. [...] [W]hen I find a way to identify how those other [forms...] have influenced what they love, [...] they listen. [...] The objectives are on the board. They know what it is we are about to delve into, so why spend time talking about those things when we can have a conversation that [...] [links those objectives to] them? (Vera 2011)

TEACHER-STUDENT RELATIONSHIPS

At first [the students] thought I [...] didn't know the answers because I would ask them questions [...] trying to get them to discover the answer. [...] It's a whole concept of ownership. Kent Sorensen, Teacher

"Who is in charge?" In this situation, the role of the teacher, not as peer or friend, but as the responsive, responsible adult in the classroom, is understood by all. The teacher appropriately shares authority by creating an atmosphere of mutual trust, openness, risk taking, and problem solving. Adjustments in instruction and changes in direction or methodology prompted by the teacher and/or students deepen and enhance everyone's learning and participation. Scott Tatum (2011) helps students take ownership of their learning by teaching them about learning preferences.

At the beginning of the year we have a several week period where I introduce [...] multiple teaching/learning styles to be used in my classroom over the course of the year. Each day, as we go through the different modes of instruction, we talk about why we're [...] [using that approach] and what type of learner I'm trying to reach. [...] We discuss how gaining understanding through multiple avenues [...] will help them be better students. This sort of meta-conversation about the mechanism of the school system they sometimes feel a victim of is a chance for them to learn to become not only responsible parties in their own education, but to start making choices as young adults. This shows up in daily interactions from how we deal with restroom usage to time management to creating the syllabus and course projects. (Tatum 2011)

PARTICIPATION IN A LEARNER-CENTERED PROGRAM

[Participation is] the fundamental right of citizenship [...] the process of sharing decisions which affect one's life and the life of the community in which one lives. Roger Hart

Involvement in real life experiences and projects in which students have ownership and investment is authentic participation. A group of students, for example, elect to be dramaturgs for the upcoming play their school is producing. They research and prepare background material to help the actors better understand the play. They write program notes and install a display of their research in the theatre lobby. They are engaged in projects akin to those of professional dramaturgs. They are also self-directed and invested because they have ownership of all phases of the project. They are participating in an authentic manner as opposed to students who write a research paper about the play for their teacher.

Sue Scarborough (2003) talks about how she includes authentic participation and decision making in her classroom.

[Learner-centered work] is in every lesson. After a monologue or scene I ask them "How did it go for you?" I start with them. [...] Empowerment of the students is a big thing with me. [...] I start very simply by not having them raise

Figure 2.2: Both teachers and students in learner-centered classrooms are engaged in reflective practice.

their hands. If they have something to say they can say it as long as no one else is talking. […] It seems so simple to adults. We don't raise our hands when we have something to say. In education the teacher has the power to decide who can talk and when. […] By giving [students] back this power […] they talk and listen […] to each other.

Roger Hart (cited in deWinter 1997, 38–39) adopted a "ladder of participation" to show the progression from synthetic to authentic participation and to characterize children's decision-making involvement in various projects worldwide. (See Figure 2.3.) Of the eight rungs on this Ladder, notice that only the top three are truly learner-centered.

For years I assumed my students were participating in authentic ways because I assigned them responsibilities and informed them or consulted them about various projects. The most dynamic theatre education programs, however, regularly embody shared decision-making and student-initiated or student-directed experiences like those on the upper rungs of Hart's model. In true learner-centered programs, students have a palpable "ownership" as Wheatley describes it (1994, 66).

ometimes […] [I ry] to shape things; nd the child will say, This doesn't make any nse, Miss Clunie. ..] We should do it is way." Gloria Bond Clunie, Teacher and laywright

DIALOGUE, DECISION-MAKING, AND REFLECTION

Dialogue – an ongoing exchange of ideas and opinions – is fundamental, as is consideration of students' academic, artistic, social, developmental, and emotional abilities and needs in a learner-centered class. With this information, teachers evaluate each student's readiness to make, act on, and bear responsibility for decisions of all kinds. Steve Seidel and his fellow researchers at Project Zero note:

> Decisions made by those in the room have tremendous power to support or undermine the quality of the learning experience. This is especially true of students, and it is important for students to be as aware as possible of the potential impact of their choices on their own and others' learning experiences. (Seidel et al. 2009, 2)

Even the language we decide to use sends signals to students about how power and authority is being used. "I want you to…" or "I need you to…" sends the message that decisions that follow are to give the teacher what she wants or he needs. Teacher-centric language like this undermines otherwise well-intentioned learner-centered work and invites teacher-pleasing or teacher-resistant behaviors. "Let's all…" or "Please…" or "Now let's…" makes clear that the teacher is making instructional decisions for the good of the group and not for his or her own convenience or need.

Level 8: *Youth-initiated, shared decisions with adults*: Hart sees influence shared between children and adults as the final goal of participation. He cites a project in a New York City high school in which students, concerned about the increasing dropout rate due to teen pregnancy, organized a coalition for better sex education in the school.

Level 7: *Youth-initiated and directed*: Youth conceive, organize and direct a project themselves, without adult interference. Except in natural play, examples of this level of participation are hard to find, says Hart, because adults have difficulty honoring children's initiatives and then leaving them to manage these themselves.

Level 6: *Adult-initiated, shared decisions with youth*: Hart sees this level of participation mostly in the case of projects concerned with community development in which initiators, such as policy makers, community workers and local residents, involve a variety of age ranges and interest groups. One project he cites is the "Nuestro Parque" project in East Harlem. Teens, young children, and parents designed a neighborhood park and involved their community in development and review of model plans.

Level 5: *Consulted and informed*: Youth are consulted extensively about a project designed and operated by adults. An example of this kind of participation is a New York television station which regularly consults and pilots their programming to a panel of children.

Level 4: *Assigned but informed*: Adults call in youth to participate and inform them how and why they are to be involved. Only after the young people understand the intentions of the project and the purpose of their involvement do they decide whether or not to take part. Hart provides the example of the children who served as pages during the World Summit for Children. They were called in as a visible presence toward compelling the leaders attending to make significant changes.

Level 3: *Tokenism*: Youth are apparently given a voice, but this is to serve the child-friendly image adults want to create rather than the interest of the youth themselves. According to Hart, this is common practice in the western world, for instance, on conference panels, where the radiating charm of children often makes a great impression.

Level 2: *Decoration*: Youth are called to embellish adult actions, for instance, by song, dance, and other affecting activities. Adults do not, however, pretend that all this is in the interest of the children themselves.

Level 1: *Manipulation*: Youth are engaged or used for their own benefit as determined by adults, while the youth themselves do not understand the implications of their involvement. For example, toddlers carrying banners in a demonstration for family rights.

Adapted with permission (de Winter 1997).

Figure 2.3: Ladder of Participation.

Decision-making flexibility is key in a learner-centered program. Teachers adjust instructional methods to accommodate students. Those who are self-directed and self-motivated might work independently, while others will learn best in pairs or groups or through more structured projects. Instruction and assignments within a given unit may vary from student to student as content is related to familiar ideas, lived experiences, and relevant social issues. Projects that accommodate a range of learning styles and decision-making abilities are built into each unit.

Reflection about what is being learned and experienced, as well as about who is making which decisions, why, and how, is part of the students' and teacher's practice. Intentional inclusion of reflection as part of the instructional process creates a dynamic classroom environment monitored by the teacher, but shaped by all involved in that learning community. "Balancing the immersion in experience and expression must be opportunities for learners to reflect, debrief, and abstract from their experiences what they have felt and thought and learned" (Zemelman, Daniels, and Hyde 2005, 11).

ORGANIZATION AND CLASSROOM MANAGEMENT IN A LEARNER-CENTERED ENVIRONMENT

How does a teacher encourage student efficacy and decision-making in a school environment that demands order, discipline, accountability, and measurable learning outcomes?

There is a clear correlation between deep, truly engaged, student-centered learning and well-executed instruction, classroom management, and organization. Many teachers are excellent directors or designers and innovative, inspired educators, but as James Stronge, Pamela Tucker, and Jennifer Hindman note:

Great driving skills don't matter when the car won't move. Similarly, great instructional skills won't matter if students in the classroom are disengaged or out of control. [...] When an effective teacher is in the driver's seat, one knows that a preventative, proactive, positive approach is in place to ensure that learning is on course. [...] Effective teachers expertly manage and organize the classroom and expect their students to contribute in a positive and productive manner. [...] [They] create focused and nurturing classrooms that result in increased student learning [Marzano et al. 2003; Shellard and Protheroe 2000]. [...] In fact, it has been noted that classroom management skills are essential in a classroom for a teacher to get anything done [Brophy and Evertson 1976]. In some ways, classroom management is like salt in a recipe; when it is present it is not noticed, but when it is missing, diners will ask for it. (Stronge, Tucker, and Hindman 2004, 64 and 66)

We all have had days when "the diners" needed more "salt," when a few students became distracted, disruptive, or disengaged and did not learn what we had intended. There are classrooms, however, where this is the norm rather than the exception. Teachers who are able to employ best practice principles are those who *consistently* create a focused, nurturing classroom environment for rigorous, challenging, and engaged learning so *all* students experience academic and artistic achievement.

In his book *Teach Like A Champion* (2010), Doug Lemov describes strategies he has gathered in our most challenging schools from some of the country's best teachers. He refers to these strategies as "tools" of the craft of teaching and stresses that diligent practice with these tools makes the difference between a good teacher and a great teacher.

I am responsible. I pride myself on not being "that flaky theatre teacher." I turn things in on time. I take care of business. I try to set a good example for other teachers and the students. Marissa Meek, Teacher

> Great teaching is an art. In other arts – painting, sculpture, the writing of novels – great masters leverage a proficiency with basic tools to transform the rawest of materials (stone, paper, ink) into the most valued assets in society. This alchemy is all the more astounding because the tools often appear unremarkable to others. Who would look at a chisel, a mallet, and a file and imagine them producing Michelangelo's *David*? [...] [A]lthough lots of people conjure unique artistic visions, only those with an artisan's skill can make them real. [...] And while not everyone who learns to drive a chisel will create a *David*, neither can anyone who fails to learn it do much more than make marks on rocks. (Lemov 2010, 1–3)

Teachers embodying best practice characteristics "do much more than make marks on rocks." Skillfully employing basic tools for learner-centered classroom and production management results in artful teaching. Dan Sullivan (2010) uses a number of tools in his drama classroom. He assigns students to groups for the year. His elementary and middle school students take turns as "the theatre manager" who monitors groups' behaviors throughout each class. Theatre managers use a white board placed prominently at the front of the room. They add checks to note when students in a group are off-task or inattentive and erase the checks when students refocus. Dan has rituals like "silent countdown," structures to get students to their places efficiently, and delineated spaces for students to sit when on the floor. He uses inquiry to teach classroom rules and develop awareness. "Does the story ask the audience to talk right now?" "What does it ask us to do?" He celebrates and acknowledges the students who are ready to work and uses students' names to redirect and focus if necessary. (Sullivan 2011).

Tal Gribbons (2011a) also sets clear standards for engaged student-centered learning in the urban middle school where he teaches theatre. In all of Tal's classes and rehearsals, he teaches students stillness and the power and necessity of stillness in theatre work and in life. This is critical for young adolescents who are often tempted toward perpetual motion, interaction, and activity. Tal invites students who become unfocused to step into the hall to "get [their] wiggles out." He often tells them as they leave, "Remember this is your safe place" or "You're better than this." Without stopping his fluid interactions with students in the room, he regularly checks outside the door until a student self-determines she or he is ready to return to the classroom and the work at hand. Students are engaged in activities related to class objectives "bell to bell." In classes and rehearsals, he asks provocative questions that require students to "take it up a notch" by thinking critically about more effective ways to present a story onstage or to solve a design problem. When engaged in a production unit, students work purposefully on clear assignments as Tal guides them to make specific character choices and offers honest and detailed feedback with interjections of humor and supportive comments. At the close of each class he asks students what they learned that day and how it relates to theatre and their lives. Holding them accountable to think deeply, he follows with "What do you think? Why? Why did that speak to you?" (Gribbons 2011a).

When a student in Eleshia Crotwell's (2010a) class swore while performing a monologue in class, she used it as a teachable moment rather than publicly disciplining the student. Since there is a wide range of subject matter and language that might make students or parents in her community uncomfortable, when choosing monologues, Eleshia has "some classroom rules about what [...] you can say and what you can't say without [first] asking me for permission."

[This girl] burst out with a big "G— D—" right in the middle of her monologue. [...] [She] didn't do it to get attention. [...] She was working so hard that we didn't stop her. [...] At the end of her monologue, I immediately addressed it and talked to the kids [...] because [...] there was a good bit of "language" [in the monologue].

After talking with them about why they have rules regarding language in the classroom, Eleshia said

Let's talk about how the playwright chose those words for a very specific reason. [...] Why is it that the playwright would chose these particular words? What was the playwright trying to convey?" We had [...] a really great lesson about the choice of words and why words are chosen and the difference between a kid trying to push the envelope because they want to say every word in the book and a kid just honestly thinking that they're portraying the character. [...] I try really hard not to embarrass anyone [...] [and to make sure] that all [...] expectations are clear in the beginning, but if someone makes a mistake, it's not my goal to embarrass them. I look at [...] "How can I use that situation to teach a concept, even though I didn't expect to be in that situation?" (Crotwell 2010a)

After he started teaching at a new high school, C. Gary Cooper (2011c) had a classroom management challenge that turned into "a really rewarding moment with a student."

[This student] "is not a gang member, but he's in that atmosphere. He's a really tough kid, but very talented. [...] The first semester [I was there] he did everything he could to undermine what I was doing [...] in the Advanced [...] Production class. [...] Finally, at [the end of first] semester, I said "You're no longer in this class. I hope that you figure out what to do and how to behave, but for right now you're not behaving in a [...] positive manner. If you want to be in a Theatre Arts II class, which is [...] a continuation of Introduction to Theatre [...] and prove that you belong back in this class, great." It was a very tough love, father kind of thing, and you could tell he was shocked. [...] He ended up taking Theatre Arts II for the second semester and I've never seen a student change so dramatically. It was "Yes, sir," "No, sir" and his academics [...] [improved] in all areas. [...] From January to May it was incredible [to see] the change. [...] He's become one of our leaders [...] in our school. [...] His GPA from junior year on is stellar. [...] He is our "best" actor [...] [and] he is never at a rehearsal [...] [without] his lines memorized. He's never at a rehearsal late. [...] He re-auditioned [for the advanced class] and was invited back. [...] [It] made me really happy that he was able to change and that possibly I said something that helped change his life. [...] He looked like he was on the road to not graduating and becoming a product of the environment that he's from. [...] Now he's auditioning for colleges to be a theatre major. (Cooper 2011c)

Brendan Kelley (2011) strives to find balance in his learner-centered practice.

One of the most difficult aspects of teaching an introductory theatre course is finding the balance between keeping a disciplined classroom and encouraging creativity. I have found that it requires a healthy mix of empowerment and strong leadership. The students need to know that they have a stake in what happens in the classroom, but I am the ultimate authority. Without the strong leadership, the students do not feel safe enough to be creative, but if they do not feel any personal investment in the class, they lose motivation. [...] I want them to be able to take responsibility and ownership of the work, but I want to make sure I am not setting them up for failure. (Kelley 2011)

An undisciplined or lackadaisical learning environment serves no one. A safe, disciplined, and democratic learning space supports student experimentation and achievement. Those who use teaching tools like masters are spontaneous and responsive to students while providing order, discipline, and security from what can be a chaotic and disorganized world. Students in these programs are then free to express themselves and show confidence, ownership, efficacy, and high achievement.

DRAMA AND LEARNER-CENTERED PRACTICE

I was [...] hesitant to work with middle school kids and have them create their own drama. I thought it would be very hokey and wouldn't have much depth. [...] I got the kids working [...] and the classes came up with important issues that they were dealing with [...] [like] the topic of judging others. [...] After about a week [...] we had the Columbine tragedy here. [...] The kids were being bombarded with the media. I had the counselors come in. [...] We talked about what could [drive] a kid [...] to the point that he would do something like that. [...] The students decided they wanted to do [their applied theatre piece] in the hallway [...] because that's where most of this stuff, all the judgment, happens. [...] [We had] the audience sit in the middle and the action [...] [happened] around the audience. These kids [created] something that [was] important and that could make a difference in somebody's life.
Brianna Lindahl, Teacher

What learner-centered teaching and directing strategies are useful for secondary teachers to know? Laura McCammon (2002a) emphasizes that when young people assume significant responsibilities and form healthy relationships with adults and one another, they are able to move successfully through adolescence into adulthood. She believes that this is "particularly true in process or role drama structures or those employing [Dorothy] Heathcote's 'Mantle of the Expert'" (Heathcote and Bolton 1995). As Laura points out, this informal drama work, also labeled "creative drama," "process or role drama," "applied drama," or just "drama," is frequently overlooked at the secondary level as a dynamic learner-centered tool (McCammon 2002a, 9). A number of secondary school theatre teachers mention regularly drawing ideas from drama and applied theatre practitioners like Heathcote, Augusto Boal, Cecily O'Neill, Jonothan Neelands, Sharon Grady, and Michael Rohd. Teacher-artists find these interactive techniques engaging for students because informal drama and applied theatre provide structures through which students can think critically, ask questions, frame points of view, make decisions, take action, and face the consequences of their actions.

A study conducted in an urban middle school with students infamous for chronic discipline problems illustrates the impact informal drama can have on secondary school students (Nelson, Colby, and McIlrath 2001). The middle school students in the study participated in a series of five drama sessions. They took on the roles of faculty members in an alternative school, as well as college students, grand jurors, family therapists, social workers, and army personnel. They explored issues of discrimination, segregation, and inequity. A drama specialist actively drew on students' lived experiences as they interacted with their teacher in and out of role. In each session students had decision-making authority, control, and power, and their voices were actively sought out and heard.

> What was unmistakable, not only to the researchers but to the administration and to the teachers in the school, was a sudden and dramatic shift in the learning behavior of this particularly challenged group of students. The cause of this change in the behavioral and social dynamics clearly lay in the power of role to free each individual's voice and allow its expression, to provide a context that empowers students to make decisions, control outcomes, and observe the consequences of their ideas in action. Finally, drama legitimizes held knowledge and allows students to build new learning on old. (Nelson, Colby, and McIlrath 2001, 67)

When we use drama like this across the curriculum and for exploration of issues of interest to learners in our classrooms and productions, we have powerful tools to liberate young people as artists and human beings. Learner-centered drama, like that described above and in the lesson and rehearsal ideas shared at the end of each chapter, are but a few examples of this dynamic approach to best practice.

DIFFERENTIATING INSTRUCTION IN A LEARNER-CENTERED THEATRE PROGRAM

Designing learning based on assessment of individual students' needs and abilities enables all students to find success. This is a hallmark of best practice in a learner-centered program. Valerie Labonski (2011a) describes how she approaches differentiation in her entry level technical theatre classes.

> Students are actively engaged in decision making when working practically on sets in my [...] classes. Students are divided into small groups and assigned a specific project related to the set. The groups and assignments are [...] based on what is an appropriate challenge for the group and what grouping is going to be the most conducive to student engagement and success. For example, some female students, if they are paired with male students, are less likely to be actively engaged in the [tech theatre] project. So when assigning groups, some students are assigned to all female groups or all male groups.

As the projects are being assigned, some groups receive very detailed, step-by-step instructions. Some groups, receive [projects] in small chunks: "Construct a 4×8 platform lid." Once that task is complete they [receive] the next step in the process: "Cut six 6-foot legs." Other groups are given more general [guidance], for example, "We need to construct a $4 \times 8 \times 6$ foot platform." The students determine the best method for assembling [the] platform. They create the cut list [and] decide upon appropriate measurements and supplies.

The culture of the classroom has been established that any time a student has a question or is unsure of how to proceed on a practical project, they ask. [...] Throughout the class period, I am circulating, checking in with groups, answering questions, and providing guidance. (Labonski 2011a)

I am at my best when "they are being loud and [...] it's messy, but they are making the text their own."
Brendan Kelley,
Teacher

As discussed in Chapter 1, in Mandy Whitlock's (2011a) program, she groups students and creates assignments that allow group members to self-determine what project to pursue from a menu of options. (See page 42.) Teachers work individually with some students, helping them select appropriate performance material, while other students choose their own material from a collection of monologues or scenes, at the same time still other students are working with peers to develop original material and perform it.

Teacher-artists also plan their production seasons with the individual abilities and background of a wide range of students in mind. Holly Stanfield has built a program in mostly blue-collar Kenosha, Wisconsin, where her team of co-teachers do a cross section of nine to twelve productions a year. Students are enrolled in after-school, credit-earning classes for each production. Her students have been invited to premiere and record student versions of Music Theatre International shows and they have performed repeatedly at the International Thespian Festival. Holly and the other teachers in the program fashion the whole season around the needs and interests of the students.

What we do is audition the kids one time in the spring. [...] We usually have an audition base of about two hundred to two hundred and fifty kids. [...] Then we look at who we have and place them in productions, so that the child has auditioned only for placement and not for exclusion. Once the cast lists are posted, the kids decide if that is what they are interested in doing, and we proceed from there with the season. [Anyone who auditions is cast.]

[...] We [...] take a look at all of the cultures that we are serving in our community, and we try to make sure that we're giving an opportunity for every child to be able to participate. [...] If the child has an interest in going on in [theatre] and would like to build a resume and really wants to be involved, we can offer that to them by casting them in more than one thing annually. If not, it can just be [...] enrichment [...] and those kids are [...] working side by side.

[...] We definitely try to cast as many kids in major roles as we can. [...] That would really give a lot of different kids an opportunity. (Stanfield 2009)

Holly describes how she individualized her work with a student, ultimately changing a costume, to help the student realize her potential.

[I taught a student who is] an amazing talent – one of [...] the best voices I've ever worked with in my life – but [...] so shy [with] this gigantic instrument [...] and she [didn't] [...] quite know what to do with it. [...] I cast her as Aida. [...] She's a little bit heavy set, so probably not the exact type for that role, so I'm sure that that was uncomfortable for her. [We were] [...] trying to work through everything [...] as far as a self-image. [...] So we went through this whole process [...] We just kept coming back and trying again, trying to break down barriers [...] [and] to keep it within a [safe] framework of what they're going to be comfortable with and what I'm comfortable with them doing. [...] [Then we got to] [...] performance mode and [...] someone would walk in and say "She's amazing," but [I knew] she wasn't released. [So] I brought in a [...] [theatre] friend [...] and she said, "I hate the dress." And I said, "I don't particularly like the dress either." [...] So, mid-week, mid-run [...] I bought a [very expensive] dress. *I* bought it. The school didn't buy it. [...] She looked really great. [...] We re-did her hair and re-did the dress and [...] she walked out and she was a new girl on that stage. Just to watch what one little thing will do [for] a young woman. [...] She gained confidence through the whole thing. And it changed her. [...] These things do really change kids. (Stanfield 2009)

I am at my best when "it's almost like they don't need me. They are working in groups [or] teams. They take initiative. [...] They retain what I am trying to teach them and demonstrate that [they understand]." Tal Gribbons, Teacher

LEARNER-CENTERED PRACTICE IN PRODUCTIONS

While teaching high school, I was invited into a rehearsal for the musical to offer some ideas for choreography. The director, head of the choral program, directed all of the musicals. He arrived just before rehearsal was to begin. He started barking at the cast and crew to get started. There were no explanations or greetings. Most of the kids onstage looked anxious, unsure, or confused about what was expected of them and why they were being yelled at. They did their best to please and appease him so he would not throw one of his legendary tantrums and storm out of rehearsal. "OK, now stand over there!" he shouted. "No, turn toward the audience and hold your chest up. No, don't look at the floor. Look up. This is happy!" [...] Later that week, a few students were in my room complaining to each other about the director. Without judgment, I simply wondered aloud why they kept auditioning for his shows if they were so dissatisfied with the experience. They looked at me blankly. "Because we want to be in the musical." It made me think.

Producing theatre for an audience is a gratifying and an essential culmination of theatre study for many young people. Productions can be especially meaningful when the experience is used as a laboratory for application of classroom instruction, investigation of dramatic or musical theatre literature, refinement of students' original or devised work, and as a forum where students' interests and concerns can be voiced. Like learner-centered classroom work, learner-centered production work engages student performers, playwrights, directors, designers, technicians, and dramaturgs in dialogue, decision making, and individual and collective action. The students' place at the center of the production process is acknowledged, valued, and nurtured. Collaboration, co-ownership, risk taking, and experimentation are hallmarks of theatre-making with middle and high school students, just as they have been in the professional practice of directors like Anne Bogart, Lloyd Richards, Marshall Mason, Mark Lamos, Zelda Fischlander, Gordon Davidson. (Bartow 1988)

Learner-centered production work is dynamic and requires ongoing assessment of students' abilities, interests, and investment. Directing strategies grow from these assessments, dialogue with students, and a clear sense of the program's purpose and direction. Learner-centered directors exhibit spontaneity and a willingness to be engaged in the creative process *with* young people. As Anne Bogart has said,

My intent with actors is to "feed them" in such a way that they arrive at the conclusion or the performance that they ultimately feel is theirs because they discovered it. What does it matter which of us put in whatever elements?
Lloyd Richards

> directing is about feeling, about being in the room with other people – with actors, with designers, with an audience. [...] [It's] about breathing and responding fully to the situation at hand, being able to plunge and encourage a plunge into the unknown at the right moment. (Dixon and Smith 1995, 9)

When some of the students in my Directing the Young Performer class at The University of Texas first experience a learner-centered approach to directing, they are skeptical about "plunging." Despite all they might have heard about professional directors who work collaboratively, some are doubtful that working this way with secondary school students can be successful. Most of them have worked with directors who started the rehearsal process with a read-through and table work typically without any script exploration or ensemble building. They then were launched into blocking sessions in which their directors told them where to move, how, and then followed by immediate memorization of lines. Now they are at the university and their concepts of acting and directing are suddenly being disrupted. Some of them feel baffled or off-balance by work that invites the company into the theatre-making process and asks students for their opinions. Others feel this inclusionary way of working is a big waste of time or an unnecessary diversion. A student once commented, "When I was in high school no one ever asked us what

I intervene very delicately, through sharing with them what I know and through releasing their imaginations so they can share what they know. [...] Then the process is a living exploration. Zelda Fichlander

we thought. We aren't used to that." Fortunately, after most of these students adapt, devise, and practice learner-centered strategies in their own directing projects – and see the outcome with secondary school students – they change their views. After using learner-centered approaches with her own high school students, this same student enthusiastically commented, "It's the only way I direct now!"

Candace Koern (2011) talks about her approach to directing in a learner-centered manner.

> I try to offer a variety of exercises and assignments. Some will excel at one thing and some another. It is amazing to see their strengths come out with exposure to new material [...] and watching their peers excel and grow.
>
> Organic blocking is king in the early stages [...] just watching where the actors' instincts take them. Beyond the technical stuff like [the dramatic action requires that] "you have to come in from this door and cross to that window," I am always open and watching how the actors can inspire me [...] and they do! [...] A great actor is a thinking actor [...] [and] I encourage them to have ideas. (Koern 2011)

Mandy Whitlock (2010) describes how her whole company is engaged in productions.

> Rehearsals begin with the [...] actors and technicians working together as a company and doing as many activities together as possible. We begin with warm-ups as a group.
>
> [...] I work with a visual touchstone for each production that I call "source work." An area of the theatre is set aside for pictures and items to be brought in relating to the script or production. Each actor and technician must contribute to the wall with research pictures or items that represent ideas, character elements, plot emphasis, mood, commanding image or objectives. Students share these objects at the beginning of each rehearsal [...] Actors present the items in character and we can ask questions about the items as a company. Items could be pictures of other companies' productions, music, dramaturgy, literary analysis, music, or 3D objects that relate to story or character. The presentation and explanation of source work items [...] give [...] students ownership of the production and serve as a catalyst for rehearsal activities that improve understanding and communication for actors and technicians. This wall [...] of the theatre creates a visual for a unified concept and understanding for the show and it continues to grow through the process. At the conclusion of the production, the company votes for who they believe was the most improved company member and they are given the source work as a souvenir of the production.

When a theater technique or stage convention is regarded as a ritual and the reason for its inclusion in the list of actors' skills is lost, it is useless [...] No one separates batting a ball from the game itself.
Viola Spolin

BALANCING ART AND EDUCATION

We were working on a scene from a show. "What should I do?" Kent asked. He was shifting back and forth on his feet and his arms, dangling at his sides, seemed heavy and awkward. Kent meant "What should I do with my body? Should I move? Look somewhere? Stand?" I said, "Well, Jeff" (his character's name), "where are you at this moment?" "In my room." "What are you doing when this scene begins?" "Avoiding my parents." "OK, here are some props to work with if you'd like. Use whatever you need. This is your room. What might you be doing right now, at this specific moment, to avoid your parents?" The rehearsal progressed with me just asking questions, sidecoaching, and encouraging him and his scene partner to try lots of different choices. They explored and improvised action and dialogue related to the scene and then worked from the script. By the end of that rehearsal, they had found staging, business, line readings, and powerful moments of action and interaction that were comfortable for them and compelling for an audience. I didn't tell them what to do, when to do it, or how to do it, like I used to do. I didn't say, "I want you to…." I just prompted them to consider the dramatic truth of each moment of the scene. I helped them generate choices for each of those moments and then we shaped their choices into playable action. *They* made the choices. They felt like actors. I was right out of graduate school, and this was a whole new way of directing for me, but, with practice, I have come to love creating theatre in this way, *with* students.

When teacher-directors discuss directing in learner-centered productions, they talk passionately and with enthusiasm about their artistry and the shared artistic process. They often discuss aesthetics, the quality of the dramatic material they produce, and their innovative and provocative use of production values. In addition, they share educational, artistic, and ethical questions related to learner-centered theatre-making at the secondary level. These questions are explored in the remainder of this chapter.

- Is directing young performers different than or the same as directing adult actors?
- What is the ebb and flow between process and product?
- What are appropriate artistic standards for work with young artists?
- What are the intersections between classroom and production work?
- What are the unique demands of learner-centered production work for student playwrights, directors, designers, and performers?
- How does a learner-centered program save time in the long run?

DIRECTING YOUNG PERFORMERS VERSUS ADULT PERFORMERS

Michael Bloom, in his book *Thinking Like A Director* (2001), reminds readers that one of the director's most important responsibilities is to determine "the story" to tell, how the playwright's ideas are to be interpreted and presented to an audience. He says, "One of the most important functions a director fulfills is determining, with the actors, and designers, which story to tell and how to tell it coherently" (Bloom 2001, 5). A director must engage the company in this process so that they collectively translate ideas into images that make meaning for an audience.

Eighty five percent of school age children are natural kinesthetic learners [yet] [...] the school curriculum offers very few [...] kinesthetic learning techniques.
Carla Hannaford, Neuroscientist and Educator

When working with experienced actors, a director can assume the performers have skills, experience, and a certain degree of training with which to "tell the story." Seasoned actors have a working knowledge, not only of the art form of theatre, but also of how to work in this art form. They understand fundamental rehearsal practices, terminology, methods, and procedures. Veteran actors know how to analyze a text, develop a character, take direction, and fully participate in a collaborative rehearsal process.

With inexperienced performers, "telling the story" requires acquisition of this most basic information and skills. Most learner-centered teachers feel young people do not effectively learn these by rote or by replicating college or conservatory theatre programs that prescribe certain techniques. Spolin (1983) captures the problems with that approach.

> Techniques are not mechanical devises – a neat little bag of tricks, each neatly labeled, to be pulled out by the actor when necessary. When the form of an art becomes static, these isolated "techniques" presumed to make [up] the form are taught and adhered to strictly. Growth of both individual and form suffer thereby, for unless the student is unusually intuitive, such rigidity in teaching, because it neglects inner development, is invariably reflected in his performance.
>
> When the actor knows "in his bones" there are many ways to do and say one thing, techniques will come (as they must) from his total self. For it is by direct, dynamic awareness of an acting experience that experience and techniques are spontaneously wedded, freeing the student for the flowing, endless pattern of stage behavior. (Spolin 1983, 14)

This sense of student actors as learners is central to best practice. Teacher-directors in a learner-centered program *teach* information and skills so young people grow in their understanding, artistry and practice of theatre. This is less necessary when working with seasoned performers.

PROCESS-CENTERED AND PRODUCT-CENTERED INTERSECTIONS

Teacher-directors engaged in best practice use both process-centered and product-centered activities as they progress through rehearsals toward performance. In the true sense of the theatre as a laboratory for applying skills and knowledge, rehearsals are times of exploration, experimentation, and discovery. Both students and directors engage in critical thinking and decision making. Using theatre games, improvisations, drama techniques, field research, art, music, and movement, they reach decisions about text and character interpretation, business, and staging choices. Design and tech students are engaged in early rehearsals and are in leadership roles collaboratively making and implementing production decisions. As in my story with Kent at the beginning of this section (see page 73), the production environment these directors create with young people is a nurturing classroom imbued with the rigors of the theatre. Unlike productions in which unguided actors are left to flounder or where directors impose every choice, learner-centered directors' shared production processes yield investment, ownership, and performances of great depth, interest, artistry, and vibrancy.

Viola Spolin (1983) is a theatre education pioneer still ahead of her time. Her writings and her work with improvisation continue to inspire, challenge, and liberate performance from dogma and tradition. As improvisation is embedded in exploration of text, theme, character, and the relation of these to students' lives, young people find their authentic voices and power as performers. Spolin speaks clearly about this relationship between process and product.

It stands to reason that if we direct all our efforts towards reaching a goal, we stand in grave danger of losing everything on which we have based our daily activities. For when a goal is superimposed on an activity instead of evolving out of it, we often feel cheated when we reach it.

When the goal appears easily and naturally and comes from growth rather than forcing, the end result, performance, or whatever, will be no different from the process that achieved the result. [...] How much more certain would knowledge be if it came from and out of the excitement of learning itself. (Spolin 1983, 26)

Blending process and product to accommodate students' diverse learning styles requires a flexible style of directing. As in classroom work, these teachers make adjustments in their directing style throughout the rehearsal process, and even within each rehearsal, to keep the process learner-centered.

In any given production, a director may find the need to move back and forth along a continuum from a director- or product-centered approach to a learner- or process-centered one based on students' experience, skills, and their greater or lesser ability to engage in the collaborative process on a given text. (See Figure 2.4.) As anyone who has directed knows, there are an enormous number of decisions of varying magnitudes that must be made when mounting a show. Inviting all company members to make each decision is ludicrous, time consuming, and impractical. Wisdom and balance are needed to determine which decisions will promote students' growth as artists and individuals. Learner-centered teacher-artists are masters at finding decisions that empower each student. This ability results from keen observation, intuition, patience, practice, and a willingness to make a mistake or two along the way. The attention to individual students helps each grow as a young person and a young artist.

I used to block everything. Then I got more courage. I stopped writing the blocking on my script. [...] I try to know what the kernel of the scene is. [...] The embodiment I more or less work out with the actors.
Zelda Fichlander

Learning from my mistakes has helped me grow as an artist and teacher throughout my career. There have been times in the past when I was teaching high school or doing a youth theatre piece that I got so into the process that I almost lost sight of the students. We would brainstorm lots of ideas, interpretations, and staging choices for a given scene and I would ask them to make *a lot* of the decisions. Some actors loved experimenting and were happy to go home, make choices, and come to the next rehearsal ready to share. Others would look at me bewildered and confused, struggling for the "right" answer. They were unused to voicing their opinions or being asked to explore different options. I had mistaken their silence for contemplation. I needed to help them learn the actor's art and feel comfortable generating choices and making decisions. In these cases, I was so engaged with *my* collaborative directing process that I had missed the fact that we weren't really collaborating. We had not developed *our* process.

After recognizing this problem, I shifted my directing style and limited the number and nature of decisions I was asking each student to make. This made the work safer for them. I might offer them a suggestion as a starting point: "How about beginning this first moment sitting at the kitchen table?" If they looked uncomfortable after trying it, I might ask where else their character might be at that moment. I would also frame choices, giving them options. Referring to an actor by his character name I would say, "Carlos, would you be fixing a

Work with the student where he is, not where you think he should be.
Viola Spolin

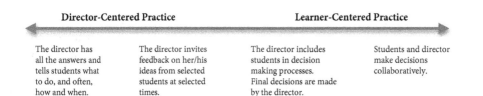

Director-Centered Practice		Learner-Centered Practice	
The director has all the answers and tells students what to do, and often, how and when.	The director invites feedback on her/his ideas from selected students at selected times.	The director includes students in decision making processes. Final decisions are made by the director.	Students and director make decisions collaboratively.

Figure 2.4: A Continuum of Directing Practices.

Figure 2.5: Those who make theatre with secondary school students must be both artists and teachers.

meal or doing the dishes at this point?" Sometimes they would come up with another alternative and we would grow the scene from there. I also scheduled shorter rehearsals with students new to the program, used more theatre games, improvisations, and ensemble activities, and I included more experienced students in rehearsals who could model decision making and explorative work. Active decision making got them away from acting in their heads, analyzing every choice, and instead got them into their bodies, moving and playing each moment intuitively and kinesthetically. At first I asked them to do less on their own outside of rehearsals, but eventually they became the veterans modeling this collaborative process.

Fursey Gotuaco (2002) talks about how learner-centered production work frees students interested in design and technical theatre to be decision-makers.

> I've [seen] how much more mature [my students] are because they've had so many [...] opportunities to make decisions and see how their decisions impact a wider circle of people around them. [...] Each show has a [student] technical director and designers. [...] They [...] work directly with the crew heads who decide everything that they need and how they can create it under budget. [...] They've got to figure out "How can I motivate [crew members] to work [...] without losing the friendship?" And for [...] them [...] power and authority [...] [is] kind of new. And [...] they've got to learn how to give and take criticism. [...] And [...] when they hit a snag [...] it's reality. It's a real problem that they've got to solve.

Patsy Koch Johns, who teaches in Lincoln, Nebraska, captures the spirit that is at the heart of this approach to theatre making.

> Theatre is collaborative. [...] It takes a director to control and orchestrate [...] but if that control becomes too egocentric, then [...] I don't think the art evolves in the right way. And the power of many is certainly more powerful artistically than the power of one [...] Maybe that's why theatre is so amazing to people [...] Maybe our amazement comes from the fact that it comes from many. I don't have to stand alone. [...] It's not a lonely art. (Johns 2002)

The power and joy that comes from theatrical collaboration with young people is a theme that emerges often in conversations with these teacher-artists.

Figure 2.6: A production of *The Secret Garden*.

ARTISTIC STANDARDS IN A LEARNER-CENTERED PROGRAM

Stanislavski is credited with saying something to the effect "There is a difference between theatre for adults and theatre for children. Theatre for children should be better." There *should* be high artistic standards for theatre with young performers. How many of us cringe to hear, "That was a terrific *high school* play" or "That was a great job for *middle school kids*." These comments create a second class of theatre and provide a justification for poor quality work. Many teachers look at these comments not as compliments but as excuses for work that is not fully realized or is otherwise ill suited to the company. Theatre is theatre. It is either compelling, entertaining, and meaningful, or it is not. This is not to say that we – like so many others who earn their living as directors – have not had our share of glorious failures. It means that we do not have a different artistic standard just because our company members are kids.

Part of the problem is the kind of plays some directors choose to produce with young people. While selection of dramatic material is discussed at length in Chapter 3, it is appropriate here to point out how poor play selection can perpetuate a culture of "high school theatre" and lower artistic standards. When directors deliberately use unprepared student-artists, limited facilities, and small budgets to produce plays created originally for Broadway, they often are setting students up to fail. Even if plays from Broadway and the regional theatre repertoire are developmentally appropriate for students to see and perform, we must carefully assess our skills, our students' needs, and our human and material resources before launching into production. The question to ask is not, "How can I do this play?" but "How can producing this play be both an artful and learner-centered experience for all involved?"

It is also an issue of how we approach the plays we choose to direct. Children never benefit when we lower or limit our expectations of them. Learner-centered directors have committed themselves to helping students define and meet high standards. They are problem solvers and solution finders who develop and improvise techniques that stretch their own artistry and enable students to learn the crafts of theatre making. Their rehearsals are learning laboratories where, for example, students discover expressive use of their bodies and voices as well as tools for developing compelling scenes and characters. These teachers regularly see other directors' work, attend classes and workshops, and adopt new directing techniques.

I want students to dream big. I [...] want them to know what it takes to make dreams a reality and sometimes that requires me to push them and make them uncomfortable and require them to work hard. And I am reminded that it requires the same of me. Lena Paulauskas, Teacher

CRITICAL RESPONSE TO STUDENT WORK

I have the utmost respect for each and every student who is brave enough to sign up for a theatre class, because it is rather scary to enter a world that puts the individual under a microscope for others to observe. I am gentle with their insecurities and adolescent angst which play a major role in how well they do as emerging artists. [...] Letting them know that their progress, no matter how small, does not go unnoticed by me is a great confidence booster. I was raised by the "silent" generation: "No news is good news, hop to it, because I said so [...], etc." I always had insecurities about just where I lined up in the big scheme of things. I never knew if I was growing in the right direction; I only knew that I wasn't screwing up. Young people need feedback! Candace Koern, Teacher

When we talk about artistic standards for work with young people, questions about appropriate critical response to their work arise. Post-performance feedback sessions can be occasions where classmates or audience members intersperse a few positive remarks with comments like "Well, I would have done it this way," or "I didn't get it," or "Why did you put her in *that* dress?"

One approach is to have students learn the role of critic. In south Florida, Julia Perlowski's students partner with journalism students for the Cappies (Critics Awards Program). Through this international project, high school students in theatre and journalism are "trained as critics, attend shows at other schools, write reviews, and publish reviews in local newspapers. [...]" Julia's school has a critics team and she has "entered [...] plays in Cappies contests in order to be critiqued by forty students on every aspect of our play productions" (Perlowski 2011c).

Engaging in meaningful dialogue about student work and understanding the importance of – and especially the differences in – the roles of critic and audience member is essential to positive student development in a secondary theatre program. Liz Lerman is a performer, choreographer, educator, and founder of the Liz Lerman Dance Exchange. She has evolved an artist-centered approach to criticism that makes audience response an opportunity for dialogue grounded in mutual respect. Her multi-step approach is equally effective for classroom work, rehearsal feedback, and post-show talk-back sessions (Lerman and Borstel 2003).

Lerman's process involves first inviting statements of meaning from responders. "What was stimulating, surprising, challenging, meaningful for you?" (Lerman and Borstel 2003, 19). This is followed by focused questions about the work posed by the artists themselves (Lerman and Borstel 2003, 19–20). After addressing the artists' questions, responders ask the artists informational or factual questions in a neutral manner.

During these feedback [sessions] I am continually surprised by how respectful, insightful, and honest my students are in their responses to each other's work. I feel that it is my job as a teacher to create opportunities like these. If you empower students as artists and thinkers, they will rise to the occasion and exceed our expectations. Valerie Labonski

Instead of saying, "It's too long" (an opinion) or "Why are your pieces always so long?" (a question that couches an opinion) a person might ask "What were you trying to accomplish in the final section?" or "Tell me the most important ideas you want us to get and where is that happening in this piece?" [...] The actual process of trying to form opinions into neutral questions enables the responder to recognize and acknowledge the personal values at play. Often these are the very questions that the artist needs to hear. (Lerman and Borstel 2003, 20–21 and 23)

My biggest goal [...] as a teacher is to have the students strive for excellence in all aspects [...] of not only [...] theatre, but [of] being a human being.
Eleshia Crotwell, Teacher

The next step in Lerman's process is to share opinions by permission. Permitted opinions follow a protocol that allows the artist to retain control of what is shared.

Responders first name the topic of the opinion and ask the artist for permission to state it. For instance, "I have an opinion about the costumes. Do you want to hear it?"

In response, the artist has the option to say "yes" or "no." The artist may have several reasons for not wanting to hear the opinion: Perhaps he has already heard enough opinions about the costumes and wants to move to something else. Perhaps he is very interested in hearing about the costumes, but not from that responder. Or perhaps the opinion is irrelevant because [...] the costumes used for the showing have nothing to do with those planned for the ultimate presentation. [...] In most cases, however, the artist will say "yes" because the process has laid the groundwork for this moment. (Lerman and Borstel 2003, 22)

I have been involved in this process as an artist and as a respondent. I have adapted it for use in my college classes and I encourage my student teachers to use it in their work. This approach can change critical response experiences from "blood-letting sessions" to opportunities for open communication and understanding. Ultimately, this approach to critical response leads to a culture of respect, better art, and better insight into others' artistic processes.

INTERSECTIONS BETWEEN CLASSROOM WORK AND PRODUCTIONS

A learner-centered approach to theatre *must* be part of both classroom instruction *and* the production process. Many teachers make conscious connections between work in theatre classes and work in the production "laboratory," their after-school theatre programs. While all produce plays, some teachers have production classes during the school day solely for strengthening these connections. Many teachers present student-written and directed work. Some schools have one theatre class while others have a sequential curriculum of many courses. Whatever the individual configuration of productions and classes, these master teachers recognize that they are always teaching. They situate themselves comfortably in the role of teacher-artist and encourage their pupils to view themselves as student-artists. To unify their programs, they incorporate improvisation and acting exercises, research, design, theatre technology, audition techniques, stage management, rehearsal etiquette, and work with text, voice, and movement in classes *and* rehearsals.

Blending performance and learning can have other benefits. Like many other teachers, Rick Garcia (2002) mounts a production with each of his high school theatre classes. He varies the kind of work produced to accommodate the skills and interests of the students in each class. For beginning level students, many of whom have limited English skills, he uses "Talk Theatre." Students write personal narratives and Rick works with them individually and collectively to produce an original performance of their poems, monologues, and scenes. This approach encourages students to find and share their voices with others, whether in English or their first language. Rick has found this a particularly effective approach in classes where students are academically challenged, feel marginalized, apathetic, ambivalent, or reluctant to participate in school. With some students, Rick works in small increments. He will coach some students one on one, moving them from one line of dialogue spoken while sitting by Rick's desk to a fully performed monologue from one of Shakespeare's plays. In this way, Rick is reaching each child in a learner-centered manner along a fluid process-product continuum (Garcia 2002). (Chapter 3 offers additional examples of work with English language learners.)

The creative melding of curriculum and performance also allows students to apply their knowledge and skills in wider circles of influence. A teacher from the state of Washington, for example, developed a theatre-in-education (TIE) class for her high school students. Students devised interactive theatre pieces about topics of concern to them. They then worked as actor-teachers, touring their pieces to area schools, engaging audience members in and out of role, and facilitating dialogue about the issues raised in the play. Teachers like Sandy DiMartino and Steve Bogart regularly devise plays with their classes to foster conversations about social change with school and public audiences (Bogart 2003a; DiMartino 2003). (See page 202 for an example of their work.)

Given the state of theatre education nationally, as discussed in Chapter 1, these teachers are the exception. The link between curricular and co-curricular work is not the norm. Emphasis and value is still often placed on productions. In more and more schools, however, the days are gone when being a great director and winning the one-act play contest can compensate for poorly managed

I want to give kids a chance who don't normally get a chance. I get a lot of raised eyebrows when [other teachers] hear who's in my shows. But once [these students] get in our department, [the teachers] don't have any problems with them anymore because they find a place [where they belong]. [...] I really like to root for the underdog. [...] I get the most joy [...] seeing those kids find a place. Billie Harvey, Teacher

classrooms and programs focused on productions that serve only "the most talented" students. That is not to say that those engaged in best practice are not concerned with or do not value performances of the highest quality. It means that because our performers are students, we must be both skilled artists *and* skilled teachers. Teacher-directors must select dramatic material and classroom and rehearsal activities that help students develop as artists *and* as human beings. Best practice directors are knowledgeable about theatre, contemporary directing practices, *and* how to teach about and through theatre. They know how best to engage and teach a wide range of young people while producing high-quality theatre.

DEVISING AND PRODUCING STUDENT WORKS

Generating or producing original performance pieces with students is a common element of best practice. Some teachers devise original plays with students using what has been called "collective creation" (Lang 2002). Others teach playwriting, or their students participate in young playwrights events. Some students create work independently or in small groups as part of a class, festival, or showcase of student work. Most often, the work allows students to reflect about and tell the stories that reveal the truths of their lives. (Resources about devising are included at the end of this chapter and sample devising projects are included in Chapter 3 and Chapter 5.)

Renee Norris (2011c) teaches at a Title I school in one of the nation's largest cities. In her Theatre II class, she taught a playwriting unit that culminated in completion of original plays by small groups of students just before their winter break.

> At that point the students could put the play to rest or they could take my written comments, the student readers' comments, and the audience comments to do revisions and prepare a final draft for entrance into a local playwriting festival. I open[ed] [...] the topic with, "I am so proud of you and your accomplishments and I truly believe that each one of you would do very well in the contest; however, it is not necessary for you to continue with this. You can take your grade and be done." I [...] [told them] what the next step [toward the contest] would be and gave them a one-week deadline [after the break] to make the revision and print the final drafts. Many students were passionate about their classmates' work and [they] encouraged each other to move forward. [...] [After the break] I asked the students [...] [who] would submit [their play for the contest] and every student raised their hands – twenty kids, twelve plays. [...] Half of those plays were edited over break, ready to print and mail. [...] Kids

When the old stories of group (communal) belonging no longer ring true, demand grows for the "identity stories" in which "we tell ourselves about where we came from, what we are now and where we are going." Such stories are urgently needed to restore security, build trust, and make "meaningful interaction with others" possible.
Jeffrey Weeks, Sociologist

were getting together to edit – without a teacher request – during Christmas. Incredible! I have two Theatre II classes, and later that day the story was the same. I was so impressed at how our process meant so much to them that they could not let it go, even over a break. (Norris 2011c)

Teachers also commission artists-in-residence to write plays for their students or to partner with students in the development of a new work. (Partnerships between schools and local artists are discussed further in Chapter 5.)

Questions about artistic quality and appropriate critical response often arise with production of new works with and by students. How does a teacher engaged in learner-centered practice address these questions?

The pressures to play "Beat the Clock" when devising or developing new material for the stage can tempt us to sacrifice artistic quality and elements of learner-centered practice. As playwright James Still commented during a visit to The University of Texas at Austin, "There is never enough time. Even if we had twice as long, it wouldn't be enough time" (Still 2003). Producing original work requires considerable organization, flexibility, and great discipline so students can move successfully through the development and production processes within the time available. That requires negotiation throughout the process regarding who makes what decisions, when, and how the company will handle the inevitable feeling that "We need more time!"

There are other challenges to consider and respond to when creating original work in a learner-centered environment. In her article, "Collaborative Creativity in a High School Drama Class," Debra McLauchlan (2001) comments on the need for balance between students' freedom and teacher-imposed structure. Speaking about a class play project she writes, "Direct teacher intervention sometimes provoked either silent hostility or withdrawal of commitment. A more positive approach was a negotiated effort to bridge differences." She also identifies the need for a "sense of shared identity" and that "[a]greement on common goals provided the most productive basis for conflict resolution" (McLauchlan 2001, 55).

Working for a balance of freedom and structure can directly affect the artistic quality of original or student-devised work. How do we develop work with or by young people that allows them to voice their concerns and interests but also allows them to look at their work critically? This is a slippery slope in a learner-centered program. Original works are often deeply personal expressions by artists and can pose special challenges for directors devising work with emerging adolescents. Interactions must allow students freedom of expression while also helping them develop their own aesthetics in relation to the range of critical standards in our field. The following incident illustrates the need for a balance of freedom and structure.

When teaching high school in Austin, Roxanne Schroeder-Arce annually produced *VOICE*, a showcase of student written work. A student playwright whose work was included in the showcase had told actors to add some unrehearsed, sexually explicit material for the first evening's performance. After seeing the performance, Roxanne reminded him that no unrehearsed material was to be performed because it is unfair to those who must call cues and perform in the play. She stressed that this rule had been discussed during the production process. She made clear that only work that had been refined, rehearsed, and of predictable artistic merit was to be performed. During the second performance, the student again added unrehearsed material. With actors still onstage, Roxanne asked the stage manager to call the actors in the next piece to "places" and to cue the lights for a cross-fade into that play. Afterwards, there was a heated confrontation by a group of students who felt the playwright had been censored (Schroeder-Arce 2002b).

In this incident, social, educational, and even moral implications of encouraging student-developed work came to light. For Roxanne it was not a censorship issue; the fact that the unrehearsed material was sexually explicit was not the primary discussion point. Instead, she chose to focus on the guidelines for appropriate theatre practice that they had all agreed upon. The guidelines needed to be upheld. A discussion was later held and students talked about their feelings. Some students expressed gratitude that she was adhering to the rules and the situation was resolved after conversations with all involved.

It is interesting to note that when this student playwright learned that Roxanne was moving to a position in another state, he was the most vocal about the future of the program, especially the playwriting project. He wondered who would carry on the showcase and encourage students to express themselves in the important way Roxanne had done in *VOICE*. It seems he realized that art comes with both freedom and responsibility and is something to be valued.

In my devising work with young performers, we consider and think critically about the personal ideas that emerge. We then use movement, improvisation, text exploration, and revision techniques to lift what might be self-indulgent contemplations, moderately humorous stories, weak portrayals, or a venting of adolescent angst to a level where the images and ideas resonate for audience members and are stageworthy and artful. Additional ideas for developing work with young artists and selected rehearsal strategies are included at the end of this chapter and throughout the book.

I utilize as much of an actor's contribution (or a designer's) as I can, and edit out the rest. I am the organizer of others' impulses. Mark Lamos

TIME INVESTMENT

This emphasis on learner-centered production work will require more rehearsal time *at the outset* than in a more traditional "read, stage, and run" model. As interactive process work leads to product, however, directors are saved a lot of time and frustration. During the last, sometimes hectic, days of rehearsals, these learner-centered directors are working with an ensemble that owns its production and understands the story they are telling. The students assume their artistic and social responsibilities to the play and to the cast. They are able to add nuances and make needed adjustments in timing and tempo to artfully "tell the story" they collectively created.

Marissa Meek directs by

> [letting] the actors move in the manner that they feel motivated to move and only change what they are doing if it is necessary to future action, interferes with the style of the production, or creates some other problem. Once a new unit or scene is blocked, we "repeat it till it sticks." I find this approach [...] [results in] lines and blocking [...] [learned] in a timely manner with little fuss [...] [and results] in a natural and easy feel to the production. Most importantly, it gives the students ownership of their characters. [...] [M]y actors also do a lot of work on their costumes and I find the reflection they engage in during that process is a boon to character development as well.
>
> Once, at a [...] one-act play competition, a judge was blown away by the costumes and asked who came up with the idea. [...] We all – cast, crew, alternates, and director – looked at each other blankly, because we couldn't remember! That's how much of an organic team effort our theatre is. (Meek 2010)

[My teacher] works with you on how to identify with your character. [...] She'll work with you one on one. She just takes a lot of time for that. Theatre Student, Bowling Green High School

Teaching and directing from a learner-centered standpoint means "front-loading" the labor-intensive aspects early in the production process. Investing time in assessing students' skills, learning styles, interests, and knowledge at the beginning of the process enables these teacher-directors to frame objectives and design lessons and rehearsal plans that maximize students' opportunities for success throughout the process. Changes in teaching style and directing practices require a *different* use of time, but ultimately not more time. Helping students learn strategies for making their own acting, design, technical, or dramaturgical choices at the beginning and throughout rehearsals means directors are not spending time during tech week reminding students of their blocking and lines, having beat-the-clock crew calls, or doing lobby displays alone. If teachers are sharing decisions, and students are becoming increasingly self-directed and engaged, then the teacher is spending less time giving orders and directions and more time being a facilitator and resource for learning. This approach enables students to feel the power of self-discovery as well as the consequences of neglected responsibilities.

In a learner-centered program, students create and take on leadership roles in a learning community where knowledge is shared, passed along to the next generation, and deepened. These are programs that relieve the teacher of the burden of micro-management and the drudgery of constantly having to re-teach how to call cues, how to operate the light board, and that it is okay to make an acting choice or have an opinion about blocking.

Voices from the field
LEARNER-CENTERED PRACTICES

EMBRACING DIGITAL MEDIA IN A LEARNER-CENTERED PROGRAM – AMY JENSEN

Amy Jensen (2011) moves easily between the realms of live theatre and digital media. She understands the role they can play in students' lives and the need to include and celebrate both in a twenty-first century, learner-centered theatre program. Amy shares her views and how she approaches these topics with future teachers in her university's theatre education program.

Great theatre teachers, by my definition, work to engage young people in learning experiences where their minds and body are used as performance tools. Their classrooms are filled with creative production and process models that are designed to help students use their drama tools to investigate the conditions of their contemporary world.

Stephani Etheridge Woodson (2004) supports this notion when she says that the best theatre classrooms value students' perspectives, understandings, and circumstances. She says that teachers should always be asking themselves questions like, "Does this [activity, play, or curriculum] illuminate the lives and social experiences of our student populations?" and "How do we let our students know that theatre is there for them and about them?" (Woodson 2004, 28). Like Woodson, I believe that we must let our students know that theatre is for them and about them. We must help them to see that theatre can celebrate ideas that are important to them, and address issues that they care about. These aspirations make it essential that twenty-first century theatre teachers think carefully about the connections between theatre and digital media.

Digital media (social networking, mobile culture, digital remix, hyperlinked multimodal content, etc.) is a part of nearly every facet of our social, cultural, and educational lives. These new realities of everyday life require that teacher-educators begin to consider how interactions with those digital tools shape our student's minds and bodies.

Like other educators, theatre teachers must be prepared to engage young people in learning processes where they are required to use and understand digital media. Twenty-first century learning models require that educators of all subject areas, but especially the arts, address digital media and employ social media and digital literacies to aid young people as they prepare to engage with others in our world.

My biggest question is what does this look like in a theatre classroom? How should theatre teachers prepare themselves to engage young learners who are fully immersed in digital media activities in their out-of-school lives? And how should theatre teachers integrate digital media concepts and literacies into their theatre curriculum and instruction?

My answer is that theatre teachers can engage students in the questions and concerns that arise out of our digital environment by embracing theatre's essential quality: meaning making. Using theatre tools (process dramas, devising, forum theatre, and other applied theatre techniques) teachers and students can engage with prevalent themes brought about through their interactions with digital media. With these tools they can begin to articulate who they are in a digitally saturated world. I, along with other theatre practitioners and educators, believe that drama teachers are uniquely suited to engage with students who consider themselves digital experts because of the inherent exploration of the human condition in theatre narratives. Australian teachers John Carroll, Michael Anderson, and David Cameron (2006) encourage us in this vein saying, "Drama teachers who understand the emerging performance conventions inherent in mediated learning communities can use them to engage their students to explore authenticity and role-based identity in new ways" (Carroll, Anderson, and Cameron 2006, xvi).

Through the processes of developing integrated digital learning experiences for K–12 theatre classrooms, I have found it helpful to consider what digital media experts describe as the essential skills for understanding and using these new technologies. For example, media scholar Henry Jenkins (2006) provides a list of competencies necessary to succeed in digital environments. His list of new skills includes:

- *Play*: the capacity to experiment with one's surroundings as a form of problem-solving.
- *Performance*: the ability to adopt alternative identities for the purpose of improvisation and discovery.
- *Simulation*: the ability to interpret and construct dynamic models of real-world processes.
- *Appropriation*: the ability to meaningfully sample and remix media content.
- *Multitasking*: the ability to scan one's environment and shift focus as needed to salient details.

- *Distributed Cognition*: the ability to interact meaningfully with tools that expand mental capacities.
- *Collective Intelligence*: the ability to pool knowledge and compare notes with others toward a common goal.
- *Judgment*: the ability to evaluate the reliability and credibility of different information sources.
- *Transmedia Navigation*: the ability to follow the flow of stories and information across multiple modalities.
- *Networking*: the ability to search for, synthesize, and disseminate information.
- *Negotiation*: the ability to travel across diverse communities, discerning and respecting multiple perspectives, and grasping and following alternative norms.

By comparing Jenkins's list against the learning goals for my theatre classroom, I begin to see where our theatre understandings, tools, and curriculum can intersect effectively and aid students in their explorations of their new world (Jensen 2011).

Voices from the field

SHARED DECISION MAKING – BRENDAN KELLEY

Brendan Kelley (2011) actively reflects about ways he can share decision making, ownership, and investment in the work with his high school students.

> One of my most important jobs as a theatre teacher is to get [students] to make their own decisions and discoveries about their characters. [...] I require them to make 90 percent of the [...] decisions about their characters. [...] "How do you want me to play this part," is always met with, "How does it make sense to you?" [...] This forces them to evaluate, analyze and synthesize, as in Bloom's higher-level thinking skills. Also, it gets them to realize that there are many different ways to solve a problem. After they present the decisions they have made in their performance, the class evaluates them. All of these skills are what Dan Pink emphasizes as "twenty-first century skills" in his book, *A Whole New Mind*.[4]
>
> I realize that true constructivists would say, "Why don't you have the students decide what they want to learn about at the beginning of the year and have them create their curriculum with you? What better way to promote intrinsic motivation?" I think that works well with subjects that have been historically taught with lectures, but [...] theatre is a different animal. The students will be presented with the opportunity to create and make something [of] their own many times in a theatre class. They need to first know that they are safe to experiment, and a structured environment at the beginning of the year lets them feel grounded in the class. If you leave too many of the decisions up to the students, there will come a point where they will not be able to distinguish the creative decisions from the managerial decisions and will get fed up with always having to make the decisions. Then you've actually stifled their motivation to think creatively.
>
> In my production work, the theory is similar to that of the classroom, but the balance is very different. [...] My job is to keep us on track and get all our boats

sailing towards the same goal. [...] I have spent years with my production students gradually shifting more and more responsibility of leadership and creativity [...] to them. [...] I have baby stepped away from responsibilities that I had taken (costumes, characterization, pressure for learning lines, even scheduling rehearsals), and let them take over more and more. For example, we performed *Our Town* this semester. I cut back on the number of after school rehearsals I had scheduled so that they could decide whether they wanted to add rehearsals back in. I did not tell them that adding rehearsals was an option, but I would ask them how they felt about the show after the rehearsals. They were nervous about the show (especially because we had lost four days to snow) and wanted [...] extra rehearsals. [...] This was their show. If they had decided against it, I would have respected that decision. However, I knew the group, and I knew that they would take it upon themselves to request more days [if they felt it was needed.] That's the "playing it by ear" part. [...] I am still trying to work out that balance between cultivating the student and cultivating the program. (Kelley 2011)

Voices from the field

"ASKING QUESTIONS IS AN AWFUL LOT EASIER" – REBECCA JALLINGS

Rebecca Jallings taught high school theatre at West High School in Madison, Wisconsin. She describes how her students helped her rethink and develop a learner-centered practice.

> I started teaching at West as a forty-year-old woman who had lived my life in a pretty white world. [...] I had [...] black kids in my Theatre I classes [and] [...] I just couldn't stand the way I was with them. [...] I was always sure I was going to say the wrong thing or do the wrong thing. So [...] I went out and tried to find books on how to make this sort of translation for myself. [...] Of course, they don't exist, or they didn't then.
>
> Then [...] the [Madison] Rep did *Fires in the Mirror* by Anna Deveare Smith. [...] I hired [...] a black actor from Chicago [...] [to come] into my class [as a guest artist]. [...] He worked with the kids in theatre and talked about issues of race. [...] At the same exact time I was starting to work on my Master's degree. [...] I was videotaping small groups as they worked on their movement projects [...] [and] would just turn the camera on and let it run.
>
> So, I'm being bombarded with all these ideas [from the guest artist] and [...] I'm looking at the tapes of the kids in my classes. [...] [In] every single one [...] the black kid is in the circle, but one step physically backed out of the circle, or half turned away from the circle. And the black kids are completely quiet. They don't say anything. They do what they're told by the white kids [...] they just don't offer any ideas. And they're just barely [...] connected.
>
> I'm thinking to myself, "I have created [a safe] environment in a theatre class [...] but [...] I have completely silenced the black kids cause they have bought into the idea that we're all going to be nicer to each other here than we are in the rest of the school." [...] It was as if they'd been co-opted into shutting up. [...] The black kids didn't want to be unfriendly. They weren't going to be disruptive

94

because they liked me, they liked the class. [...] But it certainly wasn't their stuff that they were doing; it was the white kids' stuff.

Rebecca decided to interview her students about their movement projects.

Some of the white kids were really damning of the black kids: "They didn't do anything. They just sort of stood around. We had to always call her back to work." I was just horrified. [...] [The black kids] [...] said that the project really didn't have anything to do with them and that the music they used [...] didn't relate to them in any way and [...]. "Why were [the white girls] rude?" [...] I said [...] "Did you act on that at all? Did you say anything to them?" [...] [They said] "No, we didn't want to [...] do that." [...] [One student] said "I get along with white kids okay. White kids got more money than I do. They have better lives than I do, but I get along with them. We all have the same class." [...] This was his reason for keeping quiet during class. I was [...] heartbroken.

I got my student teacher to make transcripts of the tapes [from the kids' interviews] [...] and I made a play out of it like *Fires in the Mirror*. I took exactly what the kids said in these small group projects [...] and I wrote it into a play. At the end of the semester [...] they wanted to see it. [...] I said [...] "How about if the kids who are in it view it first and if they're comfortable with it, then yes, we'll read it in class." Not only did they say "OK," but they all read their own parts.

I'm really comfortable talking to my kids now. [...] I realized that I get to make mistakes. And then you say you're sorry. You say "Explain it to me and I'll understand." [...]. You finally figure out that [as in] everything else in life, the only way you're going to get anywhere is by trying it and being ready to say you're sorry. [...] Now [...] if there's something I don't understand about what they're saying, what they're doing, I don't brush it off. I stop and say, "Wait a minute, what does that mean? Explain that to me. I'm very white. I'm fifty-four, explain that to me." Asking questions is an awful lot easier. (Jallings 2002)

Voices from the field

WHEN SURPRISING THINGS HAPPEN – VALERIE LABONSKI

When Valerie Labonski (2002) taught at Morton West High School near Chicago, she directed a production of Michael Frayn's play within a play, *Noises Off*. This experience shows the power of student ownership in a theatre program.

> It's the end of the third act. Planned chaos is ensuing on stage. As Gary falls down the stairs he clips the grocery box [with] the glass bottle of cider. The cider not only rolls down the stairs, but off the stage into the house […] [and] the bottle shatters. So [the actors onstage] have their moment of discovery with Gary at the bottom of the stairs. Then Poppy, the assistant stage manager [in the world of the play] trots out – in character – with a broom and a dustpan. She quickly sweeps up the mess and trots off. As she is doing this [the actors] all […] stop […] and, in unison and in character, react to Poppy's clean-up. A few seconds later Poppy comes back out with a mop. And they react again. It was hilarious. After the show I went backstage with a neutral look on my face and asked Maria, the [actual] stage manager, whose idea it was to send out Poppy. She […] said "It was mine." […] I told her it was a brilliant idea. Then I asked how she came to that decision. [She said she had] talked it over with [the] student tech director and [the actor playing] Poppy. At first Maria was going to clean it up, but [she thought] that would break the world of the play. Then they decided that Poppy wouldn't break [that] world […] and when it was received so well, the mop seemed like the next logical thing to do. Then I talked to the actors, who, [as if] on cue, responded "acting is reacting," which I had been saying […] throughout the rehearsal process. [Their] moment of discussion and decision making never would have happened if I had been back stage. They would have turned to me and [their] idea never would have crossed my mind. (Labonski 2002)

The students must bring their own perspective and actions to the process for it to be successful. I am not creating a puppet show when I produce a show. I want all participants to collaborate with ideas and actions.
Mandy Whitlock

96

Voices from the field

WE DO NOT PRODUCE HIGH SCHOOL THEATRE – DAVE AND DONNA BARNES

Dave Barnes (2002) and Donna Barnes (2002) both taught in Illinois at Oswego High School. Together they created a family-like atmosphere within their theatre program. Dave and Donna nurture students and build self-esteem while setting and meeting high standards in all aspects of the program. Here is an excerpt from their *Theatre Handbook* (Barnes 1999).

> The Theatre Department at Oswego High School is designed to assist students in discovering the joys of theatre while maintaining a high quality of production. Students who desire to be involved in the program should understand that while theatre can be a lot of fun, it also involves discipline and an understanding of the need to work toward quality.

> - At this high school we do *not* produce "High School Theatre."
> - We produce quality theatre performed by high school students.

> The preceding statements [...] describe two different sets of attitudes about high school theatre. The first sentence describes productions where the feeling is "Well what did you expect? They're just high school kids." The thought is an expression of mediocrity and inferior theatre. The second sentence states an attitude of professionalism. [...] The constant striving for excellence results in quality theatre and an exciting experience for all concerned. (Barnes 1999, 1)

A Closer Look
LEARNER-CENTERED CLASSES AND PRODUCTIONS

DIRECTOR OR DICTATOR? – FRANK CHUTER

Frank Chuter (2011c) is recognized for the artistry and honesty that his students bring to the stage. Frank radically changed his directing style after attending a convention session entitled "Director or Dictator."

> I remember my third year teaching, I was so very much "it's my way or the highway" that I got students quite upset. [...] One of the students got so aggravated with me that he said "F___ You!" and walked off stage. [...] I realized at that point [...] that if I am driving a student to say that, there's something wrong.

In the midst of rehearsals for that show, Frank attended the Texas Educational Theatre Association convention where "a lightbulb went off" and his "[directing] process started to change."

> I realized, "[...] This isn't about [me]. Start making it about the students. Give the students freedom to explore. Guide them, but give them freedom to explore. They're the artists. [...] Let the actor create. [...]"
>
> If you've given [students] the freedom to explore, and if you're wise enough to guide them through that exploration, then oftentimes they'll find it on their own without even realizing you were helping them. [...] I try to make things as fluid and student-centered as I can. [...] If they do something [...] that I am not a fan of [...] I give them suggestions and point them in a different direction. [...] [When I'm] really [at] my best [...] I'm not doing anything and I'm not saying anything. I'm encouraging [...] the students and [...] pushing them to think [...] [and] [...] allowing them to push each other. That's when the best work happens.
>
> [...] When they ask me a question and I don't know the answer, I'm going to tell them, "I don't know the answer" [...] and [ask] "Anybody have any ideas?"

[…] I think [it's] important for them to know […] that you're a real person and that you don't have all of the answers. […] I think that makes them respect the times when you do have the answers. (Chuter 2011c)

Using a Socratic method, Frank responds to students' work with many questions that deepen listening skills, critical thinking, and student efficacy. He also asks "How did that work for you? What worked? What didn't?" Then he asks the students to offer other ideas. In his Theatre I acting unit he uses a "vote with your feet" structure in which he makes statements and invites students to move to different parts of the room if they believe the statement is accurate, not accurate, or if they are undecided. After first repeating others' points of view, students from different parts of the room explain why they voted as they did. For example, to help students think about the critical relationship between given circumstances in a play, character needs, and action – rather than believing acting is merely emoting – Frank makes a bold statement. "Emotions are the most important element in acting." Throughout the exercise, as students consider their own and others' points of view, they both mentally and physically change their positions in the room. Students do written reflections about why they moved, where they ended up, where they started and what made them change.

Frank concludes,

Oftentimes, it's [students] talking to each other and me listening. When I'm doing all of the talking, I'm doing all the [thinking]. […] If I'm getting them to question each other, then they're thinking on a higher level and they're requiring each other to think on a higher level. […] I love […] to help them find the artist within themselves. […] I am passionate about seeing these kids grow. (Chuter 2011a; 2011c)

A Closer Look

A PLACE FOR EVERYONE – ELESHIA CROTWELL

Eleshia Crotwell (2010a; 2011a) heads the theatre program at Guyer High School in Denton, Texas. This is both a rigorous and joyful program where students are "family" and all strive for excellence in design work, classes, how they take care of the dressing rooms and prepare characters, how they strike sets, and how they speak to waiters when on field trips. Treating others with "basic human decency" is a hallmark of this program. It shows in the many "pleases" and "thank yous" from Eleshia and the tangible respect she receives from students. She snags every teachable moment to engage students in critical thinking or to share a tidbit from her considerable knowledge of theatre and life in general. As equally comfortable creating shows with high production values as she is directing the nuances of an intimate scene in class or volunteering to help a colleague, Eleshia attributes the program's success to her students' dedication to excellence and the unity that creates as they all strive for a common goal. Students who have graduated return regularly to help with projects, productions, or to mentor younger students, perhaps mimicking their teachers' generous spirit.

The biggest draw is that there is a place for everyone in the the Guyer Theatre family. Eleshia Crotwell

Because of school closings earlier in the year, in a four-day period Eleshia and her students hosted two play clinics, a one-act play contest for area schools, and a school-wide program. Eleshia had every detail organized for this busy period. While she prepared to teach a unit on period costume design to her Technical Theatre II class, former and current students wrangled cast members and sets from nearby schools that arrived unexpectedly early for the various events. Guyer students working on the clinic asked her opinions about setting up and she explained her ideas and her reasoning. If students misunderstood or did things differently, she was accepting and different solutions were found. Students exhibited a powerful sense of ownership of the program and commitment to the work and each other.

Eleshia also regularly opens her facilities to teachers from neighboring schools and districts for summer programs or special projects (Crotwell 2010a; 2011a).

As students prepared for the first clinic, in Theatre II, Eleshia introduced a period costume assignment. The assignment asked students to solve problems and apply specific content in a fun and practical way.

> The students [use] a handout which details the basic silhouette of costumes in eras from Greek theatre to the 1940s. Students [are] divided into groups of four to five and they [have] three class periods to create a costume using only scissors, tape and newspaper. Attention must be paid to the shape and details of the garment. The garment must be able to be removed and placed on again during the building process. (Crotwell 2011a)

Students also must be prepared to defend their design choices. After reviewing the instructions and rubric for the assignment with students, she taught them some fine points about fabrics and how they look onstage, illustrating with costumes from their current production. She guided students as they were trouble shooting solutions for creating fitted bodices and ruffs out of newspaper and duct tape. This was not a slapdash, undisciplined exercise in creating costumes out of paper. Eleshia used this three-day lesson to help students perceive the minutest details of costume design. Students were expected to meet high standards of achievement in this assignment. They received sophisticated design information and instructions were presented and repeated in different ways for different learning styles.

As students focused intently on building costumes, there remained a comfortable atmosphere in the room, due in large part to Eleshia's infectious enthusiasm. She moved around the room and joked with group members as she asked them to talk about their design choices.

> You order your burgers and fries with more detail than you discuss your costume designs. These are not just "ruffles." Describe the kind, use the correct names and explain in great detail [as if] to someone who couldn't see it. [...] Look at your resources – body proportion details and the ruffle [...] [handouts]. (Crotwell 2011a)

Students refered to images of period costumes posted in the room, considered the doll collection clothed in replicas of period clothing, and watched slides of previous students' costumes, which are quite remarkable. Eleshia revisited students as they worked, encouraging groups to share ideas, offering suggestions about how to create a sleeve or gathers in a skirt, and answering questions. "I don't think anyone's done that before [...] that would be [great]." She discusses a design with another group of students and suggests a sequence for implementing their ideas, offering to demonstrate the next step. She moves through the room sharing comments and compliments and encouraging students to look at the work done by other groups. To one group she asks "Are you building that [corset] on her? Great [...] Make sure you give her room to breathe. Make sure you don't kill anybody in here." She chuckles. Just before the bell rings, the student building the corset also chuckles and asks his model, "Still breathing?" She nods and smiles (Crotwell 2011a; 2011b; 2011c).

Eleshia considers what it is that draws students to her program at Guyer High School.

> I think that students are drawn by reputation, opportunity, and atmosphere. [...] I have created an extensive "ad" campaign for our program, complete with promotional DVDs, slide shows, handouts, pass-out cards, exhibitions in the cafeteria, our web page, brochures, and creating personal relationships with the community and the middle schools. I do think our shows are the first drawing factor, because that is how most people come to know Guyer Theatre. As a department, we strive to do high quality work that is at a professional level. The last thing my students or I want to hear after a production is, "That was great for a high school production!" We also have a Guyer Theatre Student Technical staff, which is responsible for tech for all events that take place in our [...] facility. [...] I believe that opportunity is a huge draw to the program. Students have the opportunity to travel, work with guest artists, attend camps, work on the technical staff, build huge costumes and sets, work with rented professional sets, perform in the [...] children's show for all the first graders in the school district, work with amazing equipment in an amazing space, and be in exciting classes. [But] the *biggest* draw is that there is a place for everyone in the Guyer Theatre family. (Crotwell 2010b, original emphasis)

A Closer Look

MAKING CONNECTIONS IS NOT ALWAYS EASY – BOBBY MALONE

Bobby Malone brings a humble yet commanding manner into every aspect of his work. He concedes that knowing how to engage students in a learner-centered way and finding connections to everyone's lived experiences is not always easy. As a dynamic teacher, Bobby recently became head of the theatre program at a new high school. He describes a Theatre I class as

> one of toughest classes I've ever taught. [...] I [had] a group that [was] pretty hostile. [...] They have never had a positive relationship with a teacher. I've learned that when I have students who are hostile [...] the worst thing that I can do is to be hostile towards them when a situation occurs. You have to, as Fursey Gotuaco (2002) would say, "be firm but fair." There was a fight that happened in class between two [...] students. [...] I didn't know what was being said, but [...] through their actions, I knew it was bad [and involved] bullying (Malone 2011b).

Bobby made clear to the students that "Mr. Malone doesn't like bullying and that fighting and bullying was not appropriate and that it needed to stop immediately." Later, the students who had been hostile in class were assigned to Bobby in a study hall situation.

> [T]he four or five [...] who usually oppose everything that I do came and sat next to me at a table where I was working, and they started chit-chatting with me. We started talking about video games. [...] [I]t was the first time there was a connection between myself and these kids. They started telling me about stuff they do at home and [...] things that they do outside of school. [...] Now [...] [they know me] as someone more like them than they thought [...] [I've been] waiting for that moment with them all year. [...] These kids are part of the same group of boys who had been fighting.
>
> [I] show kids parts of my life with which they connect [...] better and find something they respond to, that they latch onto and respect. [...] [For

some it's] not going to be theatre [but] this will aid in their learning (Malone 2011b).

Early in the rehearsal process for *Anatomy of Gray,* by Jim Leonard, Jr. Bobby brings in work from Anne Bogart's Viewpoints to engage students in the creative process. Everyone in the company is involved: actors, technicians, understudies. His purpose is to help students "find what clicks for you [...] what [...] speaks to you." As they work, he sidecoaches. "The goal is to find these characters [...] a rhythm for them, [...] what makes them different from everyone else. This is something [...] to continue to use and evolve during the rehearsal process [...] these characters that you develop today" (Malone 2011a).

Throughout the intensely focused rehearsal, Bobby pushes them to think and work as an ensemble. He typically speaks in terms of "we" or it is "our show, our work." He asks them, as a whole group, to lift an imaginary, giant brass ring.

> Let your eyes glaze over so you aren't really focused on any one spot [...] [with a] soft focus. Take everything in in the room. [...] Relax. Take outside responses. [...] Take it *all* in. [...] Pay attention to everyone else [...] the group. Take the focus away from yourself (Malone 2011a, original emphasis).

After the first attempt, he asks a student "On a scale of one to ten how precise was [...] [our] group effort?" She responds, "Three." Bobby asks her "Why did you score us a three?" and "How could we be better?" The student offers an articulate critique and Bobby agrees with her assessment. They are asked to try again. This time it is deemed by the student, "Night and day better" (Malone 2011a).

They continue moving through the room, changing direction, noticing spatial relationships, tempo, and rhythms as Bobby draws connections to the text and the diversity in the town. Based on a student suggestion, the technicians participate as the rain, light, and sound that, as Bobby reminds them, are also characters in the play. Bobby asks students to focus on tempo and make connections to the text to deepen their understanding of their character versus jumping to characterization. They add to their work as Bobby scaffolds into more complex exercises.

Later, as characters begin to emerge, Bobby asks "How are you going to make this an eighteenth-century character?" They hesitate and he asks more questions to help them. Finally, "Are you confused?" A student answers, "Yes." "Good. I'd rather have you tell me that you don't understand." Bobby invites two students to come forward and asks other students to sculpt them into poses they think represent their characters. He asks, "Does this say 1800s to you?" A student replies, "No." Bobby explains that if they think of the body in terms of silhouettes it will help them understand different periods. He adds to this by painting a picture of the town and the characters in words and silhouettes. Before taking a break, he talks with them about being perceptive to how people move in contemporary times and the need to do research about the 1800s for this play (Malone 2011a).

EXAMPLES OF LEARNER-CENTERED LESSONS AND REHEARSAL IDEAS

The Spot – Bill Hansen

Bill Hansen teaches Stagecraft, Great Plays, Group Problem Solving, Acting, Directing, and Playwriting at Lincoln High School in Manitowoc, Wisconsin. He directs and is the technical director for all of the shows. He also stage manages the eight-hundred-seat theatre when it is used for other events. "The Spot" is a series of exercises he uses in the classroom to build ensemble and an awareness of focus on stage.

> I first experienced the basic form of this exercise at [a summer intensive] for teachers with [a guest artist] from Wales. "The Spot" is (1) an exercise, and (2) a tool. As an exercise, keep expanding the student's use of body, voice, and imagination. Add more difficulty for any group or individual to keep it interesting. The exercises serve as rehearsal tools as they have become part of a shared vocabulary in the classroom or rehearsals. (Hansen 202)

According to Bill, using "The Spot" with theatre students has several benefits.
- Students learn about giving and taking focus in every scene. In a rehearsal, directors can stop and ask why a character is giving or taking focus and invite actors to try different staging ideas to create focus.
- By using this exercise, actors can direct audience focus at any given moment in large crowd scenes.
- Since students and teacher share a common vocabulary, solving problems in a show becomes much easier, quicker, and more learner-centered.

The lesson

The teacher selects a spot on the floor and each player observes five simple rules:
- Play silently.
- Avoid physical contact with others.
- Move freely about the playing space.
- Enter the spot and take focus as often as you wish.
- The game ends when all have taken the spot at least once and the players all sit down.

To take focus, one at a time students proceed to the spot, stop moving, act as if a string is attached to their upper chest that raises them up (not tip toe, just a posture change). When any person takes the spot they are asking for focus. They stay frozen until they wish to release focus, which is only after they have everyone else's focus. Performers must give focus by freezing all movement and looking at the person on the spot. To release focus, the student on the spot drops the body posture and moves off of the spot.

Variations

The following variations can be played with the whole group, then by two groups. Variations can be used in any order appropriate to the group, class content, or rehearsal needs. Reflection and discussion about what students noticed, experienced, were surprised by, is incorporated as each "round" ends and students sit.
- Change movement of the group to a specific activity.
- Change the spot elevation by using a box, chair, platform, or ladder.
- Change the spot to a specific level or posture, still frozen.
- Change the spot to a sound with a person making a sound and repeating the sound until releasing focus (still a silent activity except for the person asking for focus).
- Change from a silent activity to gibberish or talking except for the person taking the spot, who becomes silent as does everyone else.
- Change and let the person taking the spot keep talking but all must be quiet until released.
- Change to two different groups within the same space only giving and taking focus from or with members in your own group and paying no attention to those in the other group. (Use two different spots to start and, when mastered, use only one spot.)
- Students can then move to physical contact. Start by changing the spot to a person who is pointed at by anyone in the group. The person taking focus freezes and points at another player. Other players must freeze and give focus to the person being pointed at. The person being pointed at must also freeze and make eye contact with the person pointing. The person taking focus is demanding focus from one other person while the rest of the group is giving focus to the person being pointed at. All are released when the pointing stops. Vocally this can be done with "you" shouted or whispered and eye contact made without pointing. The variations from above can be combined as needed. (Hansen 2003)

Moment Analysis – A Learner-centered Approach to Directing – Brian Hall

Brian Hall has taught for thirty years and directed over 130 plays and musicals during his career. He had his own professional company and worked as a teaching

Each actor is different. To unlock his or her special gifts is the director's main goal during the rehearsal process. Mark Lamos

[I am] [...] trying different things that are out of the norm and out of [my] comfort zone, trying to get kids to think out of the box and help them understand that theatre has a more important role in our culture than just going to see a musical and then going home and not talking about it or thinking about it. Brianna Lindahl, Teacher

Figure 2.7: Rich, textured performances result from learner-centered Moment Analysis work. (Bradford High School production of *Once On This Island*.)

artist throughout Arizona. Brian taught secondary school in the Phoenix Valley and worked as a free-lance director. He was also an adjunct faculty member at Arizona State University.

During rehearsals and in the classroom, Brian uses an approach that he has developed called "Moment Analysis." Moment Analyses are done after ensemble work with the company and after initial explorations of the text. Using this method, Brian works alongside performers as they make choices regarding text interpretation, staging, business, character development, character interaction, and pacing. Performers collaborate with him and create a "roadmap" of well-crafted, aesthetically pleasing moments. His approach has proven highly effective for inexperienced performers as well as seasoned professionals.

Brian suggests beginning slowly, with one or two solo numbers from a musical, an important series of moments from a text, or one scene. As directors and performers grow familiar with the approach, students can work independently and the strategies can be extended to an entire production. Directors and performers are surprised at how quickly this work grows and how rich the performances are once everyone feels the freedom and excitement of this way of working. The work takes on an ease and naturalness and builds in texture, intricacy, and freshness.

Sample Moment Analysis of a Song

Step One: Divide the text into moments and list them

A play or musical unfolds to an audience moment by moment, like beads being strung on a necklace. Each moment conveys meaning about characters, places, and events. Collectively, these moments form the story being told. Performers and director must therefore craft each moment to tell the story and convey the dramatic truth of the play.

A moment is the smallest single action of a play. It is smaller than a beat, as we know it in theatre. A moment may be a phrase, a single word, a breath, a silent thought, a light change, a chord, a line of dialogue, or a single movement.

What to do:
- On a printed edition of the text or song text (lyrics), have performers write parentheses around words to distinguish between the *moments* they have identified.
- On a separate piece of paper, have them write the text or song text (lyrics) with one moment on each line, like a *list*.

Sample text:
"Somewhere over the rainbow, way up high / There's a land that I heard of once in a lullaby."

• Identified Moments:
(Somewhere) (over the rainbow) (way up high) (there's a land that I heard of) (once) (in a lullaby)

• List of Moments
Somewhere
over the rainbow
way up high
there's a land that I heard of
once
in a lullaby.

Ask performers to speak aloud the text inserting a slight, perceptible pause between each moment. If using this approach in class, have students compare their interpretation with someone else's. Evaluate the choices/differences among the different versions. What is clear? Unclear? Where does a moment feel too long or that it could be divided into two or more moments? When is a moment too short? Allow multiple interpretations. Next, briefly discuss the dramatic situation for each moment.

Step Two: Use questions to help performers interpret and stage the text

Both you and the performer share the quest for the interpretation of the piece. Questions focus the performers' concentration, memory, and artistic skills and put most of the responsibility to solve each task on the performer. To keep the process moving, and so you do not overwhelm the performer, you may want to offer a couple of possible answers, occasionally, and allow the performer to try one or more.

A Moment Analysis calls for a *series* of questions posed to the performer for *each* moment of the text being staged. Students can modify their division of the text into moments as you work. One of the joys of the process is that oftentimes new moments appear out of nowhere as the performer is working. Allow performers to experiment rather than jumping to "the right answer."

Work from the first moment and move in order through the moments to allow performers to internalize the text in sequence. This helps them think as the character in each moment and results in learning lines more easily and naturally.

The sequence and number of questions can vary depending on the students and the complexity of the text with which you are working. Questions are posed to *the character*, not the actor. Work in an inquiry, wondering mode rather than an answer-driven mode. Avoid asking "Why?" as that leads the actor into thinking *about* the character versus thinking *as* the character. Responses to questions are based in *the text*, not pulled from the air or invented by the actor, and are given by the performer orally in first person as the character, not written. The following is the first set of questions that can be asked while discussing the text with actors "on their feet" or "at the table." They are answered *moment by moment* for *each* moment listed in Step One.

Addressing Questions to the Character

For every moment ask:
- What is the dramatic action or situation at this moment? (Briefly discuss what is happening and what just happened.)
- Is this something the character is experiencing internally or externally?
- Is this a real or imagined moment? Is it grounded in reality, the imagination, or fantasy?
- What is the time frame? Has time stopped, is it racing, sluggish, or real time?
- What are you (the character) doing? This is answered with an action verb based on the text rather than the actor's blocking.
- To whom/what are you speaking? (For example "myself," "over the rainbow," "the world," "my past," "mom.")
- Where is this to be imaged? (Answered with one of eight circles.) (See pages 112–113.)
- What thoughts or attitudes do you have at this moment? (Answered with an adverb to "color" the moment and action.)
- What feelings are you having at this moment? (Answered with an adjective, adverb, or verb to "color" the moment and action.)
- Are these choices authentic to the dramatic truth of this moment?

Questions explored "on your feet" with lots of options for experimentation.
- Are you sitting, standing, kneeling, lying down, etc. at this moment? Try several options.
- Should you move? (If yes) Where would you move? What direction? How? Try the opposite. Try that on the line; before the line; after the line.
- (If no) How does the action verb you chose manifest itself? Does your focus change at this moment? Is there a piece of business? A silent moment?

With some performers or pieces just a few of these questions will be more than sufficient to begin to realize and stage the piece. Under other circumstances, you will want to use all of the questions. Brian notes that there will be more moments to analyze in musical theatre song lyrics and scenes, in works by Shakespeare where the language is poetic, or in Pinter where language is compressed. For other works there typically will be fewer moments to stage. Focus only on those moments that will help you and the performers create a meaningful performance and discuss moments you think will be most helpful to performers. Ask the questions that will

Tying the imagination to the action is the key. And that's where the director becomes so important in helping the actor find the right physical action so that, as the character, he can rely upon doing the action every night.
Mark Lamos

110

Figure 2.8: Sample Moment Analysis: Over the Rainbow.

Text	Situation?	Internal/External?	Imagined/Real	Time frame?	What are you doing?	Speaking to?	Circles	How? (Attitude)	Feeling?	Move?	Where?	Dramatic truth?
Somewhere	Just dismissed by Auntie Em/ Tornado coming/ Nobody under stands me	Internal	Real	Time stopped	Reasoning	Myself	2	Longingly	Unfulfilled	No	n/a	I am growing up and I want more from life
over the rainbow	Yearning for excitement/ understand-ing	External	Imagined	Same	Fantasizing	The world beyond the horizon	7	Wistfully	Same	Looking out	In the direction of the audience	I want to escape this farm
way up high	I want to escape from here	Same	Same	Same	Escaping	My place where my dreams are true	7	Hopeful	Joyful	A couple of steps	Where my dreams are	I'm using my fantasy to escape
there's a land that I heard of	Trying to remember	Internal	Real	Same	Recalling	My memory	2	Gently	Comforted	No	n/a	Same
once	I am recalling a brief moment of my childhood with my mom	Same	Same	Same	Remember-ing	My memory	1	Curiously	Warm	No	n/a	I am glimpsing what life was and could have been
in a lullaby	Same	Same	Same	Same	Same	My memory	1	Indulgently	Happy/Safe	No	n/a	Same

free them to explore and not frustrate them. Pace the questions and explorations for each individual student and the complexity of the piece.

Once a response has been explored physically, then settled on (although these choices remain fluid), the performer can move on to the next question for that same moment or follow that same question through ten or fifteen consecutive moments. Some performers need this latter approach so they feel the flow of the text. (See Figure 2.8.)

Skill directions, if open-ended, may help you and the performer get going in the same direction immediately. The performer must work to solve the task, but does not have to take as much responsibility for the interpretation as a whole. As performers work, insert skill directions to heighten or make a moment more specific, to break a moment into smaller moments, and to cull from the text more of the dramatic truth of moments.

Skill directions, or sidecoaching, like "hear that," "image that," "internalize more," "move more (or less)," may be unavoidable, but try to use them sparingly at the start, and later more for polish. Though they are effective and specific, you are still acting like the proverbial traffic cop telling the performer what to do and how to interpret. Since the director chose them, it is probable that performers may not retain any rationale for these choices. The educational value, therefore, is less than with questions.

Learning to ask helpful questions takes practice. Directors might be tempted to ask questions that are vague, director-centered, or audience or critic-centered rather than action-based or playable. With poor questions like "Who are you?" "What's your motivation?" "Why did you do that?" "Why did you gesture?" "Where's your focus?" performers can be frustrated, stall, or feel like they must mind-read to please the director or to come up with the "right" answers. In that case, the director and performers do *not* succeed in going forward together most of the time. You beat around the bush together. This is often taking your character to the analyst's couch. You end up paraphrasing the play, the text, the moment. You end up discussing feelings, actions, words, thoughts that occur later in the play's time rather than at this precise moment. *Vague questions result in vague acting choices.*

Step Three: Using Eight Circles to Place Images and Focus

The placement and use of images can answer most questions related to delivery and focus. "Where do I look when I deliver this line?" "What is my relation to the audience?" "Who do I talk to?" To image something is to use several related skills – gestures, eye focus, movement – to create an object or person that may not physically be on the stage for the audience to perceive. The actual object or person comes to mind, is remembered, is dreamed of, is imagined, is longed for, is feared, or is hated. Where images are visualized can establish the character's state of mind, relationships, time frame, and dramatic truth.

A Moment Analysis structure gives a framework [for actors and directors to move forward together]. The creative work of the performers often takes flight merely as a result of beginning with a moment structure. The question, "What do I do?" or "How do I begin?" need never be heard again! Brian Hall

Have performers imagine that they, as the character, are at the very center of an enormous bullseye which has eight rings. They select a circle for each moment as they do their Moment Analysis. Choices are modified throughout rehearsals and performances.

Circle 1: *To Your Heart of Hearts*: This circle is within you. It holds internalized places, people, objects, or ideas about which you pour your heart out exposing your most vulnerable, true self. Your deepest feelings are here.

Circle 2: *To Your Mental Self*: This circle is also within you, but is in your thoughts and mind. It holds internalized places, people, objects, or ideas about which you are thinking, worrying, or having a conversation with yourself. Your thoughts and memories of your past are here. Your hopes and fears are here. The voice in your mind is speaking here.

Circle 3: *Preciously Close*: This circle includes external, precious, very closely held places, people, objects, or ideas. The images are six inches to a foot away.

Circle 4: *Within Reach*: This circle includes external people, places, objects, or ideas you might grasp, reach, touch, travel or move toward, and achieve. Everything on stage near you is in this circle.

Circle 5: *Out of Reach*: This circle includes external places, people, objects, or ideas at a distance just beyond the ability of your character to travel, move, touch, reach, grasp.

Circle 6: *The Audience*: This circle includes places, people, objects, or ideas in the environment where the audience is. Project images and metaphorical meanings indirectly (without eye contact) into the audience's environment to include them in the scene, place, group of people, or ideas. You can use the barrier of the fourth wall metaphorically: you yearn to get out, you want to be different than you are and more like them, you want their help. For presentational style, this is also when you converse directly with the audience.

Circle 7: *The Horizon*: This circle includes places, peoples, objects, or ideas large enough to encompass more of humanity than the audience is a subset of. Your destiny lies here. The future lies here. Your plant-your-feet-determination is expressed to here.

Circle 8: *The Universe*: This circle includes people, places, objects, or ideas that are so large as to encompass everyone and beyond. The audience feels that it occupies but a tiny fragment of a larger space. Metaphorically, places, people, etc. assume a universal quality and importance. This is beyond the room of the performance and is larger than life.

Figure 2.9: Eight Circles.

Figure 2.10: Marrying the Text and the Music.

Lyric Preparation	Music Preparation
Prepare and rehearse the Moment Analysis of the song as a monologue *without* tempo considerations.	
Look for musical moments and clues to add to the Moment Analysis of the lyrics. What is the music saying about time, place, mood and images? For example: The music may reveal a moment of realization, resignation, or a mood change by a single note or a chord. Likewise, that a character is lying or having feelings they may be unaware of may be signaled by use of key changes or counterpoint melodies. Musical introductions can reveal if time has stopped, is moving to the past, future, or is racing. When exactly in the song text is there a key change? Where does the music modulate? At which points in the lyric does the music comment on the text by inserting a chord, note, or other musical device? What is being said? Find these musical moments and place them in the Moment Analysis exactly where they occur in the text.	Identify all of the vowels in the song. Sing the whole song on perfect pitch using just the vowels. Take a breath between each vowel. Sing the whole song syllable by syllable. Take a breath between each syllable. Do not destroy or distort vowels. Sing the whole song word by word. Breathe between each word. Add color, quality, and inflection to each word. Use pure vowels and dropped jaw.
Allow time for these moments as you continue to perform the monologue. In the example above, there would be a silent moment added before "Somewhere" for the music to stop time and establish what is happening for the character.	
Adjust monologue to correct tempo. Perform with musical accompaniment *underneath*.	Sing clusters of words to create images. This is the first time to pay attention to punctuation, capital letters, and rests. Final phrasing choices are made now with longer time between breaths. Use pure vowels.
Adjust the monologue for free singing so you can partner with the music.	Free singing. Sing on correct pitches with appropriate tempo *without* accompaniment.
Sing monologue with accompaniment as partner.	Sing so music is fully integrated and music appears to come from the character.
Practice, adjust, and refine.	Practice, adjust, and refine.
Repeat these steps prior to each performance.	Repeat these steps prior to each performance.

Building on his understanding of Stanislavsky's three circles of concentration, Brian employs a metaphor of eight concentric circles placed in and surrounding the character. Using these circles, as shown in Figure 2.9, can help performers answer their "Where do I look?" questions.

Step Four: Marrying text and music

For those director-teachers working with musicals, it is important to use a Moment Analysis approach throughout the process. A song can be viewed as a duet between a character and the music. Performers should prepare the text and the music separately so they come to understand the unique contribution both lyrics and music are making to the story being told. Remind the students that the music is another partner in the scene.

It is also important for students to realize that we learn lyrics in one part of the brain and the melody in another. Learning lyrics separately from the music allows students to understand and make informed choices about the whole song. If our students learn the lyrics and music simultaneously, they are either focusing on the lyrics and losing the melody, or they are singing notes without connecting them to the words. Students may struggle with the meaning of the lyrics or have trouble remembering them unless they hum the melody. (To test this, have students say the lyrics to "The Star Spangled Banner," with meaning, without mentally or audibly humming the melody. It is hard to do!) If students artfully can perform lyrics for their songs as monologues and can also beautifully sing the melodies independent of the words, then they are ready to put the song together and prepare for performance.

The Moment Analysis and music preparation occur separately but concurrently. As shown in Figure 2.10, this requires collaboration and communication between the director, choreographer, and the musical director. All involved can find great satisfaction in thoroughness and discovery at each step (Hall 2003b; 2003c; 1999).

Additional examples of learner-centered classroom work are included in Chapters 3 and 4.

IDEAS FOR FURTHER REFLECTION

Whose Program Is This?

Describe your vision of a learner-centered theatre program. Think about examples from this chapter and examples you have seen, experienced, or read about. Consider ways in which you can sustain the best of what is present in your work and how you can adjust your practice to include more learner-centered activities, approaches, and principles.

Reflect on these questions:
- Whose voices are shared in my classroom or performance space?
- Whose voices are heard and why?
- Whose voices are silenced or not heard and why?
- How is power used, brokered, or shared, and by whom?
- Who makes what decisions?
- How are students' lived experiences part of their study and practice of theatre?

SELECTED RESOURCES

In addition to the works cited in this chapter, the following offer ideas for further reading and reflection.

Gonzalez, Jo Beth. 2006. *Temporary Stages: Departing from Tradition in High School Theatre Education*. Portsmouth, NH: Heinemann.

Nathan, Linda. 2009. *The Hardest Questions Aren't on the Test: Lessons from an Innovative Urban School*. Boston, MA: Beacon Press.

Lazarus, Joan, and Wayne Brabender. 1997. *Theatre Arts Adventures*. St Paul: University of Minnesota Cooperative Extension Service and 4-HCCS.

Oddey, Allison. 1996. *Devising Theatre*. New York: Routledge.

Pink, Daniel H. 2005. *A Whole New Mind: Why Right-Brainers Will Rule the Future*. New York: Penguin Books.

Rodgers, James W., and Wanda C. Rodgers. 1995. *Play Directors Survival Kit*. West Nyack, NY: The Center for Applied Research in Education.

Weigler, Will. 2001. *Strategies for Playbuilding*. Portsmouth, NH: Heinemann.

Wolf, Jennifer, and Jan Mandell. 2003. *Acting, Learning, and Change: Creating Original Plays with Adolescents*. Portsmouth, NH: Heinemann.

NOTES

1. Margaret Wheatley is the author of *Leadership and the New Science: Learning about Organization from an Orderly Universe* (San Francisco: Berrett-Koehler Publishers, Inc., 1994). In her work in organizational communications, she found the fields of quantum physics, chaos theory, and biology to be overturning scientific theories that dominated the world for centuries. These new sciences reveal how each large and small part of the universe operates, not in conflict, but in harmony to bring about increasingly beautiful and healthy systems. She applies this understanding to her work with various groups of people and organizations.

2. On its Website, WorldBlu states "After over a decade of research into what organizational democracy is, we've discovered the ten principles that it takes to cultivate a highly successful and sustainable democratic workplace. These 10 Principles of Organizational Democracy must be put into practice on both the individual and leadership levels, and

When I ask a young actress or actor now if they sense a gap anywhere in a scene, even the smallest disconnect from one moment to another, they understand from their own experience exactly what I am asking. [...] They point out missing moments [...] and ask amazingly artistic, perceptive questions so we can fill in those gaps. Brian Hall

be supported by democratic systems and processes to have a successful democratic organization." The WorldBlu 10 Principles of Organizational Democracy™ are Purpose and Vision, Transparency, Dialogue and Listening, Fairness and Dignity, Accountability, Individual and Collective [Value], Choice, Integrity, Decentralization [of Power], Reflection and Evaluation. The WorldBlu 10 Principles of Organizational Democracy™ is a registered trademark (WorldBlu 2011).

3. Deb Alexander built her curriculum on the Goodrich and Hackett version of the play. Wendy Kesselman has since updated the script based on the release of Anne's unedited diary.

Chapter 3

Socially Responsible Practice

Theatre allows us to converse with our souls, to passionately pursue and discover ways of living with ourselves and with others. We have no better way to work together, to learn about each other, to heal and to grow.

Michael Rohd

I had a junior high student say to me, "I had a dream with you in it last night, Miss D." "Was it really me?" I said. "Yeah. We were at a grocery store, and you looked at me and said 'You can fly.' I said to you, 'No, Miss D., I can't fly. What are you, nuts?' And you said, 'Yes you can, just try.' So I had to fly through this grocery store! And I said, 'Wow, I can fly up to the top of shelves and get whatever I want.' And you said, 'Go ahead. Take whatever you want.' I said 'No, I can't do that, Miss D. It's stealing.' And you said. '[...] I'm giving you permission. You can take whatever you want.'

After he told me that, I had to go home and write it down. [...] I thought [...] 'This is going to be one of those stories [...] when life gets hard [that] I'm going to reread [...] and remember why I do this for a living.'"

Sandra DiMartino

I recently gained a new perspective on socially responsible practice in a seemingly odd setting – a hair salon. Discreetly placed on the counter in the salon restroom were fliers offering resources and information about domestic violence prevention. I asked the owner what made him decide to put these out. He said he had been approached by a local awareness group that told him stylists are in an ideal position to see evidence of abuse because of the nature of their regular, physical contact with clients. He arranged for his whole staff to attend a training session on recognizing domestic violence because he believes that making these resources available to staff and their clients is his responsibility. He said the significance of his action became clear to him when his sister visited the salon. She said she was grateful to see this literature available and then disclosed, for the first time, that she herself had been abused as a child. As the salon owner was talking to me I kept thinking, "He didn't *have* to take this action. He has *chosen* to do this." For him, social responsibility means recognizing the unique place he holds in a larger community and taking action to positively contribute to that community.

WHAT IS SOCIALLY RESPONSIBLE THEATRE EDUCATION?

Almost inevitably, when I ask theatre teachers and artists this question, I receive a question in response. "What do you mean by socially responsible theatre education?" After I share a few opinions from other teachers and artists, I ask, "How would *you* define it?" There is usually a pause, followed by an eagerness to discuss issues in their schools and communities. They talk about specific challenges their students or communities face and how they have responded or want to respond. They talk with conviction as individual theatre teachers, as artists, and as members of a larger community of educators and citizens. Most of them are endeavoring to bring about change in their own field of labor, with their own students, school, and local communities.

Angie Lindbloom characterized her socially engaged practice by describing a social justice public service announcement (PSA) project she does with her middle school students. Students watch PSAs, including examples from the United for Human Rights[1] website. They then use flip cameras to develop their own PSAs about a social justice issue they face or have seen in their lives. Angie does this project because she has "a heart for social justice and teaching [...] kids early that we live in a world where it's important to be just and it's important to accept other people." She tells students,

> You don't have to agree [with others' points of view] [...] but you should at least understand that they have a different perspective and it's okay to have it. [...] We're in the Bible Belt. [...] [I]t's hard for me to stand by and see these children [...] throw around [...] "that's so gay" and "that's so retarded" and [...] not see theatre as a medium that can change these kids. (Lindbloom 2010)

I believe that there can be no one definition of [...] [socially responsible theatre practice], but that the definition may change depending on the work, the community, and the aims of the work. Amy Burtaine, Teacher and Teaching Artist

Many teachers wish they could reach more or different students in their schools and use theatre more effectively to engage the school community in dialogue or action. They grapple with a desire to make a difference and they wrestle with questions about where to begin or how to continue. They face uncertainty about the impact their efforts have and concerns about how to expand, change, and diversify their programs while sustaining core activities at the same time. They reference their experiences and the experiences of colleagues, all the while generating as many questions as answers. For some teacher-artists, everything they do is through a lens of social responsibility and/or social engagement. For others, they offer a single project or a class in response to a specific concern.

A PATTERN OF AWARENESS AND ACTION

Looking at the experiences and steps that led these teacher-artists to their current level of socially responsible practice, I notice a pattern. These teacher-artists

- recognize there is a need of some kind in their school or community;
- acknowledge that theatre could be a viable and powerful tool for addressing this need;
- accept, as theatre artists and teachers, they are in a unique position to address this need and bring about positive change;
- identify strategies to address the need; and
- take action to effect positive change.

Kids have to make their own choices politically, philosophically, socially. I can't legislate that to them. But I can create an environment where they're empathetic in those choices. That to me is the most important idea of social responsibility. Susan Morrell, Teacher

In *The Dreamkeepers* (1994), Gloria Ladson-Billings succinctly characterizes the teaching practice that results from a pattern of cultural awareness and social action. "Teachers who practice culturally relevant methods [...] help students make connections between their local, national, racial, cultural, and global identities. [...] Their relationships with students are fluid and equitable and extend beyond the classroom" (Ladson-Billings 1994, 25).

SELF-REFLECTION AND SOCIALLY RESPONSIBLE PRACTICE

In various ways and times throughout their careers, socially responsible teachers have questioned their own practice in relation to the needs of their students, schools, and communities. Their self-inquiry can be clustered around five questions that are explored in the remainder of this chapter:

1. Whose program is this?
   - Who is my program for?
   - Who is currently being served by this program?
   - Who is included or excluded from this program?
   - Whose voice, history, culture, language, aesthetics, and perspectives are heard?
   - Who is in classes, onstage, backstage, "behind the scenes," and in the audience? Who is not?
   - Who is in the audience? Who is not?

2. What connections are made to students' lived experiences?
   - In what ways is my program responsive to the realities of students' lives?
   - How am I acknowledging these realities in the work we do?

3. What is the nature of my learning community?
   - How does the way I teach, communicate, and interact with students, staff, parents, and the community acknowledge and address their needs?
   - Is my program a community for learning, artmaking, and growing in our humanity?
   - How do I challenge and nurture students while maintaining appropriate professional boundaries?

4. How am I using the implicit political nature of theatre to engage students and the community?
   - How am I using theatre as a catalyst for civic dialogue?
   - How am I inviting multiple-perspective responses to our work?
   - In what ways does the program reach beyond the school?
   - Does this work lead to awareness, action, or change?

5. What material do we study, develop, and produce?
   - How does the material we use serve this learning community and address their needs?
   - How does it contribute to, create, perpetuate, or ignore problems?
   - What is age appropriate dramatic material?
   - Is censorship a concern?

As questions of this kind arise, some teacher-artists respond by producing plays relevant to their particular students or by developing social justice classes or projects where issues like bullying, school violence, or gender bias are considered. Middle school drama teacher Brianna Lindahl chose to address students' concerns about national and world events.

> When [the United States] went into Afghanistan [...] I created a drama called "The Good War" [based on Studs Turkel's work]. [...] The kids had a little bit of a knowledge of what the Americans were doing and that we had bombed [there] [...] so the activities really brought it to life for them. [...] They knew they were acting, but it touched a really personal [place,] [...] brought to life what was going on in the world, and made it relevant to them. (Lindahl 2002b)

Other teachers restructure their classes or programs to include students from across the school population. Many teachers engage in ongoing self-reflection and use their classes, productions, and interactions with students to heighten awareness, initiate dialogue, and move others in the school and community to action.

As a result of ongoing self-reflection, the decisions teachers and artists continue to make in terms of socially responsible practice, and how extensive or integrated their efforts are within their programs, are based on several factors that are explored in the remainder of this chapter.

- Personal priorities, values, and passions
- Focus of their programs
- Prior educational and practical experience with socially responsible/socially engaged theatre education and/or social activism
- Perception of students' needs
- Freedom to expand their programs
- Human and material resources available
- Time

Know that it's all right not to know and that the journey of knowing is what you're trying to teach your children. [...] If you're in that process of learning and knowing, as you go that knowledge will come to you. Gloria Bond Clunie, Teacher and Playwright

The glimpses of production and classroom practice I share here are based on the ever-changing, day-to-day practice of secondary school teachers-artists and are intended to characterize much larger efforts toward socially responsible theatre education. These teachers' words and accounts capture the heartfelt desires, concerns, struggles, questions, mistakes, and successes of many teacher-artists.

Amy Burtaine (2003a) has gone through several cycles of awareness and action in her pursuit of socially responsible theatre practice. For nine months, she lived in Rio de Janeiro and studied "Theatre of the Oppressed" (TO) techniques alongside Augusto Boal and his company. She later applied these techniques with a theatre troupe of youth AIDS educators she formed in Guinea-Bissau, West Africa. She returned to Brazil in 2003 to interview Boal and his Jokers about the long-term impact of their work. Amy has taught theatre at the high school level, including the Interlochen Arts Academy. She also worked extensively as a teaching artist. Amy continues to refine her views and practice of socially responsible theatre education as she works in community and university-based programs.

> I believe that all human endeavors are informed by our political, moral, and ethical beliefs. I also believe that, as participating members of society, youth need to be empowered to become socially engaged, [...] [meaning] defining and acting from one's beliefs. [...] As a theatre educator, it is my goal to bring theatre to students in ways that help them question, critically evaluate, and define themselves and their place in society. At the core of my teaching practice I believe that theatre [...] is the legacy and right of all people, not just those who are "talented," able, or economically privileged. [...] Theatre, as a tool, can become a site for performing democracy. (Burtaine 2003b; 2003c)

WHOSE PROGRAM IS THIS? THEATRE AND INDIVIDUAL DIFFERENCES

We haven't been able to keep more than seven thousand students each day from heading quietly for the exits before they've had even a chance to earn a high school diploma. [...] Barely half (51 percent) of African American students successfully complete high school, while only 55 percent of Hispanics do. [...] As a matter of social justice, we must be concerned when students are denied access to a high-quality education – one that includes learning in and through the arts – simply because of where they live or go to school. Sandra S. Ruppert, Arts Education Partnership

Confronting difference is not always comfortable. One response is to ignore the difference and pretend it doesn't matter; another response is to enter into more self-consciously complex relationships with what we perceive as different or foreign. Sharon Grady

There are many factors beyond a child's control that contribute to a healthy or unhealthy recognition of their own identity. Drama and theatre are unique tools for deeply considering differences that can shape students' development and for engendering a positive, empowered sense of self within a respectful community.

In her book, *Drama and Diversity*, Sharon Grady (2000) builds awareness about the differences that social class, race and ethnicity, gender, sexual orientation, and ability can play in a child's healthy or thwarted development. She provides an in-depth examination of each of these areas of difference as well as ideas about how drama teachers can create dynamic, respectful, inclusive learning environments that affirm each child's valued identity.

Bethany Nelson (2011) reflects on the use of applied drama and playmaking with urban youth to release understanding of identity and a sense of belonging.

Educational theorists agree that the development of identity is a critical task of schooling and should disrupt socially imposed constructs around race, class, gender, sexuality, and traditional power roles. By utilizing curriculum, pedagogy, and structural dynamics that integrate opportunities for students to think critically, explore multiple perspectives, experiment with a range of identities, and draw connections between the oppression they experience in their lives and larger social dynamics, students in schools will be better prepared to participate in redefining themselves and the society of which they are a part (McInerney 2009; Gallagher 2007; Fine and Weis 2003; Freire 1993).

Further, theorists on culturally relevant teaching agree on the importance of the establishment of community as a necessary factor for facilitating school success for urban students of color (Macedo and Bartolomé 1999; Nieto 1999; Ladson-Billings 1994). Reflecting a communal orientation characteristic of the home cultures of many urban students generates a sense of belonging for individual students, and allows them to scaffold new learning on familiar group dynamics. (Nelson 2011)

Through examples from classroom and production work, this section illustrates how secondary school theatre teachers respond to issues around identity that Grady and Nelson identify, as well as differences of language and culture, religion and spirituality, and age. Each example highlights how socially responsible theatre teachers are responding to individual differences.

THEATRE, POVERTY, AND SOCIAL CLASS

The first time I realized we might be poor was when a well-meaning lady at the [...] church my mother made us go to gave me a bag of clothes. There was an awkward silence as I stared at the bag and then at her. [...] "Thanks," I said with a forced smile, because I knew that was the expected response. [...] On the way home I threw the bag away – and vowed I'd work harder to keep our "situation" our secret. Sharon Grady

the number of children living in poverty has increased by four million since 2000. [...] By 2009, 15.6 million children were receiving food stamps, 65 percent more than ten years earlier. The number of homeless children in our schools increased 41 percent [...] between the start of the school years 2006 and 2008, before the financial crises. In 2010, in New York City alone, more than forty thousand schoolchildren [didn't] have a permanent home, more than three times as many as in 2006. Bill Clinton, quoting The Children's Defense Fund's report, *State of America's Children 2011*

I observed a young boy in a drama class who appeared to be lethargic, very sleepy, and disengaged. His teacher mentioned that she had noticed that he seemed "off" that day. At the close of class, she invited him to help her rearrange chairs so she could chat and make a positive connection with him. After class we talked about how, as teachers, we need to be alert to the impact poverty may be having on children and how we need to be discerning about student behavior and reserve judgment when children seem restless, tired, or agitated. As teachers, we may not know what is happening at home or in the neighborhood that is preventing children from sleeping at night, getting fed, or having appropriate relationships with others (Ervi 2011). Reinforcing the seriousness of poverty's toll on children, one middle school teacher explained that she made an exception and allowed one boy to rest his head on his desk during class. She knew that her class was the one place where he *could* rest, the only place he felt safe enough to sleep (Underwood 2004).

Oversimplifying or denying the impact of poverty on students' success has compounded challenges facing schools everywhere. Eric Jensen (2011) has done extensive brain research with children in poverty and connects his findings to their often low performance in school. On his website and in his book, *Teaching with Poverty in Mind* (2009), he makes a case for how poverty affects children's memory, visual and spatial skills, language development, processing and sequencing, impulse regulation, emotional development, stress, self-image, conflict resolution, meaning making, and other functions essential to academic success (2011; 2009). He presents evidence that certain educational strategies, including drama, can correct and reverse these deficits. Jensen writes extensively about how the arts stimulate development in all children, and especially in children of poverty who show marked improvement as a result of experiences with the arts at the core of the curriculum (Jensen 2001).

Bryar Cougle (2002) taught theatre and English at high schools in Virginia and Maryland before becoming the arts education consultant for the Department of Public Instruction in North Carolina. An articulate advocate for the arts for all children, he reflects on his teaching and production work with students from a rural area in the Southeast and shares strategies he used to build an inclusive, learner-centered program.

The benefits of high levels of arts participation can make more of a difference for economically disadvantaged students. Sandra S. Ruppert, Arts Education Partnership

I [...] was teaching in the rural part of Maryland. [...] We were only forty-five minutes down the road from Washington D.C. Most of [the students] had no clue that place they saw on television was near them. Many of them were poor, rural people, in many cases still with outdoor plumbing. [...] When you talked about theatre, they weren't even sure, in many cases, necessarily what that really was as opposed to television.

There was a tremendous amount of talent in that community which had not been tapped. I saw it. I knew it was there. I just had to find it and coax it [...] and I did that. [...] I [taught] kids who, in some cases, couldn't read or write. I had to find a way of dealing with that because [...] [they] were really talented kids. But they couldn't read [...] or memorize a script. So I [...] set up a peer mentoring situation where other kids taught them to read a script.

I had [...] what [some] call "the slime" of the school [working] with the valedictorians. [...] I was [...] fortunate enough in some cases to find what they needed, [...] case by case, [...] individual student by individual student. (Cougle 2002)

All of them, I think, come to you. [...] They're attracted to you for something. And for me [...] I think it was because I had something good going on. My theatre program [...] was visible. [...] It packed a twenty-five-hundred-seat theatre and [...] [was] one of the central focuses of the school. [...] A lot of kids wanted [...] the visibility. They wanted to do it to prove they could. [...] They wanted to do it for the honor and accolades they got. [...] A lot of them came from [...] broken families, and they saw the theatre as their sort of secondary family. And so their friends became their brothers and sisters, and father and mother in some cases.

I have the typical stories everybody has about individual kids who changed [...] not so much because of me but because of the opportunities they had as a result of my program. . [...] Some of them were saved, from themselves in many cases. [...] One [boy] in particular [...] [who was] [...] functionally illiterate wanted to be in the theatre program. [The] first few shows [he] didn't want to speak, just wanted to hang out and work on crew. But then [he] decided that it was time to [...] [be] in a show. So, he went and got some help from one of the other students and read for the show [and] I cast him. [...] At the time [...] he was overweight, [had] low self-esteem, [was] low achieving. By the time the third year rolled around, his grades had improved, he had lost weight [and] changed his physical appearance. [...] He didn't go on [...] [to] the university and become the rocket scientist. [...] He [...] decided he wanted to go to beautician school. He got a license, started doing hair, and [the] last time I saw him he was making more [money] than I was. But – and he often has said this to me – the reason he was able to do that was because he got enough confidence [through the theatre program] to say, "Well, let's see what I want to do with my life – and can I do it? Sure I can. I can do anything I want to do." (Cougle 2002)

Eric Vera (2011) talks about what is compelling about teaching at a Title I school.

Their stories. I know I have an interesting story to tell [growing up on the Mexican border] [...] but the hardships that they have had to face amaze me every time [they share them]. Some of them have been abused, neglected, abandoned, hurt, you name it. Yet, they wake up every day, get to school, do their best, and [...] [they] find their way onstage [...] their escape. They get to be whoever they want to be onstage and not themselves.

In my three years of teaching I have so many stories [...]:

A student who is [...] autistic [and] who is shy, not talkative, and likes to keep to himself, [but who] when he hits the stage is the loudest and best actor he can possibly be.

A student who is on her way to being a National Merit Scholar who [went from] [...] being the quietest girl in the class to being [...] [a] lead in every play and musical this season.

Football players who were told by the coach not to audition for "no damn musical," [one of whom] [...] when given the chance, ran to the stage to perform his heart out just as well as he did on the field.

[...] They teach me more than I could ever teach them. I listen to them. [...] I trust them as much as they trust me. [...] I tell them [...] I will never let them make a fool of themselves on that stage. Their stage fright goes away the minute they agree that we trust one another to make the best work we can. And with their background, trust is more valuable than money. (Vera 2011)

Even in schools historically enrolling middle- and upper-class students, changes in the economy are changing the level of poverty in the district.

We have seen a shift. [...] The parents are not always able to give their time and money like other schools in our district; but we have a strong work ethic that we instill in our kids that negates the financial restraints. (Koern 2010)

THEATRE, ABILITY, AND DISABILITY

Inclusion of students with disabilities means that all students receive equal, appropriate education together, in a setting that provides the support and services that meet their needs. Shernaz B. Garcia

It is often assumed that secondary school theatre is exclusively for the talented, gifted, and able-bodied. Most socially engaged teachers, however – including those working in fine arts specialty schools or magnet programs – make clear that their programs are for all students in the school, not just those whose performance abilities or other talents have been developed or are even apparent. In addition, students with disabilities are actively involved in their theatre programs.

Aline Knighton (2003) actively includes students of all abilities in her program. She had student taught with veteran teacher Beryl Knifton at a public high school also designated as the district's fine arts academy. Beryl taught a Theatre I class that included five students with a range of physical and cognitive disabilities including cerebral palsy, Down's syndrome, and other developmental disabilities.

Of the three types of child maltreatment [neglect, physical abuse, and sexual abuse], child neglect is most powerfully associated with neighborhood poverty status. Brett Drake and Shanta Pande

On the first day, after these students were excused to return to their classroom a few minutes early to avoid the crowds in the halls, Beryl took time to talk to the remaining students about the privilege they were going to have [learning] with these students in their class. She told them to assume that [the students who had left early] were going to be a part of all activities and that they would [all] learn from [one another]. [...] With some very minor adjustments, they participated in all activities except when their aides felt it was not in their best interest.

The thing that was remarkable to me about it had [...] to do with the able-bodied students in that class. Certainly the [...] students [with disabilities] participated and at times moved us to tears with their sensitivity and insight. [...] But in twelve weeks I never saw any student in that class treat their [...] peers with [...] anything but love and respect. [...] No student ever complained about the members of their group, able-bodied or not. The students made accommodations so that the assigned work for the [...] students [with disabilities] was within their [range of] abilities.

In a production class, we had a young woman who [...] [used] a wheel chair. She was cast in a role that could accommodate her [physical] challenges. [...] [She] [...] had to have some help on stage since she had limited ability to push her chair for herself, [but] this was easy to accommodate. She also participated in drama club faithfully. (Knighton 2003)

The diversity of activities encompassed in a quality theatre arts curriculum provides opportunities for the involvement of all students, regardless of experience, cultural background, or disability. American Alliance for Theatre and Education

At his high school near Houston, Frank Chuter teaches a Theatre Productions class specifically designed for students with disabilities. Class members work closely with student aides from Frank's other theatre classes on both acting and technical theatre skills. One student aide created a short play for the class. During their final rehearsal, as the student playwright was reviewing entrances and exits and discussing the meaning of a portion of the text, a student became agitated. Frank talked privately with him and diffused the student's escalating anger while the student aides stepped in to rehearse lines with students, discuss characters, and help them adjust their blocking to the set. A student from this class is also in Frank's Advanced Technical Theatre class to enable him to develop more life skills in this area of interest to him (Chuter 2011a; 2011b).

Mandy Whitlock (2011a) became an advocate for a boy in her program who was diagnosed as schizophrenic. She researched his challenges and learned about community services that might help him. She developed strategies for him to be successful in her classes and shared her strategies with the art teacher. As a result, he was able to pass both classes and earn credits toward graduation.

In Richard Silberg's (2011b) adaptation of *Macbeth*, a middle school student who was cast as one of the witches was hard of hearing. She taught the rest of the witches American Sign Language and together they developed signs for phrases like "fair is foul and foul is fair." They effectively signed to signal Macbeth's death at the end of the play. In that same production, a student with Down's syndrome was cast as one of the porters. "It was his desire to sing Alice Cooper's 'Welcome to My Nightmare,' which gave rise to a whole different kind of role for the porter."

> Both of these kids were involved in the [after school] ensemble from the beginning of the year and it was great to honor their special gifts at our performance [...] The crowd – and I'm talking a daytime crowd of 650 seventh and eighth graders – erupted in cheers when [he] sang his song [...] He told me that for days kids would stop him in the hall and tell him he should've gotten an Oscar or an Emmy or something. [...] Everyone is welcome into the ensemble – no auditions – just a commitment to work and play together. (Silberg 2011b)

Many of the world's [...] [children who are] disabled are figuratively beating at the rehearsal doors of the world, yearning to be part of the action. We must see that these doors continue to swing open for them. Richard Morse, Actor and Author

To draw out each student's strengths, Tal Gribbons (2010) pairs students – a student with low vision or a student with Asperger's syndrome – with students who are capable and comfortable accommodating their partner's needs. Tal had a shy student with "a profound speech [disorder]" who he insisted audition for an advanced class because he "knew she was smart and capable." After voice and diction work alongside other class members, she performed a monologue in a recent production and was "amazing!" This student is now a leader and is more involved with school and other students (Gribbons 2010).

THEATRE, RACE, AND PRIVILEGE

> *African Americans, Latinos, and Native Americans are underrepresented among high-achieving students in the United States at all levels of education and across all subjects, including the arts.* Richard Young, Arizona State University

> *Theatre curricula periodically require deliberate, focused interrogation, innovation, and reconstruction. [...] As diversity infuses and informs life, we must strive to infuse and expand theatre curricula with diversity.* Lorenzo Garcia

C. Gary Cooper (2011c) teaches in an urban high school of thirty-six hundred students where just over 50 percent of the students in the school are Latino, 30 percent are African American, almost 15 percent are of Asian or Middle Eastern descent, and fewer than 10 percent are Caucasian. "The 'majority' is the minority and [...] I *love* it." He notes that the theatre department is not reflective of these percentages because, unlike other programs in the school, "We don't break down along racial lines. We have an equal [number of students from] all of the races." Recently his students were invited to a clinic to prepare for the state one-act play competition. The clinic was held at a school that is "predominantly a white school, so our kids felt that. They really felt, 'Oh, wow, we're in a different environment than we're used to.'" Gary used that as a teachable moment and started a conversation with them.

> Look at our company right here. Look how evenly divided we are within all races. I think that's a really good testament to what we're doing. [...] A lot of different people are feeling comfortable coming into our program. (Cooper 2011b)

Students respond to accessibility, comfort, and a sense of ownership and belonging in his program. This is palpable in classes, productions, and informal interactions.

Holly Stanfield (2009; 2002) teaches in an urban high school in Kenosha, Wisconsin, a predominantly working class community between Chicago and Milwaukee. She describes the transformation that happens in her drama class in this racially diverse school.

> You start a class [...] [at the beginning of the year and the black or Latino kids] [...] all sit on one side of the room and the white kids [...] on the other. [...] [But] by the [...] end of the semester, they're all just sitting [together] and talking and have risked something in front of each other. [...] I [...] think that's maybe as important as anything else that we teach. As important as math and science. [...] Maybe more important. Because it teaches courage with other people. And I think that's something that our culture in America is sorely lacking. [...] This whole thing is about courage. (Stanfield 2009)

Like Rebecca Jallings' (2002) experience in Chapter 1 (see page 94), Tara Affolter (2002) felt impelled to address how race and white privilege were impacting her students' educational opportunities. Tara's theatre program became her laboratory while she taught theatre and English at a racially mixed school and pursued a graduate degree in education. Tara reflects on her role as teacher-researcher.

> My reason for going back to graduate school in the first place had to do with my frustrations with [...] the way kids of color with sort of harsh lives are pushed aside in schools [...] frustrations with having such a predominantly white theatre program in a multi-cultural, multi-ethnic school. [...] [I wanted] to really deconstruct that.
> [...] When I started the thesis project, my idea was [...] [to] interview kids of color – the few who were involved in the program already and kids who had been identified or maybe showed up for one audition but then I would never see them again. [...] I realized that the way I was framing the question [...] still put the blame on the kids of color. It was [...] "Why aren't you involved?"

rather than [...] "Why would you want to be involved?" [...] What were we doing as the director [and] the kids in the theatre program that could be read as exclusionary?

I [also] started [...] interviewing [white] [...] kids in the program [...] about what they thought about race, what they thought about [...] the makeup of the program. [...] They really thought racism was something of the past, "back in the day of my grandparents, maybe, but not me." [...] We had to do a lot of processing around that, [...] calling kids on some things they may not have seen in a way that wasn't too confrontational. But it made them stop and think. It opened a space for me within the program then to push a little harder. (Affolter 2002)

How are you using the voice that you have in that school? And what are you saying? What are you choosing to say?
Tara Affolter, Teacher

As Tara's program grew and more students of color got involved, she felt it was essential to look at assumptions about race in terms of casting and character interpretation. In her production of *One Flew Over the Cuckoo's Nest*, Nurse Ratchet was played by an African-American student. During rehearsals, Tara and the actor talked about the "invisibility of whiteness that's implicit in the script and what it means for [this] student to play the part" (Affolter 2002). Tara did not want the student to think she was being asked to be a white woman. Tara encouraged her to see her own identity as an African American woman as part of the character's identity. Tara comments that "the literature out there is still [...] colorblind white. [...] I [...] refuse to do a show [...] unless [...] you say 'All right, let's look at what is assumed about this character.'"

For me, [what's important is] making the theatre a place where kids can come and [...] see someone like themselves in a role. [...] See [...] it's not just a white kids' thing. It's not just a program for stereotypical theatre kids. [...] We [...] did *The Piano Lesson* by August Wilson [and we] did *Prelude to a Kiss* at the same time because *Piano Lesson* is an all African American cast, and [...] I don't teach at an all African American school. [...] I don't want to be exclusionary on any level. (Affolter 2002)

Tara offers some suggestions for including students from across the school population in the theatre program.

I think that one of the first things you do is you ask. It's as simple as "Would you like to do this? Would this be something you'd be interested in? [...] Your English teacher said... I saw you in the hallway... Not being afraid to talk to kids and not just isolating. The other thing that's really important is to not just bring a lone student in, unless they're particularly solid. [In my] English classes [...]

sometimes [I'll say] just a gentle "You really ought to try this, and bring so and so with you so that you're not isolated, [so] you don't know anybody."

I think you start with the audition process. Offering a couple of different audition times [...] [I] try to run my auditions like theatre workshops. [...] We might do some kind of physical [...] warm up [...] not too weird, with enough people [...] that [students] realize pretty quickly that no one is looking at them. [...] The key [...] for kids that are new [...] is to not make it too funky or weird or they won't come back. [...] You can't do that right off before kids trust you. [...] I walk around encouraging them.

Occasionally, we'll do some sort of structured improv activity [...] usually based on [...] the play. [...] [We have a] big enough group [...] so nobody feels [...] on the spot. At some point, I do have them read something for me, and I'm as close to them as I can be without sitting onstage with them. [...] Usually just something simple. [...] Just me and the kid and the other director [...] one at a time.

The first two weeks are crucial to making kids feel safe, making them feel like they're a part of something, not just this outsider trying to break in. [...] And this part's tricky. I've got a core group that identifies themselves as "The Theatre". They're the theatre clique. [...] [I am] busting up that clique and using the pillar of that clique at rehearsals to [...] [eliminate the] exclusionary feeling. [...] [I use] double casting [...] [to have a] built in "somebody else" [and] I pair them for double casting, [...] building in that kind of time so they can talk about character. We set it up so they're a built-in community [...] early on. [...] They care for each other. [...] I make a concerted effort to make sure people understand that not everybody has rides – and this isn't along racial lines. [...] [I ask] "Who can carpool?" (Affolter 2002)

[After] opening night [...] they come back. "That's the best thing I've ever done!" [...] Slowly [they] bring a friend and bring a friend. I'm not saying I'm where I want to be yet in terms of diversity and its facets [...] but I'm getting there.

Socially responsible theatre is [when] you realize that [...] there are a lot of ways that you can reach out, even within the mainstage [...] [model]. [It means] having your students become socially responsible and work towards, in my case, social justice and [...] equity in their own school. [...] The other layer to social responsibility is, "What are you saying to the adults, the families, parents, staff that come see this show?" [...] The social responsible piece looks at the bigger picture. [...] "Is it just another show? Or is there more to it than that?" (Affolter 2002)

I personally recruit kids who I think need to be in theatre. [...] Most of the time they want to do it; [...] they just want someone else to ask them and boost their confidence.
Lena Paulauskas, Teacher

THEATRE, LANGUAGE, AND CULTURE

They told me the small pastries we made were called "butterflies." My Mamá called them "buñuelos." They said my mother was wrong. She said they were called buñuelos in México. They told me it was the "Rio Grande." My Mamá told me it was the "Rio Bravo." They said she was wrong. In México it is the Rio Bravo, she said. They told me Columbus discovered America. My Papá said, "How could you discover something when civilizations were already here?" They said my father was wrong. They told me that the Aztecs and Incas were savages that ate people. Mis Papas told me that they were astronomers and mathematicians and farmers and writers and warriors, and they took baths, too. They told me my parents were wrong, their stories irrelevant. They told me to stop asking questions. They told me to stop putting the accent on my name. They told me to stop doing my math the way my father showed me. They told me that I should be more like the other boys and girls. They told me that my parents were wrong. They never stopped to think that maybe they were wrong. Mónica Byrne-Jiménez

It is […] important to note that differences are not the same as deficits. English language learners (ELLs) come to us with much more than a desire to learn English. They come with knowledge of other places, languages, literacies, customs, and cultures. They come with optimism, energy, and unique perspectives. Through interactions with ELLs, teachers and classmates learn many things that enrich their lives and that help prepare all students for increasingly diverse workplaces and communities. The Knowledge Loom, The Education Alliance at Brown University

While preparing a theatre curriculum project, one of my preservice students questioned, "Why do we always start theatre history with the Greeks? Why not start with the Mayas?" A theatre program seems an ideal place to liberate young people from the boundaries of an English-only, Euro-centric curriculum, freeing teachers and students to ask questions and explore ideas beyond the limitations of spoken language or a single culture. Teachers engaged in best practice seek out resources and professional development experiences so they can effectively interact with each child in their program in learner-centered, culturally sensitive, and socially responsible ways. The Knowledge Loom (2011) at The Education Alliance at Brown University is one resource for teachers to share and explore ideas and information.

Like all children, English language learners [ELLs] vary in their nutrition and care histories, family structure and stability, household composition, parental education and socioeconomic status, neighborhood and community resources, exposure to literacy, life experiences, knowledge, cultural norms, abilities, and dispositions.

ELLs bring with them varied cultural experiences that have shaped their notions of appropriate adult-child interaction. For example, children from some cultures may ask questions of adults and display knowledge by volunteering answers, whereas children from other cultures may have learned to show respect for adults by listening quietly. Some children may demonstrate the desire for closeness with the teacher through physical proximity and hugs, while others may expect to have a more formal or distant relationship with their teacher. Some ELLs seem independent and mature beyond their years, having developed high levels of social and linguistic competence through helping their families, caring for younger children, and interpreting for their parents.

ELLs differ from each other in their previous literacy experiences. Some may be familiar with literature genres, informational text, and the analytic activities prevalent in U.S. classrooms. Others may be more familiar with religious texts or functional uses of literacy such as recordkeeping and letter writing. Styles of narration and writing vary across cultures. For example, a chronological narration of events is highly valued in U.S. schools, while in other settings narratives are judged on imagery, poetics, word play, contextual details, or other criteria.

Many English language learners […] go through a "silent period" during which they listen and observe more than they speak. During this silent period, ELLs benefit from opportunities to participate and interact with others in activities that use gesture, physical movement, art, experiential activities, and single words or short phrases. (The Knowledge Loom, 2011)

In settings in which many cultures are represented and different languages spoken, theatre teachers effectively have used movement, visual images, and music to create works that explore commonalties and differences in language and culture. In other instances, they stage plays that give voice to otherwise silenced children. A theatre program is a place where the differences of language and culture that walk in the door with each child and every teacher can be celebrated.

John Heinemann (2002) and Patsy Koch Johns (2002) had an experience in their school that brought about tremendous good and fostered inclusion and an open sharing of cultures.

We did *The Rememberer* [by Steven Dietz]. […] We have about twenty-five Native American [students] at our school and there's a class called Native American Scholars where [students] get to look at Native American culture. […] [The Native American students] were really the consultants for the production. They were all involved. Some actually auditioned and were in the show, but many of them [...] talked about [...] [their experience in their nation] [...] even though [where the play is set is] [...] a nation in the Northwest. They had stories to tell, and kids really had a chance to sit down and talk with each other about [...] their culture. [...] These students [...] had never really had a voice in our school.

That play was a very powerful experience not only for the actors onstage [...] [but for the entire school community]. We have twenty-something first languages spoken at Lincoln High, and we [display] [...] the flags [of all of these nations]. Second semester [...] [some Native American students] noticed there were no Native American nation flags there. [...] Then they did this assembly – a whole ceremony – in front of the school. They blessed their flags [...] [and] spoke about their nations. [...] They never could have done that without the experience of having *The Rememberer* on that stage first semester [...] Then, second semester, they're up there telling their own [...] stories! (Heinemann 2002)

I admire teachers and artists who are multi-lingual and able to easily interact with students in languages other than English. I also admire those English-speaking artist-educators who employ innovative strategies for teaching theatre to students who speak the many other languages heard in our schools today. Some theatre teachers devise projects that include a cross section of students who represent different cultures or who all speak different languages, while others choose to give voice to one or more groups within the school population. Several teacher-directors develop or produce bilingual plays, while others have learned new languages in order to teach their students more effectively.

In the mid-1990s, Roxanne Schroeder-Arce (2002b) moved to the Texas-Mexico border town of Laredo to begin her first teaching job. There she was cautioned by her colleagues not to learn Spanish or allow students to speak Spanish in the school.

A flock of teachers and counselors began to advise me. "Don't let them speak Spanish in your classroom. They'll take advantage of you," and "They get to hear Spanish all day. They should speak English in school. This is America." Despite the advice, I welcomed the Spanish lessons my students offered, and my interest surprised them. Every day, the last fifteen minutes of class, someone would play teacher, and I played student with the rest of the class. [...] [Then] I began seeking plays that were culturally relevant to them. We found a couple, we wrote a couple. (Schroeder-Arce 2002a)

Roxanne became fluent in Spanish and felt welcomed by Mexican Americans in the community. She wrote several bilingual plays for professional production and later became education and then artistic director at Teatro Humanidad, a bilingual theatre in Austin, Texas. She writes about the challenges she has faced as a white woman doing this work.

> I have been careful for quite some time, as a white, female, English-speaking teaching artist in classrooms full of a multitude of cultures, colors, languages, genders, and other orientations. Yet, where does this notion of "being careful" come from, and what does it mean? As an educator, why does consciously discussing my or my students' cultural identity feel like walking on ice?
>
> [...] I am realizing that the ice I walk on – that we all walk on as "other" – may never melt completely and become firm ground. If the ice were to melt, I could never learn to skate on it, to benefit from the cultural and linguistic challenges I face as an "other." [...] Maybe this is how it should be. (Schroeder-Arce 2002a)

The majority of theatre teacher-artists in the U.S. are not of the same race, ethnicity, or culture as the students they teach. Being honest in our interactions with students whose language, culture, and race are different from our own can be scary and intimidating. Rather than "faking it," Gary R. Howard (2006) talks about learning the "dance" of culturally responsive teaching.

> Learning the dance of diversity is not easy for white Americans. There are complex moves and many ways to lose the step. Before my lessons could begin, I first had to break out of cultural encapsulation and isolation. [...] I began to see myself as Blacks, Hispanics, and others outside my group saw me, both collectively and personally. I had to face the history of white dominance.
>
> In order to continue the lessons and learn the more difficult steps, I had to acknowledge my own complicity and privilege, as well as the racism in myself and my family. I had to learn to move with some degree of grace and style to these new rhythms, without stumbling over guilt, denial, or the rejection of my own whiteness.
>
> Today, as the dance of diversity continues for me, I want to take more time to think about the music. Where is it coming from? [...] I find myself listening more now for my own inner music. [...] I am less patient with our diversity jargon and the surface strains of the old multicultural tunes, which sometimes push us to impose our own assumptions rather than waiting for the larger truths to emerge. I want to explore the more subtle tones of the music now, the nuances and complexities created by our vast differences and similarities as human beings. The lines we have drawn around race and culture seem too simplistic to speak to the incredible diversity of our actual lives.
>
> I know the dance of white identity will continue to change and deepen for me. [...] Each new step I learn brings me closer to my unique place on the dance

floor, helps me find my personal harmony, and guides the creation of a new way of being white, one that is both authentically connected to my own history and finely tuned to the rich mixture of sound and beat that is multicultural America. (Howard 2006, 26–27)

THEATRE AND ENGLISH LANGUAGE LEARNERS

Richard Silberg (2011a) teaches at Martin Luther King Middle School in Berkeley, California. Children of new immigrants from Latin America, Tibet, Nepal, Yemen, Palestine, and other Middle Eastern countries are classmates with children of international students, visiting professors, and children of wealthy, well-educated local families. Eleven different home languages are spoken in his classes: Spanish, Portuguese (Brazil), Arabic, French, German, Russian, Nepalese, Mandarin, Japanese, Tagalog, and Tibetan. Of the one thousand students enrolled at King, more than 53 percent are on reduced lunch. A mix of skills and languages, urban kids and newcomers, "brilliant kids [and] gang [members on the verge of] dropping out" arrive in his classes and after-school theatre program as a "rich population [...] to teach" (Silberg 2011b).

Earlier in his career, Richard taught multiple subjects including history-social science, English, science, and math. He also became certified as a language development specialist with an emphasis in literacy. About three years ago, Richard was "just teaching drama." At the urging of his principal who wanted to do what was "best for the school," Richard created and implemented a drama class specifically for new English language learners (ELLs) and those who were fluent in English but "needed a bit more." The intent was to support students' use of everyday English while developing their "academic fluency" in English, something essential to achievement in school and beyond (Silberg 2011a).

In drama, Richard masterfully integrates content from the students' other academic classes without compromising the integrity either of the art form or the language instruction. His drama lessons reinforce use of "playground English" as well as academic English (2011a; 2011c). Richard meets his classes in the hallway and tells them the "silent task" that they are to do as soon as they enter the room. Knowing what his ELL drama students are studying in their history classes at this point in the school year, Richard asks them "to make ancient Greece together." After silently creating a complex tableaux involving everyone in the class, they use English to describe what each student is doing. Richard then tells them their drama goal for the day and their language goal. They hear and speak a new academic English term and write journal entries in full sentences from a prompt incorporating the word and related to the topic of ancient Greece. When doing drama about American history, Richard would use a prompt like, "How did the British *acquire* the colonies?"

He uses words like "acquire," "analyze," "compare," and "contrast" – language critical to success in school but not something new English speakers would hear on the playground. These activities scaffold into complex drama work.

On another day, Richard lays nearly one hundred hats out on tables. Each student "chooses a hat and describes that hat in complete sentences. They then create characters based on the hat and devise scenes that these characters can inhabit." After [...] performing for each other, on the board Richard shares

- words/concepts/ideas that Mr. S. heard or observed;
- words/concepts/ideas that Mr. S. thought of;
- words/concepts/ideas that students thought of or observed.

Students write these down in a separate part of the journal and they then talk about the words and their drama work.

By learning and practicing English as used in school, by thinking and writing critically, and by creating drama together, students improve academically and artistically. While the high school in Berkeley has the highest achievement gap of any school in California, Richard's drama program has been an instrumental part of closing the achievement gap at the middle school.

Richard's love of learning is contagious. "I love to learn. [...] One thing kids get from me is that learning is the greatest thing you can do" (2011a). A detailed lesson Richard developed for these students is included on page 204. Rick Garcia's work with English language learners can be found on page 83.

THEATRE AND GENDER

There was a child went forth every day
And the first object he looked upon, that object he became
And that object became part of him for a day or a certain part of the day,
Or for many years or stretching cycles of years. Walt Whitman

I think that probably just by being a woman who teaches stagecraft I'm [...]
breaking down a lot of stereotypes. [...] They walk in the door, and they're like
"Uh, you're our stagecraft teacher?" [I] always [...] wear a skirt the day that I
teach the saws [...] just to help remind them that "You know what, girls can do
this too." I think it's a way of teaching without ever having to say a word. Valerie
Roberts Labonski, Teacher

Jennifer Chapman (2002), a theatre artist and teacher, has investigated the development of girls' role identification as females. She has questioned how the

141

characters we ask adolescent girls to play onstage might impact their own gender development. Jennifer wrote an article about a high school production of *Damn Yankees* (2000). Her ideas have particular relevance to a discussion of gender and socially responsible theatre education.

From behind the curtain came the actress. A fifteen- or sixteen-year-old girl dressed in a sequined, red dress that generously reveals her voluptuous figure. She paraded the stage in heels and stockings, belting her song "Whatever Lola wants [...] Lola gets," her hips signaling the downbeats to the music. Gradually she moved off the stage and into the house, interacting with the audience as she sang, making playful eye contact with willing male observers, and cooing to the supportive laughter and applause that met her.

[...] I felt uncomfortable, embarrassed, and generally ill at ease at the sight of a "pompom girl" (as stated in her bio) performing a character who promised the audience sexual pleasures if they could give her what she wanted. Throughout her song, "Lola" is explaining to a weak male soul that he will not be able to defend himself against her sexual prowess. She breaks away from the action on stage and continues her story/song to the audience, enticing them with her sexual power. Her job is to collect souls for her willful keeper/protector/employer, the devil. Their interactions spark laughter throughout the play, but it occurred to me that Lola's subservient position was demeaning and might not seem so funny if the characters were more realistic.

I left the theater confused by my negative reaction to a scene that everyone else in the audience appeared to enjoy. I was also concerned that my reaction was somehow related to this teenage actor's recognition of her sexual self. Shouldn't teenagers be allowed to express themselves as sexual beings who have the ability, experience, and maturity to understand those experiences? Yes, definitely. But what about when that means objectifying a woman's body and portraying it as a sexual vehicle for power and control? And what does it mean that the young woman is heartily applauded for playing this character?

My experience at *Damn Yankees* caused me to reflect on the importance of providing adolescent girls with roles and entire plays that challenge traditional constructions of female gender, express some element of their own life experiences, and provide a vehicle for self-reflection and growth. [...] If theatre is to provide an opportunity for a creative exploration of self, then we must be considerate of the unique "selves" of adolescent performers; I don't think this has to be contradictory to enjoying the process of creating a play. The challenge for theatre practitioners, teachers, and scholars is to expand the repertoire of plays for high school students to include more pieces that can achieve both. (Chapman 2000)

Eighty percent of girls aged thirteen to eighteen list shopping as their favorite hobby. [...] One-quarter of fourteen-to-seventeen-year-olds of both sexes [...] reported either sending or receiving naked pictures of someone else. [...] Fifty percent of three-to-six-year-old girls worry about being fat and 81 percent of ten-year-olds fear getting fat.
Stephanie Hanes

Figure 3.1: Both girls and boys assume leadership roles in a gender-fair theatre program.

Sexualizing children – inappropriately imposing sexuality on children (American Psychological Association [APA] 2007) – and age compression – when young children adopt behaviors previously reserved for adults or older youth – coupled with declines in middle school girls' interest in sports or academics, because seen as unfeminine or not sexy, (Hanes 2011a) are troubling trends and areas of concern for those in theatre education.

Sexualizing younger and younger children is not primarily about sex, it is about money, as evidenced by marketing group NPD Fashionworld's annual expenditure of more than $1.6 million on advertising thong underwear for seven to twelve-year-olds. Abercrombie and Fitch and Amazon.com started carrying a line of bikini tops and padded bras for children as young as five. (Hanes 2011b) In a culture in which children are manipulated for gain by marketing and retail giants, we need to examine our theatre programs for signs of sexualization, objectification, or marketing exploitation.

When a student portrays a sexualized character, we are asking them to depict that

- a person's value comes only from his or her sexual appeal or behavior, to the exclusion of other characteristics;
- a person is held to a standard that equates physical attractiveness (narrowly defined) with being sexy;
- a person is sexually objectified – that is, made into a thing for others' sexual use, rather than being seen as a person with the capacity for independent action and decision making; and/or
- sexuality is inappropriately imposed upon a person. (APA 2007)

Ethical, socially responsible theatre teachers in this era think deeply about how popular culture and the performing arts themselves applaud and reward the "sexy babe" and the "hot stud" images while imposing adult behaviors on young people. They avoid or interrupt those depictions through discussions, process drama projects, research, post-show talk-back sessions, and dramaturgical work. As they select and cast shows to study or produce, they analyze the representations they are asking students to read, see, and enact and consider the impact on the development of adolescents' identities as a result of studying, playing, or seeing characters that are objectified or sexualized.

Most teachers have seen onstage experiences for both males and females positively inform students' offstage perceptions of themselves and others. Asking teens, however, to enact behaviors that would, under other circumstances and by most community standards be deemed inappropriate – without opportunities to discuss these depictions in rehearsals, talk-back sessions, or dramaturgical materials shared with audiences – is not socially responsible practice. In addition, examination in a secondary school program of depictions of gender, as well as

[For] a teenager growing up where I'm growing up and in the generation that I'm in [...] [theatre] is an outlet for me. [...] It [...] has shown me that whoever I am, wherever I am [...] it's okay to be who I am. High School Theatre Student

The most common reason for a female character to even be there [in film or television] is eye candy. They don't have a job and their function is to be sexy. [...] Kids need to see entertainment where females are valued as much as males. Geena Davis, Actor and Activist

gender bias, is an area ripe for further consideration by teacher-artists as well as researchers (Chapman 2002).

Fortunately, there are organizations and performing artists who are drawing attention to gender representation in the media and the arts. The Geena Davis Institute on Gender in Media (2011) "is the only research-based organization working within the media and entertainment industry to engage, educate, and influence the need for gender balance, reducing stereotyping, and creating a wide variety of female characters for entertainment targeting children eleven and under." These efforts, along with the work of parents, educators, legislators, and girls themselves, can make a difference in the images young people see and are asked to perform.

Many teachers intentionally strive to make their theatre programs gender fair and to be sure that neither gender is silenced nor dominates (Metz and McNally 2001; Bishop 1992). There have been theatre projects, prompted by the work of Piper, Ornstein, and others, which have examined multiple views of what it means to be female. (A sample lesson from such a project is included in Chapter 5 on page 288.) Bishop points out, however, that "gender-fair education refers to curriculum and teaching methods that adequately support and meet the needs of *both* girls and boys" (Bishop 1992, 7, emphasis added). While there have been research studies, articles, and books written about boys (Bennett 2011; James and Thomas 2009; Thompson and Barker 2009; Kindlon and Thompson 2000; Garbarino 1999; Pollack 1998), interestingly, I found no teacher-artists who have developed performances or classroom work exploring the paths from boyhood to manhood, celebrating multiple views of what it means to be male, or depicting a fuller sense of being a boy. In the effort to be gender-fair and empower girls through gender-specific theatre projects, boys may be underserved or disenfranchised. As one middle school boy remarked to me, "Why does girl power mean putting boys down? Why can't we just lift everyone up?"

Despite increasing awareness of gender in education, subtle gender bias still slips into our classrooms in ways beyond the curriculum or production season. The most ubiquitous – calling everyone "guys" – permeates our culture and teaching practices. Preservice students often argue that this – like Disney's depictions of females or Glee's depictions of high school arts programs – are innocuous, clearly fictional, or merely gender neutral; that is until I call the male students "girlfriend."

THEATRE AND SEXUAL ORIENTATION

At a time of heightened public attention to the scourge of bullying, the experiences of LGBT youth in many schools – "high performing" or not – provide heartbreaking reminders that they especially need support in school. In a school of 1,000 students, up to 100 will be gay, lesbian, or bisexual; ten will be transgender; and one will be intersex (biologically neither male nor female). If their lives are average, eighty-seven of them will be verbally harassed, forty of them will be physically harassed, and nineteen will be physically assaulted in the next year because of their sexual orientation or gender expression. Sixty-two will feel mostly unsafe going to school. Thirty will harm themselves in what may be suicide attempts. Abe Louise Young

Gender identification in a theatre program is related in some instances to recognition of differences in sexual orientation. I taught drama to teachers at a theatre institute one summer with Jason Ewing, a drama teacher from Evanston, Illinois. Jason was using *From the Notebooks of Melanin Sun* (1996),[2] to demonstrate how a book could be used as a springboard into drama for older elementary and middle school students. Two teachers borrowed and read the whole book, which later in the text includes the heterosexual awakening of the young protagonist against the backdrop of his discovery of his mother's homosexuality. The teachers were taken aback by the material and concerned about how parents and administrators would respond. While Jason had no intention of using the entire book in the classroom, he acknowledged that some students might be interested in reading it since his drama work with the story leaves off just before the mom brings a visitor home for her son to meet. In his interview with me, Jason describes *Melanin Sun* and the way he handles sensitive material in the classroom.

I use the piece in such a way [...] that I [...] give them just a little bit of dramatic information and then let them make choices. [...] I don't do the [story] in a linear fashion. [...] At first it's just getting to know who these characters are and really doing a character study. [...] What is it like to live in Brooklyn in the summer on the third floor in Hell's Kitchen? And what is it like to live in a community where you hear all these different languages and you see kids bouncing up and down [in the street] on box springs? [...] What is it like to be a kid who doesn't feel comfortable with all the other kids? [...] It's really interesting to me to see what comes from those dramas.

We hear the history of how Mom got this family of two into this neighborhood. And it brings up issues of the father who's not there, and how do you define father, and should people feel sorry for kids who don't have fathers because they don't know any different? So, it brings up a lot of good issues that students can talk about.

In [...] [the] part of the story [where] Melanin's mother tells Melanin that she's bringing someone home for dinner [...] and she wants Melanin to be there, he says, "Wait a minute, you're not getting married are you?" So she's [...] concerned that his paradigm is going to have to be shifted. [...] [W]hat's interesting to me is to see what scenes they come up with. I call it the "Guess who's coming to dinner?" scene. (Ewing 2002)

Jason goes on to discuss why and how he chooses to use controversial material in the classroom.

> I've been really careful [...] when I pick literature [for drama work]. I make sure that either the literature has won an award, has been reviewed by the American Library Association, or is a current book [in a library] somewhere in town, so that it does not appear that I am [...] forcing beliefs or forcing cultural mores onto students. [...] I'm really careful in how we talk about this. But you know, we have [local, state, and national] standards that talk about current events. [...] And the teachers do current events in their classrooms, which gives me the entranceway to do things with that in the drama classroom. (Ewing 2002)

Jerry Smith teaches theatre at Salem High School in LaGrange, Georgia. He feels sexual orientation will naturally emerge as a topic in a theatre program.

> With our kids [...] one of the things we try to do is deal with gay issues because we certainly have gay students in the building [...] and in the department. I think what theatre allows us to do is [...] work through, in a conscious setting, things that we would only subconsciously think about. [I]n the guise of an improv, you can say some of those things that you might think but you sure would not say standing in the middle of a commons area. Or you might get that interesting look on your face when someone says something about someone gay. And there is then the opportunity to [discuss] that. (Smith 2002)

Nancy Wilkinson's theatre students became socially engaged in response to incidents of sexual harassment in her school.

> This year [there were] [...] problems for some students [who] are gay. [...] One boy was beaten up at a dance because he brought a guy. Another boy had his car [...] vandalized because he's gay. [...] So when we did *What Is Your Dream* [...] for Martin Luther King [Day], we incorporated the whole gay issue – not just [...] a dream for being ethical and having dignity and inclusiveness for all races and religions – [but also] for sexual orientation. Now that would not have been a focus five, ten years ago when I was teaching theatre, but it is right now, at least [...] this year. So we dealt with it through that piece. (Wilkinson 2002)

Patsy Koch Johns, who teaches with John Heinemann in Lincoln, Nebraska, explored issues related to sexual orientation when she directed *The Laramie Project*. That production, like their production of *The Rememberer* (see page 137), had a profound impact on both faculty and students.

It's not being LGBT (lesbian, gay, bisexual, and transgender) that causes the problems. [...] The problems are the outcome of intolerant actions and speech by peers, parents, teachers, clergy, and strangers. Youth Contributors, *How to Respect and Protect Your Lesbian, Gay, Bisexual, and Transgender Students*

There is not a day that goes by that I do not remember the story of Matthew Shepard and *The Laramie Project*. A student enters my room [who] [...] has to tell me a story that relates to the experience they had while working on the show. I encounter situations that require the courage to stand up and repeat what I learned – that violence begins small – with the words we choose to say to each other every day. Directing, acting, analyzing, studying *The Laramie Project* altered many lives [...] I believe, for the better. It gave us all a keen awareness of our own personal power to change the world with our small everyday actions. That power can be used to do good or to do evil. (Johns 2003)

There are other aspects of sexual orientation to be considered. For a majority of teachers, public knowledge of their sexual orientation is not an issue affecting their practice. For others, especially those who are gay, lesbian, or transgendered, knowledge of their sexual orientation can present challenges, such as harassment, rumor mongering, isolation, ridicule, and inappropriate or unwanted sexual advances. Jennifer Chapman (2002) reflected about the importance of dialogue about this issue, especially among teachers. While in graduate school at the University of Wisconsin-Madison, she and another graduate student were commissioned to devise and present a performance ethnography piece entitled, *Wearing the Secret Out: Performing Stories of Sexual Identities* (Chapman, Sykes, and Swedberg 2003). This performance piece is a thoughtful, stylized dramatization of verbatim excerpts from interviews with gay, lesbian, and bisexual physical education teachers. The piece has been shown at professional associations and to the intended audience of preservice teachers where it stimulated discussion about problems teachers face in their interactions with colleagues, parents, and students, as well as appropriate responses to these challenges.

Open conversations among peer theatre teachers about challenges they may encounter related to their own, a colleague's, or a student's sexual orientation – or assumed sexual orientation – and candid discussion of these concerns prior to and after entering the work force, can help prepare teachers for positive interactions with co-teachers, staff, students, and parents. Dialogue enables everyone to thrive in a safe and respectful work environment.

THEATRE, RELIGION, AND SPIRITUALITY

There is a principle which is a bar against all information, which is proof against all arguments, and which cannot fail to keep a man in everlasting ignorance. That principle is contempt prior to investigation. Herbert Spencer

Hate crimes and religious intolerance, unfortunately, are not things of the past. I know of incidents where children are subtly excluded from social gatherings when their friends' parents learn they are not the "right" religion. When one of my students was in high school, he experienced overt religious discrimination. Some people in his community learned that his mom identified herself as a pagan. They reacted with violence, setting a fire on the walk to the student's home, and burning hateful messages in his front yard. My student had been harassed on the way to school and at school. These behaviors, and the attitudes leading to them, beg for interrogation, discussion, and action.

Seth Wax (2005) presents four models of personalized spirituality in the work place and includes the presence of spirituality in the performing arts, specifically in theatre and music. In his paper about religion and spirituality for Project Zero, Wax offers James' understanding of spirituality.

William James (1903/1985) argued that [...] ["the spiritual"] consists of attitudes, ideas, lifestyles, and specific practices based upon a conviction "one, that the visible world is part of a more spiritual universe from which it draws its chief significance and, two, that union or harmonious relation with this 'spiritual more' is our true end." (Wax 2005, 382)

Other than the occasional holiday decorations, in many K–12 and higher education settings there is a palpable silence around issues of spirituality and religion due, perhaps, to concerns about separation of church and state. This silence may be confusing or disconcerting to young people for whom their faith or their family's spiritual beliefs are a vital part of their identity. Assumptions about organized religion in general, stereotypes about specific faiths, confusion between spirituality and religion, and uncertainty about legal issues can leave educators unsure of how to respond to issues that might come up in school. Young people, "religious" or not, can become vulnerable to criticism and misinformed about students or the faculty with whom they must work closely.

D. Michael Lindsay (2003), a consultant for religion and culture to the George H. Gallup International Institute reports on findings from a recent Gallup Youth Survey.

The spiritual hunger among teens is remarkable. Millions of teens attend church and youth groups regularly. Teenagers express a burgeoning interest in learning about other faith traditions, yet most remain faithful to their own orthodox beliefs. They are persuaded that faith is an important component in their lives, and many of them want to deepen their religious understanding.

[...] The Gallup survey showed that 92 percent of teens consider their religious beliefs important to them. A third say faith is the most important influence in their lives. That number goes up to 52 percent for African-American teens. Close to four in ten say they pray alone frequently (42 percent) and read the Bible at least weekly (36 percent).

[…] Ninety-five percent express belief in God, and 67 percent have confidence in organized religion. Over half (55 percent) call themselves "religious," with an additional 39 percent referring to themselves as "spiritual but not religious." (Lindsay 2003)

Many adolescents, like many adults, have a spiritual hunger which can be defined as a desire to understand what truly governs the universe, a desire to be of purpose, to make connections and feel included, to make sense of seemingly senseless events, and to gather our best hopes and see them fulfilled. If students – or the adults in their lives – do not recognize that their restlessness, rebellion, or need for privacy or constant stimulation may be unfulfilled spiritual hunger, then young people will try to fill themselves up with material things – drugs, alcohol, sexual activity, shopping, eating, video games, social networks, and other "foods" readily available in our culture. "Nutritious" theatre programs – those engaged in best practice – can offer adolescents a place to feed their spiritual hunger, a safe harbor in which to question, explore, find meaning, and make a difference in the world without imposing specific religious or denominational beliefs. Professional educators, like those whose stories are shared here, can make misinformation and incidents of prejudice or religious discrimination opportunities for inquiry, tolerance, expanded appreciation, and a nourishing opportunity for spiritually hungry young people.

After September 11, Jason Ewing (2002) and his class

did a lot of talking about stereotypes, a lot of talking about why it is that cultures are perceived in certain ways. […] I brought in some Muslim literature. I brought in some literature from Africa that was not Judeo-Christian in its beliefs. I brought in books about animism. And we looked at them and said, "Wait a minute. How does this change our beliefs [about others]?" (Ewing 2002)

Deb Alexander had occasion to interrupt some misconceptions about Judaism while teaching her middle school students. They were discussing *The Diary of Anne Frank* (Goodrich and Hackett 1958), and Deb was talking with her students about anti-Semitism during the Nazi era.

I chose to tell them the stories that my grandparents had told me about surviving the Holocaust. I also used several visuals to tell Anne Frank's story. Halfway through my presentation, one of my students asked me, "Are we all Jews?" At first I thought he was being a smart aleck, but then I realized that he had no idea

These are incredibly powerfu[l] and empowering moments that happen [unexpectedly] in classes. If I don't throw whatever we're doing out the window and address them I think [I'm] being irresponsible. […] My charge is to educate. That's what [I'm] supposed to be doing. Rebecca Jallings, Teacher

what a "Jew" was. It turned out only five members of the class knew that Judaism was a religion. I needed to back up and explain Judaism. Now I was in very sticky territory because I didn't want to be teaching a religion lesson. Students asked, "What does a Jew look like?" "How can you tell if you're Jewish?" and "Hitler looks like a Jew." This actually led into an entirely new lesson that proved to be an excellent experience for both the students and myself. We ended up tying the discussion into the Martin Luther King, Jr. holiday and the oppression of African Americans in the United States. (Alexander 2002)

Abi Pierce found her eighth graders eager to learn about others' beliefs.

We chose the theme of labels and stereotypes and [they] developed a story that centered around a Muslim teacher and her diverse class. […] I saw a few students step up as directors and others got excited about writing and scripting the show; a couple were all about finding sound cues and one student made an excellent editor. They were so accepting of and encouraging to one another. I was […] happy with the final product, but I will never forget the process and all the moments we had as a class leading up to it. […] We learned a lot about each other through the process and shed some tears together. (Pierce 2011)

With his Theatre Ensemble in Berkley, California, Richard Silberg (2012) devised *Curiosity will be rewarded: Inside the Hagia Sophia*. The play presents a group of young people from the United States trapped in the building after an earthquake. Through extensive rehearsals, research and discussion, students explored and presented themes connected to religious conflict and possibility. Richard describes the play.

It is a meditation and response to this historic and sacred building, originally built in 532 AD, located in Istanbul, Turkey. It is a building that has been an Orthodox Christian church, an Islamic Mosque, and now is a secular museum. It has been ravaged by earthquakes, graffitied by Vikings, and sacked by Christian crusaders. Now partially covered mosaics of Christian history and theology are side by side with Islamic tile work and huge circular calligraphy panels honoring Allah, Mohammed, the first four Caliphs of Islam and the two grandsons of Mohammed. [...] It doesn't take much to make a case that the building is a reflection of both the conflicts and possibilities that have been and are still present throughout this region and, by extension, [have] imposed [themselves] on much of the modern world. (Silberg 2012)

Holly Stanfield, a teacher and a performing artist from Kenosha, Wisconsin produces provocative theatre pieces and musicals with students. Two of her recent

Figure 3.2: Socially responsible theatre education includes producing plays with complex, controversial themes relevant to students' lives. (A scene from *Parade* directed by Holly Stanfield.)

shows touched on the subjects of prayer, religion, race, and other areas of difference. In the first, she staged Mark Twain's "The War Prayer," written originally for choirs, symphonies, and soloists. The same year her students also did *Parade*. This musical is set in Atlanta and is based on the 1912–13 Leo Frank case. Holly describes the show and why she chose to produce it.

> A Jewish man [...] [is] [...] railroaded and accused [of] a young girl's rape and murder. Eventually he's lynched. [...] The show approaches race issues, Black/ White [issues and] Judeo/Christian issues, North/South issues, [and] male/ female prejudice issues. It goes through the whole gamut of issues that we faced at that point in our history. [...] It gave] us [...] an opportunity to discuss some of those things in class and let the kids think. [...] And I think they're old enough to think. [...] I think they want to. Some of them don't. Some are going to be really uncomfortable, but this is an elective. [...] If they want to come and meet us at this level, and they're ready for that discussion, then they'll come. (Stanfield 2002)

The restorative, nurturing and healing effects of a quality theatre program – whether through socially engaged work, or inclusion of disenfranchised students, or democratic, learner-centered instruction – is, as Jo Beth Gonzalez (2011) said, "a spiritual experience." (see page 181). In *Theatre: Its Healing Role in Education*, Richard Morse (2009) writes

> what greater gift can we provide for our young people than in conveying a proper estimation of who they are? Certainly a vision of their true natures and capacities forms the underpinning of all else [14] [...] With a little boost from us, our children open the windows of thought to a different world, where alienation, frustration, and violence are replaced by connection, self-esteem, and the celebration of community. (Morse 2009, 244)

THEATRE AND AGE APPROPRIATE PRACTICE

[Students] understand that a high school is a certain kind of an audience. [In improvs] I don't want to hear about drugs. I don't want to hear about sex. [...] [T]his is the way we need to do things because [they're] still kids. Holly Stanfield, Teacher

Some teacher-artists wrestle with balance when it comes to socially responsible practice. A number have decided that emphasis on current events or social issues should not be the *primary* focus of their programs. This perspective is based on a perceived need to protect the social and mental well-being of students and to focus primarily on theatre study and theatre-making. Fursey Gotuaco articulates the challenge of trying to strike a balance.

> Sometimes [...] something happens in the real world, and I'll discuss it, pull it in [...] do something with it and process that. And then there's another half [of me] that says, "You know, this must be the one place where they get to get away from all that." [...] I think there's a balance to be had. I think that theatre is the best tool in the building to make them come to grips with their emotions and the realities of the world [...] but [...] theatre is also probably the best tool in the building to give them an escape from the pressures that they feel in the world. (Gotuaco 2002)

Others, like David O'Fallon (2002), former director of the Perpich Center for the Arts in St. Paul, feel that we cannot be naïve about who is sitting in our classrooms.

> They're caring for siblings. They're working at Burger King. [...] They're doing the bagging at a supermarket. They're involved in very heavy family issues [...] sometimes with a lot of responsibility for home life. And then they come to school, and we treat them like they're six-year-olds rather than working with them to enforce their sense of responsibility and growth. [...] At the Perpich Center [...] we tried to [...] give kids more choices and responsibility and let them live with the consequences of some of their choices. (O'Fallon 2002)

Until I started writing this book, I had not thought about ageism as having anything to do with teaching young people. Yet, as I visit schools and observe and interact with teachers, artists, and students, I grow more convinced that there are important age-related questions to consider. What is age appropriate in a secondary school theatre program? What is too much, not enough, or the right combination of exposure to contemporary societal issues for children who are eleven to nineteen years old? What is the balance between what is age appropriate, what is socially responsible, and what is curricularly relevant? In centuries past, thirteen-year-olds were fighting wars and having babies. For many of our children, sadly, this is the truth of their life today. They are daily facing gang warfare in their neighborhoods and/or the consequences of early sexual activity in their own lives and the lives of their families and friends. While some American children are able to grow from childhood to adulthood under the nurturing and attentive care of mature, well-balanced, responsible adults, we cannot assume this is true for all of our students. How do we acknowledge, address, accommodate, and reflect this truth in our theatre programs?

It is our nation's shame that we continue to neglect our children's emotional lives and murder their dreams. I hope and pray that one day soon society will accept the truth that artistic process needs to become an integral part of every human being's daily life, especially our young. Robert Alexander, Director, The Living Stage

Teachers and artists are working to find answers to these questions in their classrooms and productions. Many assert, as does Staley (1988), that adolescence extends into our early twenties. Akin to the identification in the last century of adolescence as a life stage, researcher Jeffrey Jensen Arnette identifies an unsettled period of "emerging adulthood" from the late teen years through the twenties (Henig 2010). If this period is indeed a new life stage, as Arnette asserts, how we teach and interact and what we produce and study during the high school years is now more important and more complex. In the long run, questions of this magnitude must be answered, not by theories, formulas, or examples in a book, but as Bryar Cougle suggests, "individual student by individual student" (Cougle 2002).

Patsy Koch Johns eloquently summarizes the need for theatre education programs to teach and to acknowledge that our children are part of a diverse world.

We're all in our own little worlds. And that's what theatre is about, taking you into somebody else's world and making you see the world through their eyes. Once we get in our little house and we make our little breakfast and dinner and we get in our little cars and go to work [...] it's like Mr. McGoo. We become near-sighted – and if everything is all right in our little world, then it must be all right in the rest of the world as well. Theatre takes us out of our world into other worlds. I think it gives us an opportunity to mind travel, and then [...] to become better human beings, more responsible human beings because we're responsible, not just to our little microcosm but to the whole entire world. [...] We're educating young people to be responsible to the world [...] not just their world. (Johns 2002)

MAKING CONNECTIONS TO STUDENTS' LIVED EXPERIENCES

The program at Lexington High School is structured so that we always take it back to the kids' lives. For example, if we're doing a piece on status [...] we always look at status in their lives. What that does is make the process circular for the kids so that they understand they're not just looking at something on the stage or characters or something in the movies. They're actually looking at things that play out in their lives. Sandra DiMartino

Another aspect of socially responsible theatre education is how students relate to the material studied and produced. Not only do teachers and directors draw from and connect curriculum to relevant aspects of students' lives, they consciously select topics and material to interrupt assumptions and to cause a shift in students' understanding of themselves, others, and our world. While some teachers make clear that not everything they do relates directly to students' lives, they emphasize that there are natural and relevant connections to be found in most lessons and productions. Students working on *Romeo and Juliet,* for example, may not be considering suicide or facing gang violence, but they can identify with having a crush on someone, defying or being thwarted by authority figures, or being part of a group that is either privileged or excluded from certain activities. Links like these can open discussion and engage students in theatre-making and reflective learning.

As many teachers have learned, merely working with plays that might somehow relate to students' lives does not automatically result in a shift in understanding about the world or a change in behavior. We must deliberately help students find connections between what happens onstage and what happens in the world. This transfer of insights from a class or production to a student's life and vice versa is a goal of both drama and formal theatre and must be facilitated by a skilled teacher-director.

One cannot help but wonder how we identify transfer of knowledge and experience or transformation of thinking and behavior based on our classroom and production work, especially when one of our goals is a shift in students' understanding of themselves, their fellow humans, and their world. Assessment and evaluation models, even portfolios, document impact over fairly short periods of time and often do not capture the transfer of new understandings to larger, out-of-class lived experiences. If transformations happen out of our line of vision and sometimes long after students have left our classrooms and rehearsal halls, how can we determine what has transferred and so refine our curriculum and artistic interactions? Jo Beth Gonzalez often ponders about transfer of theatre experiences and the related joys and disappointments (2002a). In her article about transfer and transformation, she wonders aloud about what many of us sometimes have felt in our hearts.

> In my darkest moments, I regretfully sigh and wonder if any play has the power to truly influence teens to change their lifestyles or attitudes. [...] I know that adolescents are egocentric and they learn to situate themselves in society by taking risks to discover boundaries. I know I should accept the discontinuities and accept the impossibilities of full understanding. I know I should expect the impact of our work with students to be inconsistent, so I must come to terms with contradiction. I should be happy for moments of connectedness. (Gonzalez 2002a)

Some teachers are concerned about connectedness and what some may call "failed transfer." This is when students separate ideas explored in their theatre study from their lives – those frustrating moments when, for instance, after a thought-provoking rehearsal related to gender bias, a student leaves and then speaks rudely and disparaging about boys (or girls) in the parking lot with friends. Jo Beth calls these "mis-connects" versus "failed transfers" and feels they are to be embraced as part of democratic, learner-centered practice. "The particular plays that we select for our students to explore through production give students the opportunity to examine their own lives, but students must choose to make the effort" (2002a). She concludes,

> As I and other high school theatre teachers coach students to discover meaning in the plays they participate in, we will find the challenge to guide students no less difficult, but we might accept those resistances as part of the process of teaching. [...] We welcome "breakdowns" for the fresh insights they may bring to our understanding of our students, to our curriculum, and to ourselves. (Gonzalez 2002a)

We cannot fairly determine impact from a few students who have not chosen to transfer ideas from a play production to their lives or have done so selectively. Assumptions about impact, positive or negative, should not distort our work or serve as excuses for "business as usual" or for an unwillingness to raise difficult questions with students and audiences.

BUILDING A SAFE LEARNING COMMUNITY

> *For children to learn well, schools must act as centers of community rather than outposts of domination.* David Levine, Robert Lowe, Bob Peterson, and Rita Tenorio, eds., *Rethinking Schools: An Agenda for Change*

> *As a high school freshman, I dressed differently than many of my classmates and faced ridicule for it. I was withdrawn from much of the [...] school until I joined the [...] theatre department at the end of the year [...] I was quickly accepted into a group of friends that actually praised me for my need for individuality. What was even better was that this department was molded [by] some of the coolest teachers I have ever met. Their constructive criticism allowed me to open up and help add to the department [...] I hope one day to teach in a public school in the same way my high school mentors have.* Ben Gooding, Preservice Teacher

One overarching aspect of socially responsible theatre education is that sense of belonging – of being noticed and valued – that students feel at first contact with a healthy theatre program. Students in these programs often speak of their secondary school theatre program as a "community," "home," "family," and a "place where I feel I belong." The programs they are speaking about are open to all students in the school, especially those who feel they do not fit in anywhere else.

Peter Block (2008) describes community as "the structure of belonging" and writes that "[t]he essential challenge is to transform the isolation and self-interest within our communities into connectedness and caring for the whole" (Block 2008, 1). Block also speaks of the need to be accountable to a community by intentionally building relatedness and structuring belonging (Block 2008, 11). As theatre teachers, we are in a unique position to notice and respond to students' isolation and self-interest and influence how our students see themselves, their peers, and connect to the world in which they live. Being accountable and willing to accept this influential role with maturity and sensitivity is best practice.

Jan Mandell describes how she assumes that role in her program in St. Paul, Minnesota.

> What we're about is unity, diversity, talent, [and] respect. Those are kind of the key words for us. [...] I work with racially diverse kids. [...] A lot of [students] are not used to revealing themselves to people of other races, backgrounds, sexual [orientations]. They come in with all kinds of barriers in terms of what adults are about in their lives. [...] The very first thing I say to the kids is that it's my challenge to get you to trust, and I'm for real. [...] I tell them how I came to this work and why it's important to me and then we go into a variety of theatre exercises that develop safe space for an individual and for a group. Safe space is also something that you have to continually work on; it doesn't just appear and then it's there. You tell certain things to your family or to your folk that you don't reveal to other people. [This] [...] also makes for a really volatile classroom because as soon as everybody knows everything about you, if any violation happens, it's much bigger than just an argument in any kind of class. [...] By knowing your kids, you really get a sense of [...] what to do. (Mandell 2002)

It is impossible to calculate the impact one teacher can have on a student's life. I recently read an account of a young woman who overcame depression and isolation because a teacher took an active interest in a book she was reading (Markowitz 2003). But how do teacher-artists create community and carry principles of learner-centered instruction and socially responsible practice into their whole theatre program and the school community?

Bobby Malone talks about being flexible, responsive, and finding teachable moments to build a safe learning community.

> You look for these openings [...] where you know that those kids are listening. You're [...] in their element, something they're really interested in [...] a moment in their life that [...] you know without a doubt that they're taking in what you're saying or what's happening. [...] You're not necessarily teaching

For students whose home cultures have a strong community orientation and who are primarily denied a sense of positive community ties in the white, middle class dynamics of their schooling (Macedo and Bartolomé 1999; Ladson-Billings 1994), the establishment of community in school settings is crucial. Bethany Nelson

Figure 3.3: A theatre program can be a safe place for students to talk, be heard, and feel appreciated.

[...] about [...] [theatre]. You're teaching them about life and how to interact with one another and how to cope when things are good or bad.

[...] I had a senior [...] my second year teaching [...] and she was [...] the sweetest girl, hardest working student [...] always there to help. [...] In the spring of her senior year, her brother, who was a year younger than her, committed suicide. [...] This is not a [...] kid that you would ever expect [...] would do this. [...] As a teacher you plan and you have your curriculum and you have schedules and you have due dates and then something like that happens and all of that goes away. [...] How could you talk about [...] scene work or theatre [...] when you know that the person in your class is grieving as badly as she was? And [...] all the kids surrounding her [...] lost a friend [...] [T]his is the first time they've ever felt loss that close to them. And so being careful not to make [the class] a counseling session, it [turned] into more of a support group. [For example, for] the next two weeks [in] theatre class [...] [because] we knew the kids weren't eating [...] we made sure that we had [...] stuff to make sandwiches and chips and drinks. [...] We felt we had to support those kids where they were not going to support themselves. [...] You have to feel out the kids, where they're at, what's going on in their lives and you really have to respond to that.

That's an extreme situation. I hope a lot of people don't have to go through it [...] but then you've got the [...] kind of situations that happen daily in your classroom. [...] You come into that classroom and in your head [...] everything's going to work out and everybody's going to want to do what you've got planned today [...] but there's always a handful of kids [...] [who are] going to challenge you in some way or another or somebody's pet's going to die. [...] I've had a kid come and tell us before a show that she just found out that she was pregnant. [...] That will throw your entire rehearsal off! [...] How can you tell a kid to take the stage when you know that they're battling something [like that]? She told us [...] before she told her mother. [...] We brought in all three of the theatre directors [...] (after we asked her if she'd be comfortable with that). [...] We had an alternate fill her place [at rehearsal]. [...] Our stage manager ran rehearsal [...] and we spoke with her. [...] We comforted her and helped her make a decision to tell her mom. [...] Again, that's one of those curve balls that as a teacher you're going to get every single day. [...] You judge whether or not you can continue what you've planned or not and once you've made that decision [...] [you] think on your feet [...] [about] what's going to benefit the students the best from that point on. [...] Those are the moments that make a teacher, knowing you're going to fill many roles and knowing when and where is the appropriate time to change those roles during the day, during the class, whenever they happen. (Malone 2011b)

The first time I walked into a theatre was the first time I was wonderful at something. Patsy Koch, Teacher

160

Jerry Smith (2002), who teaches in Georgia, notes that "teachers spend more time with kids [...] than parents do." His program also operates as a community and includes parents in appropriate ways.

[It is important] [...] for parents to understand how their kids are working their hands off. [...] I [also] think our students learn a tremendous amount from the fact that parents are here. They're welcome to be here. They're not forced to be here. [...] Our parents are in and out of rehearsals. They feed us the week and a half before a show. [...] I would not have a program, it would not be educationally sound, if that part of the community wasn't involved.

I believe that without parents involved, you don't have the full conversation. [...] Sometimes, that's a negative conversation, which is fine. [...] I love it when a parent wants to challenge. [...] Then there can be a dialogue. [...] We, as a school community, we, as a theatre community, have to be open to the dialogue, not be afraid of it, but be open to it. (Smith 2002)

Like so many other teachers, for Holly Stanfield (2002; 2009) creating a safe and respectful community and making long-term commitments to students is central to her program.

The rule [...] [is]: It has to be safe. That's it. Which means [...] when you get into [...] improv [...] some of the scenes [might become hurtful]. [...] Kids know when you're laughing cause it's funny or when you're laughing to be mean. [...] So, if you're laughing to be mean, you can drop the class now. That means you just aren't mature enough to do this yet. You can come back again. I'll love you either way. We'll talk, and your parents and I will talk, but you can't do that here. [...] If kids are going to grow in a community, that's just not possible. And it's kind of a collective sigh of relief when they really realize that [this] class is going to run that way. And they all make the decision, "Okay, I know I can't do that, so I won't." (Stanfield 2002)

A CULTURE OF CARING

This one kid [...] comes from a terrible home life and he always used to be a problem [for the other teachers]. [...] Now he's acting and he adores it. He's not been in ISS (in-school suspension) once since he started doing theatre. He's kept his grades up to As and Bs and he hasn't been sent to the office in a year. Billie Harvey, Teacher

We all have treasured stories from students about the impact our theatre programs have had on their lives. Both teachers and students attribute much of this impact to the fact that their theatre programs are safe havens for students in socially, emotionally, or physically hostile school environments.

I describe this phenomenon as the intentional creation of a culture of caring in schools that can be "outpost[s] of domination" (Levine et al. 1995, 234). These caring communities are fostered and nurtured by theatre teachers who are able to love in the largest sense of the word. Their love is not personal or inappropriate or overreaching, but an unconditional love for children as valuable human beings. They seem to effortlessly express this larger love in joyful, selfless interactions that embrace all who enter their classrooms or theatres. Some teachers are more formal in their interactions than others, some more playful, but all extend genuine caring and human kindness to the people they teach and with whom they work. Teachers engaged in this way often speak of teaching as a calling, a way of serving others.

Candace Koern shares,

> I love my job and working with young people [...] [and] actually caring about how another human being is doing [...] the path they are taking. [...] I was a mischievous teenager myself, so I can relate to even the most challenging students [...] and I work to build relationships with all my students. I try to talk to each of them personally each and every day, even if it is only a "what's up?" And I am honest with them. If there is a problem, I address it directly. If I have made a mistake, I admit it. (Koern 2011)

There are many moving examples of theatre teachers who have noticed a need and responded with the right word or action, thus helping a student to feel noticed, cared about, and "at home." In one of his first years teaching, Brendan Kelley put on the musical *Honk!*

> The student who played the mother of the ugly duckling had a father with cancer. One night close to the performance date, she and a friend asked if they could take some of the kids to his hospital room and perform some songs, because he was not going to be able to come to the show. I said, "Of course!" A few days later, the student's mother found me and said that the day after the students came to perform for him, the father had died. She told me that he loved watching them sing. I went to talk with the student, and I told her that if she needed anything, even if it was letting her out of the show, to let me know. She said that she needed to miss a rehearsal, but she still wanted to perform.
>
> The mother [in *Honk!*] has a song that goes "Every tear a mother cries is a dream that's washed away." She sings that on stage all by herself when she thinks she'll never see her son again. The student had a beautiful voice, and when it

came time for that song every night I teared up [...] because I could [...] tell that she was singing the song to her father. I did not have a lot to do with the students making the decision to sing to her father [...] but it was one of, if not the most, moving experience I have had as a theatre educator.

[...] I have made the conscious decision to teach out of love. I try to find things I admire about each student, and I let them know about those things. When they push back with caustic or sarcastic remarks, I try to remind myself that those are the kids that probably need a model for a healthy relationship more than anyone. This is my goal. I do not always succeed. Sometimes I get angry with some students or feel like giving up on them. The next day, though, I try again. (Kelley 2011)

Teachers in these programs make apparent to students that *what* they teach and produce and *how* they teach and produce directly relates to the students' lives and their interests and concerns. They are consistent in showing compassion and encouraging reflection, inquiry, and ownership in their classrooms, in rehearsals, and all other interactions with students. The ongoing alertness to students and their needs and open dialogue characterize their learner-centered, socially responsible classrooms and enliven their entire theatre programs.

Frank Chuter characterizes teaching itself as a call to serve others.

Helping somebody is what I'm supposed to do. [...] I'm put on this planet to teach and [...] to inspire and to love other people and I [...] believe that [...] people need to know that they're loved and that they're cared for."

Referring to Frederick Buechner's quote – that your calling is "where your deep gladness meets the world's deep need" – Frank adds,

[Teaching is] where I'm most happy, my deepest gladness. Theatre is great and it's wonderful and I love doing it [...] but I don't do it because I want to teach kids how to be better theatre students or how to be better actors. That's a byproduct of what I'm doing. (Chuter 2011c)

Rebecca Jallings (2002) highlights the gap a theatre program can fill in students' school experience.

One of the things the kids say in their final exams a lot is [...] "This is the only class [...] I've ever had where I learned everybody's name." [...] A retired teacher [...] who I really respect said that what happens in a classroom between the kids in the class and the teacher, [...] that community of people, is mystical and sacred. [...] I think she's right. On a good day it's mystical and sacred. You can't leave out pieces of it. And you can't expect people to have a mystical and spiritual and sacred experience in a group of people whose names they don't even know.

BUILDING RELATIONSHIPS WITHIN THE PROGRAM

Lara was very shy, very reserved, as a ninth grader. She was taller than most all of her classmates, including the boys. [...] [She] didn't carry herself with any air of confidence. [...] She had rounded shoulders and her arms were crossed most of the time, closing herself off to others around her. When she entered the theatre department, she didn't seem to fit in [...] until [...] a senior [student] costumer in the department extended her hand to include Lara on her costume [crew]. [...] We started to see changes take place in Lara. Little by little, pieces of Lara's shell started to crack. [...] Lara is [now] a senior at Carnegie Mellon University majoring in design [and her] costume designs [...] will be seen on the Carnegie Mellon stage [....] [...] There is a place for everyone in theatre. Carlin Gilseth, Teacher

I learned (the hard way, through experience) that [thinking of or] labeling a kid as "bad" or even a class as "bad" doesn't help. You can't hide the truth from them. They will see right through it. Lena Paulauskas, Teacher

How do these teachers and students build this safe place within schools and with students, faculty, staff, and parents who work and frequent the school? As artist-teachers, many of our interactions with students occur outside of our classrooms or rehearsals during crew calls, drama club or Thespian events, fundraisers, or informal gatherings. Through our formal and informal interactions with students, colleagues, parents, and community members, we establish a culture that makes clear that our program is inclusive or exclusive. We create a community that either invites or discourages authentic participation by all students.

Teachers invent ways to make their theatre programs inviting places of discovery and celebration. Doors are open when work is going on; audition workshops are held and new students are invited to attend; social needs of the adolescents are addressed through celebrations of accomplishments; clean-up days, field trips, and service projects are planned; welcome-back and end-of-year festivities are hosted for current and prospective members of the program; and students serve as formal or informal ambassadors to students new to the department.

Opportunities to be of service in the school and community allow teenagers to move beyond themselves while still being anchored in the safe harbor of a community that values theatre, artmaking, and their individual contributions. All of these interactions among and between students and teacher-directors characterize principles of best practice. An inclusive, learner-centered culture is at the foundation of these programs.

Many teachers are also active in the life of their schools, giving students opportunities to work with faculty, staff, parents, and other adults in the school community. Laurel Serleth (2002) used theatre to build community within her urban school. Working with the drama club, she devised a piece based on the dreams of all those in the building. Students collected dreams from other students, the custodians, teachers, and administrators. The night dreams and nightmares of the school population as well as their daydreams, hopes, and desires were staged in a bilingual, eclectic performance for the whole school.

In Fursey Gotuaco's former high school, the principal thought of him and the theatre program almost as an extension of the administration. The principal turned to Fursey (2002) and former co-teacher Jenny Lutringer (2002a) for advice and solutions to issues in the larger school community. Brianna Lindahl (2002b) brings her drama skills into service for her school as well. She developed a process drama and used Boal's (1985) Forum Theatre techniques in workshops and programs with faculty and staff.

Sandy DiMartino (2003) found a way to respond to an administrator's concerns while unifying students and teachers at her high school in the Boston area.

> This year we held a Renaissance Fair. [...] Our goal was to have more of the adults [teachers and staff actively] involved in the school. [...] We had adults singing and performing and reading Tarot cards. [...] It brought kids and adults together in a way they wouldn't normally be brought together. [...] One of my agendas [...] was to make [...] connections so the adults had [...] an understanding of the types of students who were working with us and also of the work involved. [...] Also, the principal has spoken with me about ways in which to [...] help connect the community more because the adults in our school are all [...] separated from each other. [...] One of the other agendas was just to help the adults see each other and connect. [...] The feedback was overwhelmingly positive. (DiMartino 2003)

The rehearsal process becomes part of a bigger experience, the creating of a community of actors who are being put in touch with another community, the community of the world of the play, which in turn makes a larger connection to the community of people who come to see it. Gordon Davidson

Creating an environment in which students can safely explore ideas and challenges that will help them grow into healthy adults is an admirable goal. It can also serve a larger social purpose by allowing young people to practice healthy interactions with peers and adults and to imagine life beyond high school.

Steve Bogart teaches with Sandy DiMartino at Lexington High School near Boston. In his Drama of Social Issues class, students devise and perform two original pieces for the school during the semester. In their improvisation classes, he and Sandy challenge students to be socially engaged and to look at their actions from multiple perspectives. In one lesson, they invite students to journal about and then improvise a conflict they had with an authority figure. In this paired improv, students play the authority figure and coach the actor playing them. As a result, they have seen students change their perspective and initiate new relationships with adults. (See the "Conflict with Authority" lesson, page 202.)

Others see theatre programs serving an intervention function, redirecting students into productive activity. In her 1999 essay responding to the shootings at Columbine High School, Holly Giffin discusses how theatre programs might help our young people imagine multiple solutions to the dramas they live out each day at school. Betty Staley (1988) furthers this idea by stating that "Through drama, adolescents are able to try out roles; experiment with anger, confrontation, sensitivity, compassion, and sacrifice; and to vicariously experience what happens to people in different life situations" (Staley 1988, 14–15). It is far too speculative to consider if tragic events have been avoided because someone got involved with or stayed active in a secondary school theatre program. It does give me pause, however, and hope for more research in this area, when I hear of young people who avoid involvement in gangs or abstain from drugs, alcohol, or other dangerous behaviors because they are in a theatre program where they feel "at home."

I don't care whether it's math class or phys. ed, you don't pass up a chance to talk about issues of ethics and morals and empathy. [...] I'm a teacher. Theatre happens to be my discipline; but I'm a teacher. That's what I do. Rebecca Jallings, Teacher

SOCIALLY RESPONSIBLE INTERACTIONS WITH STUDENTS

Education as the practice of freedom – as opposed to education as the practice of domination – denies that man is abstract, isolated, independent, and unattached to the world; it also denies that the world exists as a reality apart from people. Paulo Freire

There are typically more informal interactions between students and theatre teachers that occur during crew calls, between classes, at rehearsals, over lunch, on field trips, and after school than occur during classes. Many teachers feel that the very nature of our work – the exploration of controversial, amusing, or provocative issues, the investigation of intense emotions, the dynamics of human interactions within the company and the school, and the sheer number of hours spent with young people – demands setting personal boundaries and shared understandings of protocols and procedures. Teachers develop handbooks that spell out everything from the philosophy of the program, to audition procedures, to shop rules, to rules for field trips, to appropriate student-student and teacher-student interactions. Bryar Cougle (2002) comments about why this is important:

I think [...] part of the reason that teachers experience a lot of burnout [is] because [...] you get very close to kids. If you work closely with students, both instructionally and after school – which also is instructional but on a more personal level – you can't avoid [it] [...] because kids bring their stuff to you,

166

and you end up being a part of that whether you volunteered for it or not. So the work becomes [...] professional work that you have to deal [with] on a very emotional level with kids and with your own self sometimes. [...] Aside from the physical work of being a drama teacher, and the mental work of being a drama teacher, and all the things you have to attend to just to teach every day and keep an after school program going, [...] then you heap on top of that dealing with individual kids who need something from you or need something from [...] the environment you have created [....] That's hard. That's a very hard job. It's a balancing act to keep it all going and not step on any toes, not to get in any trouble. (Cougle 2002)

There are teachers who *have* gotten into trouble because they have not created a safe, respectful environment for students. I know of a teacher who swears at students and refers to them, to their faces, as "a–holes" and "losers." I am told he keeps his job because he is a great director. We all have heard stories like this, of teachers who actively socialize with students, share intimate details of their personal lives, supply alcohol to students, get mired in the personal minutiae of students' lives, or who leave students unsupervised, working alone on ladders or with power tools. Many new and veteran teachers also have confused the love students feel for the theatre with personal love for them.

So where do you draw the line between being a compassionate and caring adult professional and being a friend, confidante, lay therapist, or buddy? Despite signs and protests of maturity, secondary school students are still children who need teachers who will offer protection, guidance, and sound professional judgment. A number of teachers counsel that drawing boundaries for students shows respect for them. They advise:

- Never confuse your job with yourself. Kids love the work, which is different from you in the work.
- Recognize the power you wield and use it with benevolence toward all. Favoritism is more about your ego than their learning. To quote from *Spider-Man*, "With great power comes great responsibility."
- If students begin to disclose information to you that puts them or others at risk, let them know that you, by law, will have to share this information with a counselor or other appropriate person. Offer to go with them to the counselor's office.
- Do not share your own secrets or personal information with students unless you want it shared with others. Not only will students tell others what you say and do, they will embellish and distort the truth intentionally or not.
- Learn your district's policies and your school's procedures for liability and crisis management. Work with administrators, parents, teachers, staff, and students to

amend policies and procedures so that they address unique circumstances that may arise in your program.

- Never be alone with a student in a room with the door closed.
- Take the work seriously. Do not take yourself too seriously.
- Make a life for yourself outside of school. It will make you a better teacher.

THEATRE AS A CATALYST FOR DIALOGUE: CONNECTIONS TO THE COMMUNITY OUTSIDE OF THE SCHOOL

We need to bring the neighbor back to the "hood." Grace Lee Boggs

A teacher at the high school nearest to the World Trade Center [...] gathered the writing of the students who witnessed history firsthand. Their school was used as a law enforcement command post, and many of the students, unable to return to their school, turned to art, theatre, and photography and writing to express their emotions. [They wrote] monologues, based on interviews with students, faculty, and staff, [and] put a hopeful perspective on a monumental tragedy, demonstrating the remarkable spirit of our nation's children. Jeanette Larson

The examples in this book clearly depict theatre programs where classroom and production projects serve as catalysts for dialogue, community building, and new connections to ideas and individuals. Teacher-artists work intentionally to connect the school with the larger community and the community with the school as part of their socially responsible practice. A number have devised pieces and offer productions in community venues and area schools.

Tory Peterson (2002) illustrates one example of engagement with community. He teaches in St. Paul, where he uses his curriculum to link students to issues in other Minnesota communities. Students conduct interviews with community members and then create original theatre pieces based on their research. He describes one project in particular:

My students are reading *Main Street* by Sinclair Lewis this summer. [...] When we meet in the fall, [we'll] talk about [...] the issues raised [...] [and] then I will turn my students loose in small-town Minnesota – whichever small town they choose to go to – to look at economics, labor, cultural diversity [...] [and topics] in Lewis's play [like] provincialism, institutionalism - so it's all [...] connected. (Peterson 2002)

Deb Alexander (2012) has created community connections through the musicals her middle schoolers are to present each year. When she was about to produce

Annie, Deb pondered how the project could have deeper meaning for her students and herself. Following the themes of adoption and finding a loving home, she contacted the local Humane Society and created a joint project that was advertised to the school and surrounding community. An "orphan" (rescue) dog was selected to play Sandy. After the Sunday matinee, other dogs from the Humane Society, including Sandy and all of her puppies, were adopted by audience and community members. Admission to performances were donations of dog food, dog supplies or cash donations to the Humane Society.

Deb's productions move her middle school students from concrete to abstract thinking and focus on ways to serve others. At the time Deb was deciding to produce *The Wizard of Oz*, the community was becoming polarized over the proposed development of a new bike path and discussions of bicyclists' rights were in the news. Her fifth graders suggested basing the design concept around Miss Gulch's appearance on a bicycle. Deb and the students designed the yellow brick road as a bike path and designed elements of the production to move on wheels, such as the monkeys, Glinda, the Wicked Witch of the West, and other characters and props. Weaving the connections further into dramaturgical and design work, cast members each decorated a used bike to reveal aspects of their characters. Having very little storage at the middle school, Deb used found objects and scrap metal to create sculptures onstage for the Emerald City and other locations. Audience members were invited to bring used bikes to the performances. After the final performance, all of the bikes were donated to the Yellow Bike project which repairs used bikes and provides them for public use. All of the set and prop pieces were recycled.

Before beginning on her current production of *Godspell*, Deb and the students discussed the themes of the play and ways to engage the whole school. Since the production was around Earth Day, they decided to make this a green production and use only recycled materials focusing on love and loving the earth. Working from students' ideas, she found an architect and designed a set to be made of student donated canned food held in place by wooden frames and chicken wire. Deb contacted a local company that rents platforms, step units, and other set pieces. Her students will paint the pieces and the company owner will work with them on assembly. Since the stage is in the gymnasium, each time a class comes in for gym, they can see more of the set being built from food they have donated. After strike, all of the food will be given to a local food bank and the costumes and props, built from second hand items, will be given back to thrift stores. (Alexander 2012)

Joint community-based projects can bring groups together to address significant issues. On page 283, Gillian McNally describes an interdisciplinary arts program that served as a catalyst for artistic and cultural self-realization and important community dialogue.

CHOOSING SOCIALLY RESPONSIBLE MATERIAL TO TEACH AND PRODUCE

True personal freedom and self-expression can flower only in an atmosphere where attitudes permit equality between student and teacher and the dependencies of teacher for student and student for teacher are done away with. The problems within the subject matter will teach both of them. Viola Spolin

Socially responsible theatre education means that the material produced with students challenges them to think critically, stimulates their imaginations, and encourages them to consider the nature of what it means to be human.

There is a range of subject matter, periods, styles, and structures in the scripts teachers produce. Many are well-crafted examples of the art form, scripts that provide rich use of language, character, and structure. A number of the scripts discussed by teacher-directors are deemed worthy for production because they provide opportunities for students in the company, and people in the audience, to grow emotionally, socially, and artistically. Plays with themes that are relevant to performers and audience members and with protagonists who live in the same world – or are challenged by the same concerns performers are facing – provide avenues for understanding self and others. Directors often note that production material related to students' lived experiences, whether classic or contemporary, while being relevant, should not stoop to the derivative, sensational, contrived, or merely trendy. Instead, dramatic material that challenges the performer intellectually, emotionally, and artistically excites students to a greater understanding of the power of the theatrical form and the power of their voice within that form (Lazarus 1986).

Communities and schools have mostly unspoken standards of what is appropriate for students to perform and see. In addition to work that has artistic merit and student relevance, there are other criteria for choosing dramatic material to be studied or performed. Depicting illegal and risky behaviors in the classroom or onstage without showing authentic consequences is neither honest nor socially responsible. With discussion and reflection, socially conscious theatre productions can reveal, for example, that drinking, drugging, being sexually active, bullying, or using weapons have consequences. If we produce plays or musicals in which fifteen-year-old girls play strippers or lovers to married men, or young boys play alcoholics or enact male stereotypes, are we not giving tacit approval to this behavior? It is our responsibility to help students understand characters' behaviors in a real-world context. Quality dramatic literature depicts realistic consequences for characters' actions and raises questions about characters' choices. If we produce works like *The Who's Tommy* – as one high school did because "we have the voices and want to offer this challenge to our students" – how can that be sufficient justification in the face of children seeing and representing pedophilia, bullying, discrimination, drug use, child abuse, neglect, bigotry, and other unsavory behaviors – all without consequence? Concern for young people's social, emotional, and developmental well-being – as well as their artistic development – must weigh heavily in script selection. Unless we hold our personal artistic ambitions in check, unless we

---

When working with sensitive or controversial material, teachers engaged in best practice take thoughtful, intentional steps.

- Help administrators, parents and students understand your rationale for choosing to produce a work that may be controversial or contain sensitive material. Work though appropriate channels to garner support for the project.
- Discuss assertions, assumptions, and stereotypes embedded in the text with students.
- Encourage students to think critically about the implications and consequences of characters' choices. Help students consider the characters' actions within the world of the play *and* within the real world.
- Look at the ideas the play presents from multiple perspectives and determine the production style and interpretation. Do these correlate with the story you and the students want to tell?
- Remember you are neither a therapist nor counselor. Invite content specialists and trained social workers, counselors, or mental health professionals as partners or resources at your rehearsals and classes. Include professionals familiar with the issues presented in the play to help facilitate post-performance sessions.
- Make hotline information and resources readily available to company members if the topics being explored might affect students' mental, emotional, or physical health.
- Invite parents and administrators to open discussions about the play and your rationale for its selection.
- Alert parents/guardians to any incidents or discussions that concerned or upset students whether in the classroom or rehearsal. A letter, e-mail, or call home allows everyone to be alert in caring for students' needs. Communicate with your principal and school staff about any such incidents and keep a record of that communication for yourself.
- Alert potential audiences to the nature and age appropriateness of the material.
- Include dramaturgical information about the piece and the production in the program and/or lobby displays.
- Schedule outreach sessions and prepare study guides and resource materials about the play for classes in the school and for feeder schools who may be invited to see the play.
- Plan talkback sessions with the audience after each school or public performance.
- Prepare students to serve as dialogue facilitators.

Figure 3.4: Working Responsibly with Controversial or Sensitive Material

consider the child engaged both in the artmaking and in the audience, we do a disservice to our young people, to their healthy development, and to the art form.

This is not to advocate for a Pollyanna season that has been purged of all controversial material. On the contrary, socially responsible programs actively tackle topics and produce plays that relate to the realities of students' lives with teacher-artists handling controversial material in a socially and artistically responsible manner. (See Figure 3.4.)

Dramatic material that is age appropriate may deal with difficult, controversial, or sensitive issues in a fashion that allows audience members and performers to consider new perspectives and consequences for actions taken by characters. Plays that raise questions or offer multiple perspectives on situations are intriguing to young people. Theatrical works need not resolve difficult issues or leave audiences with happy endings to be appropriate for study or performance.

Since socially responsible teacher-directors select the material studied, performed, and produced for their own, unique communities, there is no one set of rules that everyone follows. There are, however, important questions to consider when reviewing a script. (See Figure 3.5.)

- Is there a relationship between the story being told in this script and my students, school, and community?
- What is the playwright's intent in terms of the audience for this piece?
- Is the perspective presented that of a young person or an adult?
- Is the protagonist someone with whom young people can identify?
- Does the play respect the world of young people and respect the audience by presenting the material with artistry and depth?
- Will the imaginations of the young people in the audience be engaged? Will they be engaged intellectually and emotionally?
- Is the content such that the performers can understand it?
- Does it relate to their life experiences in ways that they could recognize?
- Are there elements in the play that glamorize, trivialize or promote risky, illegal, or morally questionable behavior without showing the consequences of such behaviors?
- Does the play respectfully address ideas relevant to diverse audiences and performers?
- Are the ideas in the play presented realistically, symbolically, metaphorically, abstractly? Is this a style that can be accessible to young people? Can young people relate to the metaphors and symbols used?
- Are there aspects of the play that will need to be cut or edited to make it appropriate for the performers or audience? Can you get permission to make changes? What impact on the structure of the play will these changes make?
- Do I have concerns or doubts about the appropriateness of the material? (If so, have others read the play and pose your questions to them.)

Figure 3.5: Questions to Consider when Selecting a Script

FINDING TIME TO LOOK FOR SCRIPTS

Given the workload of most secondary school theatre teachers, finding age-appropriate dramatic material suitable for their students can be a challenge; it takes time and requires becoming familiar with a lot of scripts and talking to colleagues about their experiences with dramatic material. As Roxanne Schroeder-Arce suggests (see pages 194 and 311), it can be tempting to produce only those scripts we have seen, been in, directed before, or heard about from other teachers. Two teachers interviewed expressed dismay over colleagues they know who have developed a four-year season of plays. Those teachers direct the same plays over and over again every four years regardless of who is attending the school or involved in the program. To offset this temptation, some teacher-directors work with playwrights-in-residence, commission new works written specifically for their students, or take advantage of new play development projects through professional theatre education associations. Some involve students in play reading and/or play selection. Other teachers have a regimen of reading a certain number of plays each month or over the summer. Other teacher-directors create a list of titles that they think would fit the needs of students and the program in the coming year. The student play selection committee then chooses from among these plays and determines the season. Sometimes teachers from other disciplines, administrators, and parents are involved in play selection.

This all takes time, but primarily it takes a willingness to do things differently. It means inviting students and teachers from throughout the school into dialogue. It may mean acknowledging a limited knowledge of plays relevant to students whose ethnic, racial, and cultural backgrounds are different from one's own – and then asking for help. It may mean acknowledging having limited knowledge of plays relevant to students whose backgrounds are different from one's own – and then asking for information and others' perspectives and ideas. It means, as Rebecca Jallings says,

> [I]f there's something I don't understand about what [...] [students are] saying, what they're doing, I don't brush it off. I stop and say "Wait a minute, what does that mean? Explain that to me." Asking questions is an awful lot easier. (Jallings 2002)

CHALLENGES TO SOCIALLY RESPONSIBLE THEATRE PRACTICE

Don't let the hard boots of your idealism trample the tender shoots of your accomplishments. Georg Locher

Each community, school, and class, and each student within each class are constantly changing, and so must our responses to the issues and concerns we all face. Being socially engaged and responsive to the needs of students and the community can seem overwhelming in the face of the responsibilities of running a secondary school theatre program. I know, at times, I have lost my perspective and vision for a program or lost heart that the work was making any difference. Sometimes I have been challenged by others who have a different vision for my work. I am inspired by the attitudes that enable teacher-artists to continue in their journeys toward socially responsible theatre education. It helps me to remember that it is our own movement on the journey toward or away from best practice that should be considered. Figure 3.6 offers teacher-artists' suggestions for facing these challenges.

- Be willing to begin and keep going. Do what you can.
- Remember that socially responsible work is not just voicing or focusing on problems; it should raise questions and point to solutions and positive action.
- Do not be daunted by the skeptics, cynics, or naysayers.
- Do not be intimidated by the self-appointed champions for the rights of any group who criticize you in that 'damned if you do and damned if you don't' way.
- Remember, education is messy.
- Do not be afraid of mistakes and missteps; they are inevitable. Learn from them.
- Have your own cause, talk about it, but do not demand or expect everyone to join you. Be glad you do not have to make everyone else's cause your own.
- To the extent you are headed in the same direction toward positive change, work with others who are willing to speak up about things they care about.
- Remember everyone is on a different journey. Find common ground with others, be inclusive, and work with people who think differently.
- Manage your time. Get out of the building and see daylight. Do something to care for yourself every day.
- Keep perspective. Not everything is an issue and not every issue can or needs to be addressed through theatre.
- Laugh. Find humor in your life and joy and hope in your work.

Figure 3.6: Embracing the Challenges of Socially Responsible Theatre Education

AT WHAT COST? TAKING CARE OF YOURSELF AS BEST PRACTICE

When I taught high school, there were many days when I barely saw the sun. I left for school before sunup and returned long after sundown. I worked Saturdays and carried work home for Sundays. Between shows, I was always reading scripts or getting ready for the next show or project. I had few interests beyond my students, my program, and theatre. I performed and directed professionally and did theatre work with kids in the summer, jumping right back into my program in the fall. I worked constantly, did not sleep as much as I should have, and ate far too much fast food resulting in substantial weight gain.

I wish my compulsive work habits were the exception, but sadly, this is the norm for far too many theatre teachers. In many academic settings, being a "workaholic" is celebrated and rewarded, and in theatre education it is often the expectation – but at what cost to students and to the teacher-artists themselves?

Some teachers find that it is hard to balance school and family life. While they love what they do at school and can see how important their programs are to students, they also acknowledge a downside to their work life (Lazarus 2011). One teacher has a preschooler and nursing infant at home. Both she and her husband are performing arts teachers. During productions, her children's caregiver brings the children to school twice a day so she can nurse the baby and have meals with her son and daughter. Another teacher was approached by a group of freshmen who wanted to come in during lunch so they could do improvs together. She gobbles her lunch down between classes so that she is available to them when they arrive during her lunch break. Since her students cannot afford to attend expensive summer theatre camps, another theatre teacher works for free in a summer program she runs at her school. Other teachers spend their own money buying expensive set or costume pieces that the school cannot afford. Many drink coffee or caffeinated drinks all day long. For some teachers, their work schedules makes it difficult to see family and friends or to meet people to date, while others confide that their work was a contributing factor in their divorce.

In addition to just having time for oneself, a number of teachers report that time to prepare new lessons, to attend the theatre, to read plays and books, and to attend professional development programs, or to work with others in the school or district, would make them more effective teachers. There are teachers who, given their production schedules and despite their best intentions, are teaching things the way they have always taught them or are giving attention to productions at the expense of their classes and students. Unfortunately, there are others who have become lax about classroom management or teaching stimulating lessons "bell to bell." We all have heard of theatre classrooms where students listen to MP3 players, text, make phone calls, chat during class, or watch movies while the teacher works on the production or focuses on a few "talented" students as others stare aimlessly into space. Some teachers stay too busy to organize their workspaces so they become dumping grounds for production and instructional materials, supplies, and equipment. Many teachers want more time; however they acknowledge the problem is not necessarily time, but one of setting priorities, clarifying one's core values, and embedding them into a program that does not completely consume the teacher (Lazarus 2011).

An increasing number of teachers who love their jobs are voicing a need to be with their families or friends – or just to be alone – to have time away from school, students, and theatre so they do not burn out. These teachers make adjustments in their teaching schedules and some decide to do fewer shows, divide tasks with other teachers, or move into other positions with fewer demands. Candace Koern (2011) chose to work part time because

> Our district is now requiring heads of theatre to teach six of seven classes [each day]. [...] I felt like I couldn't do the job justice under those conditions. (I have three young children of my own.) [...] I have found great joy in being a better teacher to my [three] classes [...] [and] directing a show [...] second semester.

While moving to a part-time position might not be a possibility, there are other options for sustaining best practice while caring for oneself. C. Gary Cooper (2011c) found working so many hours was taking a toll on his family.

> It was great [...] that in only six years we had had a lot of success [...] and I was happy. But at the same time, in order to have that success, I literally lived [at the school]. [...] I wasn't seeing my family. [...] I was never seeing my children. And so for my family, I [...] went to the junior high [...] and [pursued a graduate] degree [in educational administration.]. [...] I knew I would still have [long] hours as an administrator but [...] [not] the hours [...] that a theatre teacher has.

After two years, a former administrator approached Gary to head the program at another high school in the district.

> I told him if I come [...] I am going to balance it with my family. [...] I told [the other two teachers] as well, "I *will* balance this. I will not have it where I'm neglecting family at home," and they understood. [...] There are some days that [...] I say, "Okay, rehearsal is over at 4:30. I have to go and pick up my son at swim [team]. I'm going." And they all understand. (Cooper 2011a; 2011b, original emphasis)

Other teachers work long hours for limited periods of time or do not work in theatre or with youth at all in the summers. Teachers who have clear understandings with colleagues about their workloads comment that they have more energy, are more effective, and bring more to students from their balanced lives. They also garner respect from administrators who understand they cannot take advantage of the good will of the theatre teacher.

It is a very delicate balance, especially when your program may be the thing keeping a student in school or providing the learning students need to pursue a theatre career. Each of us has to answer some hard questions: What is the right balance between serving students and caring for myself? How is my work life part of my whole life? Does my work life reflect my core values and vision of a full life? Do I love my students *as* – not *instead of* – myself ? How does my work life harm rather than help me and my students? Quoting Douglas Steele, Thomas Merton (1966) highlights a startling view of overwork.

> There is a pervasive form of contemporary violence to which the idealist fighting for peace most easily succumbs: activism and overwork. The rush and pressure of modern life are a form, perhaps the most common form, of its innate violence. To allow oneself to be carried away by a multitude of conflicting concerns, to surrender to too many demands, to commit oneself to too many projects, to want to help everyone and everything is to succumb to violence. The frenzy of the activist neutralizes work for peace. It destroys the fruitfulness of the work because it kills the root of inner wisdom which makes the work fruitful. (Merton 1966, 81)

I hope, as a field, that we will consider these questions and so remain wise, fruitful, and forward moving.

Voices from the field
SOCIALLY RESPONSIBLE PRACTICES

STRANGERS IN A STRANGE LAND – LUIS MUÑOZ

Luis Muñoz (2011) is director of the University Interscholastic League (UIL) theatre programs for the state of Texas. He oversees UIL education, professional development, and performance and design activities from the local level to the state one-act-play competition. Luis is an award-winning director and a dedicated professional educator with a clear vision for bringing change to secondary theatre education through openness and inclusion of those not yet being served.

The latest U.S. census shows that the number of Latinos in the United States grew at a rate of 43 percent between 2000 and 2010. In the last twenty to thirty years, a demographic traditionally found in the southwest border areas of the United States has made its way into Boston, Atlanta, New York, Denver, Washington state, New Orleans, and many other areas of the country that were not considered traditional Hispanic population centers in the past.

As these changes become more and more apparent, theatre teachers will begin to find that the makeup of their classes and casting pools will change too. We will be faced with the challenge of getting the students to involve their lives in our programs and, more important, of getting our programs involved in their lives.

A recent study by the National Education Association (NEA) showed that a decline in minority children taking arts classes began in 1972. This coincides with the "back to basics" educational movement. By 2008 the change was dramatic. The number of Latinos taking at least one arts class had dropped from 47 percent to 28 percent of students.

James Barton, one of my teachers at Texas State University, used to say that theatre was an opportunity to "try on life." There is no better time in our history to look for opportunities and strategies to involve these young Latinos in our art. It is the time to utilize the power of educational theatre to give these young students an opportunity to develop the confidence, the language skills, and the passion not only to "try on life" but to take on life.

Many of these children are "strangers in a strange land." They are barraged by daily news about immigration issues, negative political characterizations, cultural stereotypes on television and in film and, for those who are recent arrivals, by a language they have not mastered. They are in need of a sense of belonging and self-worth as they desperately look for a safe haven.

The theatre arts classroom can offer some incredible solutions. I am of a strong opinion that we, as educators, need to seek out these students. Their lack of contact with the arts, as demonstrated by the NEA study, will necessitate that we actively recruit these students into our programs. There is no better time than now to look at the possibility of introducing multicultural or dual-language theatre into our theatre programs.

I want to clarify that by multicultural I do not mean plays about Latinos performed by Latinos or plays about Asians performed by Asians. Rather, the only way students can "try on life" is by having plays about Latinos performed by anyone, plays about Asians performed by everyone, and *I Remember Mama* performed by anyone and everyone. Empathy is a skill that has no better classroom than the theatre. By trying on life, our students gain a global understanding of others. We try on life to understand life. We try on cultures to understand cultures and through that understanding become better world leaders, doctors, counselors, inventors, and, yes, artists.

The idea of dual or multi-language theatre is an educational tool that can offer its own rewards. Experimentation in the area of multi-language theatre or bilingual theatre had its Renaissance in the 1970s. My personal experiences with the Teatro Bilingue at Texas A & I University involved productions of *The Fantasticks, The Sandbox, A Hatful Of Rain, Historias Para Ser Contadas, Milagro En El Mercado Viejo* in English and Spanish.

The companies were comprised of monolingual and bilingual college students. Some members of the company were fluent in Spanish, some were fluent in English, and some were fluent in both. Monolingual English speakers learned Spanish and monolingual Spanish speakers learned English. Many were very uncomfortable during parts of the rehearsal process. Word memorization was simple, but for many it resulted in meaningless sounds. It took what Professor Joseph Rosenberg, the company director, called "pantomimic fidelity" to truly achieve meaningful performances. Joe Rosenberg once wrote, "Pantomimic fidelity is accomplished when the actor arrives at the point where the word becomes filled with meaningful imagery. Pantomimic fidelity was also to serve the important purpose of coming to the aid of an audience for whom the language was also posing problems." This part of the process resulted in long-term benefits for the participants. I came to realize later in life that it was that cultural immersion, that "trying on of life," that search for truth or "fidelity" that made us better people.

It is this immersion in culture through language and action that can give those "strangers in a strange land" and the "local natives" a better understanding of themselves, each other, and the world around them. If we as teachers do not know the language, then be the student. Embrace the potential that this is providing. It is easy to remember that "kids are kids" and that the color of their skin, their special needs, the longitude and latitude of their birth, or whether they choose to say "hello," "hola," or "cháo" does not matter.

This new classroom demography demands that we cast aside the norm. Re-envision "theatre" and see if it can work. Give every kid a chance and throw us a curve. It'll do us all some good. (Muñoz 2011)

Voices from the field

RECOGNIZING SPIRITUALITY IN A HIGH SCHOOL THEATRE PROGRAM – JO BETH GONZALEZ

Several years ago, my high school was victim to a rash of male teen suicides – seven, as a matter of fact – over the course of three years. After the first suicide, I received permission from my principal to stage the award-winning one-act play, *Eric and Elliot* (Dwayne Hartford, 2004). The play metaphorically honors the search for hope following suicide. I partnered with our county's Suicide Prevention Coalition and we made preparations to present the play and a post-show talkback for the community. As this process developed, more suicides occurred. Instead of shutting our project down, our administration supported additional performances and talkbacks, albeit under revised conditions (Gonzalez and Donnelly 2008).

Upon reflection, staging *Eric and Elliot* was a spiritual adventure. During a conversation with the playwright in which we discussed metaphors and symbolism in the play, Hartford explained that in his mind, one of the characters was a Christ figure. The cast and I thought we had thoroughly dissected the play. How had we missed that strong imagery? Were we truly oblivious to the allusion that Elliot, the older brother who has committed suicide, returns to life explicitly to teach his younger brother Eric how to hope? Or as a teacher am I conditioned to skirt references to Jesus Christ, knowing that my principal discourages me from staging shows like *Godspell*, *Children of Eden*, and *Joseph and the Amazing Technicolor Dreamcoat* because of their blatant Biblical content? In my classrooms and rehearsals I avoid deep discussions about religious dogma, for I fear privileging one religious denomination over another, or being accused of proselytizing or creating a situation where students will proselytize. But is any public school dogma free? I look at the typical holiday repertoire of our school district's vocal and instrumental programs and resoundingly answer "no!" Yet, as we learned, *spirituality* was a powerful component of the *Eric and Elliot* project. I believe – intentionally or not – spirituality is a powerful component of every theatre endeavor my drama students and I take on.

The government legislates that public school employees adhere to the separation of "church," i.e. institutions that impart religious dogma, and state; it does not legislate separation of spirituality and state. So how is spirituality different from religion in relationship to high school theatre? The American Counseling Association describes spirituality as "a capacity and tendency that is innate and unique to all persons. It moves the individual toward knowledge, love, meaning, hope, transcendence, connectedness, and compassion" (Hancock 2010, 165).

An acute need for *connectedness* prompted support for our performances of *Eric and Elliot*. The play spoke to the spirit of our community and our common humanity. Deborah Conklin, pastor of Peace Lutheran Church in Bowling Green, Ohio, asserts,

> that "spirit stuff" is the exploration into what it means to be human. Spirituality involves "whatever it is that is seeking acceptance, inclusion, beauty, justice, equity, love, acknowledgement, identity, and contribution," for the human heart seeks these in order to live. (Conklin 2011)

A broken heart searches for healing. The need for healing in our community compelled our administrators to support the play and talkbacks because the project was designed to help our community heal its broken hearts.

Our work as theatre teachers is inherently spiritual because theatre exists to examine the human condition. Unlike conventional education, "in which the things you learn today often cannot be applied to daily life but must be stored away for future application" (Ryoo et al. 2009, 137), high school theatre becomes a refreshing oasis that immediately permits theatre teachers, by way of the work itself, to spiritually awaken our students. To participate in the development and performance of a quality high school play is an expression of spirituality.

Theatre educators engaged in best practice commit to social transformation for individual and collective good and so can be considered "spiritually conscious." They are subscribing to what some scholars define as *critical spiritual pedagogy*, which encourages critical thinking and self-reflection by teachers. As in learner-centered practice, in critical spiritual pedagogy, students and teachers "openly legitimize and challenge their experiences and perceptions of our complex society that is riddled with power imbalances, in order to find their own truth and create a better world in the image of that truth" (Ryoo et al. 2009, 134). Staging a play allows audiences "to find their own truth" that addresses and attempts to make sense of issues pertinent to the lives of the community, such as September 11, Hurricane Katrina, the 2011 tornadoes that ripped apart communities in Mississippi and Alabama, and my own community's struggle to make sense of multiple teen suicides. This leads to spiritual awareness, and awareness leads to healing – to a change of thought, heart, and ultimately, behavior. As a testament to the potential for change that critical spiritual pedagogues strive for, five years after our performances of *Eric and Elliot*, our county's Suicide Prevention Coalition held a celebratory event both to recognize those who are working hard to spread awareness of suicide prevention and to share that these efforts are reducing suicides in our region.

Theatre education that awakens the spirit does not exist, however, in a vacuum. The culture of a school supports the efforts of a critical spiritual pedagogy when it is a *permission-giving environment*, one in which participants are engaged, affected, and changed because a shared experience supports and connects them.

Two of my drama students were in a junior-level honors English class when the topic of homosexuality arose and, as their teacher described it to me, a desire on the part of the students to solicit student participation in a Day of Silence – a date designated to support teens who identify as gay, lesbian, bisexual, or transgendered – emerged quite organically. With permission from our school administrators, the two juniors linked with two other drama club members to promote the event school-wide. Interested students were required to sign up and inform their teachers and, with permission from both faculty and administration, an entire quarter of our student body participated in the 2011 Day of Silence. The culture of our school, as conventional as it is, nevertheless is fortunate to have a principal who understands that pockets of permission empower students. This permission-giving environment empowered students to transcend stereotypes and to demonstrate unified compassion for others. It was a spiritual experience (Gonzalez 2011).

Voices from the field

THEATRE IN THE MIDDLE: BIG ENOUGH FOR EVERYONE – BETSY QUINN

Acknowledging the challenges her students face and the realities of middle school teaching, Betsy offers insight, perspective, inspiration, and a vision for theatre's powerful impact on young people.

Middle school drama education lives at the crossroads. It exists where creative drama meets theatre, where childhood meets adolescence, and like all great art, where self meets others.

As in many high schools, middle school theatre classes are collections of students who are in upper-level high school math classes, in the middle of a divorce, homeless, the center of attention, outcasts, abused, privileged, in gangs, talented performers, gifted athletes, brilliant artists, unable to read, on medication, extremely social, and painfully shy. *Unlike* most high school electives, theatre classes in middle schools are often required courses. Classes are filled with students who may or may not want to be there.

How can a required middle school theatre class be differentiated enough to meet the needs of all of the students at the same time? Fortunately, the art form itself is differentiated and collaborative by its very nature.

Students entering my class for the first time occasionally tell me that they do not like drama. My response is always, "Really, you don't like drama? But drama [...] is big enough for everyone. What *do* you like to do?" Often their response is something like, "I like to draw" or "I like to write, I hate acting." "Perfect! You are a designer or a playwright, not an actor." When working with such a wide range of students, we need to meet students where they are, make them feel safe and empowered, and then take them further than they ever believed they could go.

Creating a safe, respectful space for exploration and reflection is the first responsibility. This is important at all levels, but absolutely crucial in middle school when students are self-conscious and completely focused on the opinions of peers. I am absolutely convinced that any misbehavior in the drama classroom stems from fear. Students would rather get in trouble than be embarrassed. Those teachers who are able to figure out why students are so afraid and make them feel safe have very few discipline issues in the classroom. In order to do this, teachers must sincerely listen to students and make sure they know they are valued.

Through the years, I have listened carefully to my students as they reflect about the art of theatre. Their answers almost always follow three patterns. The first is like this quote from an eighth grade girl: "The art of theatre brings people together and can make you feel like one big family." She intuitively understood that theatre is not an individual art form, but rather a collaborative journey in which there will be many voices coming together to enact a story or explore a theme. Like in any family, there must be sacrifice, commitment to a common goal, and most importantly, love. We may face challenges, but we will face them together. Students almost always talk about the sense of community that is built through the art form.

In addition to the community-building nature of drama, students will often reflect about their experiences in one of two conflicting ways. Many say, "It helps me express myself. It makes me who I am. It's me being me, even when I'm someone else." Others say, "I can be somebody else and gain stuff from that person I'm pretending to be. I think that it is really fun to act, especially if you are pretending to be a character that is nothing like yourself." Both of these quotes came from students in the same eighth grade drama class. How can the same activities evoke such different experiences? This is when careful listening matters. Some students like theatre because it allows them to be who they "really are." In a middle school, students often have to pretend to be something they are not in order to fit in or perhaps they have to sit still and be quiet most of the day. In the drama classroom, many feel as if they are able to actually be themselves, move around, and express their opinions without fear of ridicule.

In contrast, other students feel as though the art of theatre allows them to escape from their problems and be someone else for a while. How often do we see quiet students take the role of the antagonist and absolutely come to life? They are able to have experiences in their imaginations that they would never get in the "real" world. They are able to walk in the shoes of their character and see the world through the eyes of another.

Students and teachers who share rich drama experiences and common vocabulary can translate these experiences into the very culture of the school. Being the drama specialist, I interact with all of the students in the building, and this allows me to be a valuable resource to the administration and the community in ways that might be surprising. Often when two students are in a conflict and are ready to fight, we have a conversation about the audience that goes something like this:

"Would you even consider fighting if there was no audience?"

"No."

"Then why are you letting the audience get their entertainment at your expense? You know that people love conflict [...] that is what makes good drama. The problem is that they are in class and you are in the office."

By establishing a safe environment for middle school students in their drama classroom, we can frame other situations in theatre vocabulary and allow students to step out of tense situations and reflect on them with some objectivity. Drama techniques also can be used to role play. Years ago a seventh grade girl was being bullied by a new girl. She was so enraged that she ended up hitting the bully and got herself in trouble. Her mother tried getting through to her, but was hitting a brick wall. Finally, the mother brought her to my room after school to see if I could talk to her. Instead of talking, I suggested that we play the scene. The girl played the role of the bully and her mother played her. The girl was able to walk in the shoes of the bully and the mother was able to model how the situation might be handled differently. We didn't need to talk about it because right after the scene, the girl said, "I get it! I shouldn't have reacted the way I did." Drama allowed her to figure it out for herself. (Quinn 2011, original emphasis)

We build a community where kids can grow in their "humanness." Jerri Castlebury, Teacher

Voices from the field

THEATRE TEACHERS AS TEACHER LEADERS – LAURA McCAMMON

Laura McCammon (2011a) teaches preservice teachers and here highlights the importance and wide range of benefits that come from serving the field and the school as a teacher leader.

> Many theatre teachers I know are more than just teachers and artists; they are also teacher leaders. They are members of planning teams working to improve teaching and learning in their schools; they coordinate theatre festivals and tournaments; and, in these troubling economic times, they advocate for the arts.
>
> What *is* a teacher leader?
> Successful theatre teachers who are creative and caring educators with effective classroom and production skills employ leadership skills. A teacher leader, on the other hand, is willing to take these skills outside the classroom. "Teachers who are leaders lead within and beyond the classroom, identify with and contribute to a community of teacher learners and leaders, and influence others toward improved educational practice" (Katzenmeyer and Moller 2001, 5).
>
> What do we know about teacher leaders?
> After reviewing the literature on teacher leadership (McCammon 2008), I developed this list of common characteristics of teacher leaders. It is notable that the literature focuses on teachers as instructional leaders and not necessarily on leaders within a profession:
>
> 1. *Teacher leaders are good teachers and have classroom competency and credibility.* Not only are they good teachers, but they have earned the respect and trust of their colleagues.
> 2. *Teacher leaders have good interpersonal skills and can collaborate with others.* They know how to listen to others, recognize and celebrate differences, and use problem-solving skills to enable colleagues to feel encouraged, supported, and challenged.

3. *Teacher leaders take on a variety of roles.* These roles are usually organized around instructional rather than administrative leadership and depend on the desires of the teacher. They range along a continuum from formal (e.g., department chairs, members of school improvement teams, festival organizers) to informal (e.g. mentors to new teachers, advocates for new teaching methods.)

4. *Teacher leaders overcome barriers.* These barriers result largely from the traditional hierarchical structure of schools and the culture of teacher isolation. [...] Those who choose to lead, however, have strong beliefs in themselves and are committed to a broader view of their work.

5. *Teacher leaders can learn by doing and reflect on their experiences.* They are lifelong learners who promote this attitude in students and colleagues.

6. *Teacher leaders have a strong passion for teaching and belief in themselves as effective teachers.* Because they are good teachers, they often have strong beliefs in themselves as effective teachers and a high sense of self-efficacy. This enthusiasm for their work enables them to be energy creators with a sense of moral purpose, emotional intelligence, quality relationships, quality knowledge, and physical well being. (McCammon 2011a)

Theatre education needs teacher leaders both within and beyond the classroom. When teachers see themselves as leaders, they will have a greater sense of satisfaction in their work, better self-efficacy and empowerment, and are more likely to stay in the teaching field (Barth 2007).

If I hope my students will be teacher leaders, then they need to see that there are multiple opportunities both within and beyond the classroom and that their competence and confidence in leadership skills build together over time.

Because I believe that all teachers can be leaders, I challenge all my students to be teacher leaders. Some have natural leadership abilities that just need encouragement; others are often unaware of their potential. Sometimes just saying to a student "You can be a teacher leader" enables them to see another side of themselves and to start looking for ways to build leadership skills. It's important, too, to build in leadership activities both within the classroom (e.g. a team teaching assignment or class project) and also beyond the curriculum. These include outreach and service activities that we conduct such as theatre festivals, touring Theatre for Young Audiences productions, opportunities to serve on departmental committees, etc.

While I hope that the preservice teachers I mentor will be teacher leaders, what I really hope is that they will understand who they are and will ultimately be their own best selves:

Like the Tin Man looking for a heart, the Scarecrow looking for a brain, the Lion looking for his nerve, or Dorothy looking for home, I know that developing the heart, head, and hands of leadership is a risky and complex endeavor; these characters' experiences highlight the importance of having someone who can guide them to look deeply inside themselves to discover the attributes they already possess (Bowe 2007, 321–22; McCammon 2011a).

Voices from the field

A PARENT'S PERSPECTIVE – JUSTINE JOHNSON

Justine Johnson (2003) was active in her theatre program as a high school student. She reflects about the impact of that experience on her as a student, adult, and now as a parent of a high school theatre student.

I tried out for my first play the fall of my first year [...] and I actually got a part. It wasn't a very big part, I didn't even have lines, but as I heard many times "there are no small parts, only small actors." After that I was hooked. [...] I worked on every production during my high school years.

My director-teacher at the time played a big part in my experiences. [...] She also spent quite a bit of time with us [after] school. We knew she cared about us. [...] We knew she was our instructor, that she had authority over us as any other teacher would, but she didn't lord it over us; she treated us like the adults we were becoming. [...] As we became independent [...] from our home [...] we were safe in our drama family. We were able to be individuals and learn how to be self-sufficient participants in a social situation that was safe. We learned responsibility as we each had tasks that were integral to the production; however small in themselves, [they were] still a part of the whole.

Some of my best friends in high school were those I met during drama. When you spend so much time with people, they become like family. [...] There are some I still keep in touch with, even after thirty plus years. I even correspond with my instructor.

I believe my experience in drama in high school helped me become the person I am today. It was a positive learning experience that afforded [...] good practice for the "real" world. [...] Now I have a teenager in high school [who] is delving into the drama department. [...] I hope he [...] can gain as much as I did. (Johnson 2003)

A Closer Look

SOCIALLY RESPONSIBLE
CLASSES AND PRODUCTIONS

NO LIMITS – RENEE NORRIS

Renee Norris (2011a; 2011b; 2011c) stays very much in tune with the needs of students in her large high school where there is "an edgy, urban feel in the school population." Haltom High School is in the Dallas-Fort Worth area. Students live in nearby trailer parks and apartments and are considered low SES [socioeconomic status]. Those factors, while significant in the lives of students, are never seen as limitations (Norris 2011a; 2011c). Renee places students at the center of her unique, socially engaged program. From her intensive focus on college readiness, to the carefully crafted projects that always include real-world applications, to the generosity, kindness, and respect shown colleagues and students, Renee Norris' program represents "alternatives ripe with hope and rich with possibilities" (Hock 1999, 78).

> Students arrive the Monday before spring break and are greeted at the door with a hug, a handshake or sometimes a high five. As they walk in, the [...] [black box] space is set up for the day's activities. [...] Every class period begin[s] with [...] some kind of interesting vocal response [...] to get every student settled and focused on being in theatre [...] [and to] allow them to remove thoughts of the class or [a] hallway interaction prior to our work. Once that concludes you see me engaged in their lives. Every activity requires me to make eye contact with every child, to make them all feel part of the excitement. (Norris 2011c)

On Mondays, Renee makes those connections to students lived experiences with "hi/lo's," when students share a high and/or low point from their weekend. Students talk mostly in light, breezy ways while Renee listens carefully, remembers and inquires about relatives who have been ill, students who had weekend school events or work projects, and is alert to anyone whose life has changed since they last saw each other. "[Each] class is very [...] [student]-centered and all of my students feel special in my class[es]. [...] Student leaders in class [...] take roll [and] do vocal warm-ups" (Norris 2011a).

Renee is not only a gifted educator and director, she is a remarkably generous teacher and colleague. For years, Renee would come in early two mornings a week and, without pay, offer a class in college preparation. She recently got a grant for this class including salary money for her, which she donates for scholarships to "underclassmen so that they can do seminars and camps" that they could not afford otherwise.

> I love working with kids to get them into college. [...] Most kids do not know how to start this process and I work with students who rarely have parents who went to college. [...] I create small groups during their ninth- and tenth-grade years where I do career counseling and open the doors to all of the wonderful things that they can do for two years independently and during the summer to build their resumes. By their junior year, I hold classes two mornings a week for portfolio building, college online researching, and monologue and song selecting. [...] I have developed a summer [...] readiness curriculum that includes college students and professors coming to talk over breakfast on Mondays. [By fall of] senior year [...] they have all built portfolios to take to their interviews. [...] I work with them on their monologues and they do research. [...] For all of my junior and senior production class students, I have a guest in once a month to share a topic in the industry and to promote college studies.
>
> This part of what I do is what drives me. I believe that it is my role to prepare my students for the next stage in their life, first by being a positive and healthy role model and second by providing them with everything they need to make college happen. I take them on college visits, we go to loads of college plays, we sit in on classes, and we fill out applications together. I help them explore ideas for essays and then help them through the process of writing and submitting. I educate parents on their role in the process and in many cases fill in for them. (Norris 2011c.)
>
> The results are impressive and I see more and more success each year. I send care packages to them in their freshman year of college that includes a season pass to shows at school. I have [...] theatre alumni over for dinner every [winter break] [...] and we all sit down and say our hi/lo's just like Mondays when they were in high school. This year was especially fun when [...] three of them announced [they were going to] graduate school. [...] I chose to make college readiness so important many years ago because each year the underclassmen watch what it takes and learn and celebrate with the seniors. [...] Then, when it is time for them to begin, they are less frightened [and] so are the parents. (Norris 2011c)

No matter what challenges her students face, Renee always seems genuinely delighted by them and being with them – to be teaching, coaching, directing, or helping a student or colleague "find the artist within themselves" (Norris 2011b).

If you have come to help me you are wasting your time, but if you have come because your liberation is bound up with mine, then let us work together. Lila Watson, Australian Aboriginal Woman

A Closer Look

REACHING THE "UNREACHABLE" – BRIDGID THOMAS

Bridgid Thomas (2011) teaches at the Del Valle Opportunity Center, an alternative high school. Bridgid writes "that a teacher should always see themselves as a student." In this blog entry, she writes about a pivotal learning experience she had while student teaching at a high school in the border town of McAllen, Texas.

> One of my [...] theatre classes was especially challenging. Many students came to class, plugged into an iPod, and closed their eyes. Some had been told that if they took the class they'd get to build things, and they'd been rebelling after a unit on playwriting. Before I met the students, I'd selected a play by a Mexican-American playwright that involved puppets (that they would design and build) and themes of immigration that I hoped they'd relate to. Fiasco. So I threw out my lesson plans and started over. I had a [...] [conference] with my mentor and [...] bilingual playwright, Roxanne Schroeder-Arce. I ordered a few copies of her play, *Sangre de un Ángel* (Schroeder-Arce 2010). The play is based on the true story of a family in east Austin. [...]:
>
>> When his mother has had enough, her older son, Juan, and his family offer to take in his teenage brother, *Ángel*, thinking he can guide him to make stronger decisions about school and his future. Despite the efforts of a stable home and loving family, *Ángel* resists the help, looking to his troubled friends and their gang family for approval.
>>   He is lured back to attending school by a caring auto-mechanics teacher who gives him responsibility and the opportunity to rebuild a classic 1957 Chevy. Eventually, *Ángel*, begins to open up to his family and a hopeful future, but trouble follows him home when angry young men come looking for him – with a gun. (Dramatic Publishing 2011)
>
> I'm pretty upfront with my students. I don't speak Spanish, but I hoped, since 95 percent of my students did, that the themes and opportunity to experience a story of their own culture and language would pull them out of their apathy and help them see that I respected them.

[…] As we read, some of the students started opening up about their own experiences with gangs. One young man, "R", confided in me, after we had paused in our reading, that he had once been in a gang. He realized that he […] [had] a responsibility to take care of his family, especially his mother, and he got out. It wasn't easy, and his former friends in the gang beat him badly. He said if he fought back, they probably would have killed him, but he took it, knowing it was the only way out. Now he goes to school eight to nine months a year and works in the fields all summer to save money to go to community college and help his family. Much like *Ángel*, he liked to work on cars and hoped to go into collision repair.

Reading the script together out loud opened up some other surprises. The characters in the play speak bits of Spanish and English, and this really excited some of my students. "L" was normally very quiet, or at least not participating, but when he found out some of the characters were speaking Spanish, [he] quickly volunteered to read. He'd come in to class each day and shout, "I want to be Paco!" After class, he came up to me and asked, "Miss, can we read more Mexican plays?"

Each day we'd come into class, read [a] little of the script, then talk about it. After a few days, I had a special treat for them. I asked, "How would you like the opportunity to meet the playwright and talk to her about the play?" They were in shock. I had shared with Roxanne the progress the students were making and asked if she would be willing to Skype in during class and talk with my students. She was more than excited at the idea. When the day came, the students surprised me over and over. They got really excited about asking Roxanne questions in Spanish and hearing her respond. I then asked "R" if he'd be willing to share his story with her. He was a little reluctant at first, but then went down closer to the camera and started to open up. A few minutes later, "L" got up, walked down to the front of the room, sat in front of the camera, and said matter-of-factly, "I want to tell my story." What followed none of us saw coming. He told us that he had served three months in prison […] for murder. He had been at his house with some friends and fellow gang members when a group of guys came and set in motion a night that changed their lives forever. His brother got into a car and "L" climbed in and started chasing after some of them. His brother ended up killing someone with his car. "L" plead[ed] no contest and served three months in jail. His brother, the driver, will be there for a very long time. Now, like "R", he leaves […] school early to work in the fields each summer and tries to steer clear from the gang life he left behind.

When we came to the end of the play, we were short on people to read, so I was reading for the grandmother. I came up to a long section that was entirely in Spanish. Totally intimidated, I asked if one of the girls would switch parts with me. Before she could say anything, "L" walked up behind me and said, "It's okay, Miss. I'll help you." One line at a time he would read it in Spanish, and I would repeat it.

Sometimes as teachers we think we need to know everything, or as members of a community we think teachers should always be the experts. How empowering it was for him when *he* got to be the expert. (Thomas 2011)

A Closer Look

BREAKING THE CYCLE FOR "UNREACHABLE" STUDENTS – ROXANNE SCHROEDER-ARCE

I asked Roxanne Schroeder-Arce (2011) to write about her experience from the perspective of Bridgid's mentor and the playwright for *Sangre de un Ángel/Blood of an Angel* (see pages 192–193). Roxanne also offers a larger context in which to consider influences of language and culture in a secondary school theatre program. In Chapter 6, she speaks about breaking the cycles in theatre teacher education that perpetuate disengagement from students' cultures and languages (see page 311).

In Chelsea, Massachusetts, theatre teacher Amy Czarnowski teaches at a school that is 74 percent Hispanic. She told me there was an absence of Latino/a plays in her graduate work in college. This led to her offering her students the same canon of plays about white people that she had seen as a graduate, undergraduate, and high school student. After seeing a tour of *Sangre de un Ángel*, she decided to produce the play. This was the first Latino/a play Chelsea High School had ever produced. The play was, in fact, the first Latino/a play that Czarnowski had seen, and the same was true for her students.

Most often, it is not a lack of willingness, but fear and a lack of information and resources, that lead theatre teachers to recycle the white canon. I have, however, seen promise and progress on this issue.

Throughout the nation, bold theatre educators like Amy Czarnowski select plays that reflect the demographic of the school and community they serve rather than the canon they have learned or based simply on their own cultural experience. This practice brings more diversity to their programs and fights against the idea that theatre is an elite art form to be created for and by white people.

Additional promise for breaking the cycle is seen at Framingham High School where theatre teacher Donna Wresinski directed *Bocón*, despite her lack of Spanish-speaking ability and fear of representing the culture "wrong."

Most recently, I saw progress in the work of [...] Bridgid Thomas. While student teaching in this school with predominantly Latino students, Bridgid found that upon offering the youth an opportunity to engage with material they related to, they opened up and invested in their theatre class. In the case of Bridgid selecting *Sangre*, it was also the youth culture reflected in the play that caught the students' attention. Hearing the story of her student who had been involved in gangs and gone to jail filled me with so much emotion because it was so reminiscent of the real-life story dramatized in the play. Of course, I was saddened by [the student's] story, and the story of his brother still in prison, but then, in reflection, I was also thrilled that he had accessed a piece of theatre that made him think and feel and want to share. So many students in theatre classes around the nation take a theatre class and are never touched – what a missed opportunity to engage them and make an impact on their lives.

Interestingly, Bridgid's cooperating teacher, herself a Latina, was surprised when the Latino/a students started to share personal stories after reading *Sangre de un Ángel*. When in high school and college, had she herself been able to read, perform, and see dramatic material that represented multiple cultural perspectives related to students' lives, would she have been less surprised at the impact of this play on her students?

Certainly, not only Latino/as benefit from opportunities to engage with Latino/a plays. All students need access to a variety of stories to enrich their understanding of different cultures. Several teachers in predominantly white schools have asked if I am comfortable with them producing my plays that depict Latino/a characters and stories. I encourage these teachers to produce my plays and others that tell a variety of stories and ask young actors and audience members to empathize with characters whose lives are similar and different from their own. Teachers and students are often surprised that emotions and histories transcend cultural boundaries. I also remind these teachers of how often students of color are asked to play white while the reverse situation is not nearly as common. This is often due to the fact that teachers more readily ask students to see the world through their eyes rather than adjusting their own perspective to look at the world as any given student might. Happily, I see evidence that this, too, is changing. (Schroeder-Arce 2011)

A Closer Look

ESTABLISHING A SOCIALLY RESPONSIBLE CLASSROOM – BETSY QUINN

Betsy Quinn (2011) is a middle school drama teacher at Haven Middle School in Evanston, Illinois. Her program is literally a haven for children in this large school with a widely diverse student population. Betsy is also an adjunct professor at Northwestern University and is as masterful in her work with college students as she is with middle schoolers. On the first day of class each year in her urban middle school, Betsy Quinn (2009) gives "The Talk."

My first-day talk with the kids [...] [is] really specific. The only rule I really have in [my class] [...] is that we have to be respectful. We have to be respectful to people in or out of this classroom, individuals and groups, verbally and nonverbally, and playing or for real.

[...] [T]he [very] first time I meet the kids I [start by saying,] [...] "Don't say any words, don't make any sounds, but show me a *disrespectful* audience" [...] [and] they do. I say [...] "Now, show me a *respectful* audience." I say, "That's what I expect to see in here. If I say to you, 'You're being disrespectful,' and you say to me, 'I didn't *say* anything.' You're in trouble. You just proved to me that you don't have to say a word to be disrespectful." All of a sudden you see the light go on and the kids are like, "Okay, she's onto us." That's sixth grade.

[With] the seventh and eighth graders, [...] the ones that I've had before, I talk to them at this point [...] saying [...] "Now, I want you to show me the subtly disrespectful behavior that you see in an audience, so that a teacher wouldn't even know it's happening." [They do.] "Exactly. We are not having that in here... Why? Because you have to get up here everyday. And what if I do this, [imitates the subtle disrespect] what does that tell you? 'She doesn't like me, she doesn't like my work...' So, I'm not having that. We will be respectful."

"Number two, I don't want you to disrespect individuals or groups. I don't want to hear, 'That's so gay' or 'He's so gay.' We're not having that [...] out of respect for my friend. [...]" And I tell them the whole story about a friend of mine from high school who killed himself because he was gay. And there are a lot of snickers [...] "And we're not having that [...] because of the *prejudice* that exists in this world against gay people." And when I use the word prejudice in Evanston, it's so loaded with [all of the] diversity issues here that they really get it that I'm not having that prejudice against gay people.

"We're not having the word 'retard' in this classroom or 'That's so retarded. [...]' My godson Quinn [...] was born with Down's syndrome [...] and when he was born the doctors told us, 'Let's not have his heart surgery because he is retarded. He's not going to have a good quality of life.' And [then] I pull out a picture and say, 'Does this guy look like he has a good quality of life? [...]' Of course he does. I don't want to hear that. It's an insult to my family and it hurts my feelings. I don't think we're going to have any problems with that."

"I can tell that you're all respectful and that boys won't disrespect girls, girls won't disrespect boys, we won't disrespect any religions, or races, or cultures by stereotyping. I don't want a certain type of person being a cab driver or someone who runs a 7-Eleven. We're not having any of that in here." Now this is all the first day.

I say, "But here's the hard one for you. There's no *play* disrespecting in here. I don't want to hear, "We were just playing" or "She's my best friend. I always call her that. [We're] not having that because [...] sometimes people say they're playing and they're not really playing [...] they're really for real. Or sometimes it starts out playing, and then it gets serious. So those are the reasons we say nothing disrespectful at all. Other than that, don't chew gum, don't be late. [...]

"And I know the work is not going to be a problem, because you'll love the work. [...]" Then I say, "How many people want to get an A? I'm the type of teacher who thinks you should all get an A because I taught it to you. What kind of teacher would I be if I say, 'I think 25 percent of my class will get Ds. [...]' No, it's 'Do it again, fix it. [...]' You won't all get an A, but that's what I expect from you.'" That expectation is set up the day they walk in.

[...] When the kids come in, I put them in assigned seats [in] alphabetical order [...] because in a middle school it actually makes them feel safe. [...] What if I had a fight with my friend at lunch, and I walk in and I always sit with her, but now I have nowhere to sit in the classroom. It takes out the "Who will sit next to me?" And it also takes out the gender and racial divides that you would see if they picked their own seats, or in the sixth grade, the elementary school divides that you would see.

Then we do a really fun activity to learn names and to kind of do a pre-assessment – a game of group juggling [...] where you say [someone's] name and you throw the beanie baby. [...] If there is any disrespect in that game [...] I'll [...] [address] it. We were playing group juggling once [...] and this kid [...]

who [elsewhere bullied] another kid in the class [...] [whose] name was Nathan [...] threw the beanie baby and said, "Gaythan." And I said [quietly], "Hand in the beanie babies please. [...] Please take your assigned seats." And they all moved back. [I didn't] look at the kid who said it, [but] look[ed] at the rest of the class and [said], "Raise your hand if you don't understand why you're sitting in your seats." [No one did.] "I am not having disrespect in this classroom. Any questions? Everyone back to the circle." So that's the way that [I] would handle [...] that extreme of a case. Or [...] if the game is going on, I might just stop and say, "We're not having it." [...] The kid who is doing that is trying to test you to see if they're safe in [the classroom] [...] almost always. They're not doing it for any reason except, "If she tells me to cut it out, then no one will be able to pick on me." It seems counter-intuitive, but that's actually the reality in middle school.

My first day of teaching, a six-foot [tall] kid [...] stood up at the last minute [before the bell]. I'm three months out of [grad school], I'm twenty-four years old, and he says, "I'll give you ten seconds to let us out of this classroom. Ten... nine..." They were [about to go] to lunch [...]. "Eight, seven..." And I said, "When everyone is seated, I'll dismiss you." [...] And all the rest of the class said, "Man, sit down, sit down! We want to go, we're hungry." "Six, five..." He was the only one not sitting. He slowly lowers [into a chair], "Four, three..." still counting, [he] just barely touches [the seat], and I say, "Goodbye everyone." [...] He ended up being the giant in *Jack and the Beanstalk* that year. [...] He ended up taking drama class [again], and no other kid in the whole school ever did that. But the principal came to me and said that it "was the only class that he was successful in [and] his mom wants him to take it again just because it was the only thing he was good at." He was testing me [that first day] to see if he's safe in [here]. And because I held my ground and wouldn't let him get away with that stuff, he could relax. So that's really how you create [a safe space]. [...] And it takes time, it absolutely takes time.

There are kids who come in and I say, "You're making my class feel unsafe [...] Because you're creating a whole ethos of fear in here, and we're not having it." [...] You make the kids who feel the least safe the most safe. [...] And that's on all sides – socio-economic, age, gender – it's just about what's inside the person. (Quinn 2009, original emphasis)

A Closer Look

SOCIALLY ENGAGED PRACTICE – JULIA PERLOWSKI

Julia Perlowski (2011a; 2011b; 2011c) teaches theatre, English, and reading in Florida at Pampano Beach High School, a magnet school for international business and technology that is now also known for its theatre program. Julia has attracted so many athletes to her program – "[we] get them in the theatre and they never go" – that she now plans productions around the baseball schedule.

In recent years, Julia has been recognized in Florida and by the Children's Theatre Foundation of America for her work. She was selected by the U.S. State Department to participate in a two-week collaboration with teachers and students in Mumbai, India, followed by a two-year collaboration through digital technologies. She also received the Sontag Prize in Urban Education, a program of targeted academic support for students in need in conjunction with the Boston Public Schools, Harvard Graduate School of Education, and Harvard Business School (2011c). Julia believes

> in being a role model to students for how to work and live. I love the life I live and I live the life I love. I want the same for my students. I believe that they must see me work hard and meticulously with commitment to artistic practice and my fellow human beings. (Perlowski 2011b)

Julia reflects on other important aspects of her practice: Brainstorming is [...] important to me and I [...] [am] always looking at how we are brainstorming – kinesthetically, verbally, visually, on paper – without "the cop in the head!" (2011a). When working on a show or a class project, Julia is always looking for the next question in the last answer. Students working in groups do "bodily brainstorming" to create shapes that have a connection to the script – a circle or triangle perhaps. There is discussion and they then embody key objects from the script – the dagger from *Macbeth* for instance. They discuss these and then physically create images of themes or motifs from the play – "disconnectedness" from *One Flew Over the Cuckoo's Nest*, "ambition" from *Macbeth*, "willfulness" from *Much Ado About*

Nothing, "loyalty" from *Romeo and Juliet*. Julia says they own the images and deconstruct them, and ideas are put on paper and kept on the wall.

> I learned I needed to ask [...] better questions and [...] leave the ownership [...] to them. [...] My job is to continually retool questions to push my students further into their own identified areas of inquiry. If, for example, my students present me with a piece of improvisational theatre around a theme or issue and I don't "get it," I might ask them to complete the following sentence: "The thing I am trying to communicate through this piece of theatre is..." If their answer does not match what I see in the theatre piece, *their* job is to retool the theatre piece so that their message is communicated clearly from the stage. [I'm] questioning, letting them create, and then [we] deconstruct it. [I ask], "What you're saying is [...]" "What are we seeing that could be a positive view of ambition [...]?" [As] the teacher, [I] serve only [to] exploit the buried perspective in that tableaux.
>   [It's] a constant struggle – how much control and structure [to provide]. The answer lies in knowing your group of kids. [...] [I'm also] interested in finding relationships between characters [...] [a] solidness between and among the characters and the students. (Perlowski 2011b, original emphasis)
>   Often the questions and discoveries come from Julia's students. During a recent rehearsal of *Much Ado*, Benedick tells Claudio, "You are a villain." The young man playing Claudio stopped to ask why Shakespeare did not write "thou" instead of "you." We all stopped. Before I could open my mouth [...] the young man playing Benedick said, "Thou" is too good for Claudio. Benedick hates him at this point. He is not even worth a "thou!" This was thrilling for me for [...] [many] reasons. The students noticed a change in language and commented on it; the students talked about Shakespeare as the creator; they talked about text in terms of craft; and the students critically thought through the text. Having students work this stuff out for themselves is the best you can do.
>   During an improvisational game, a rather shy girl was asked if she would like to go to the movies. "No" she said, and then quickly looked up at me and said "Sorry! I blocked." She proceeded [with the improv saying] "No, but let's go wash Dad's car!" This [too] was thrilling for me. She thought she failed because she had blocked. Actually, she succeeded because she caught it *in the moment* and pushed through it. She became a reflective practitioner in that very moment. (Perlowski 2011b, original emphasis)

Julia's students are engaged in writing original plays, and Julia is deeply committed to a socially engaged focus in her program.

Last year [we] developed a Leading the Witness Theatre Project[3] with striving ninth grade readers and Kindertransport [Holocaust] survivors. Through this project, I [...] devised theatre with two generations and [two] historical periods [...] [and learned how] theatre activity [can form] [...] relationships between teens and older adults. This year, my Drama I students worked with Diane Samuels's script *Kindertransport*. The [elders] from last year advised us on language [and] the emotional impact of this history. (Perlowski 2011c)

Julia is also exploring a theatre project for pregnant teenage girls where they "may envision their futures in light of their newfound responsibilities. The girls will be able to jump into the drama to subjectively explore their options and critically think about their choices." (Perlowski 2011a)

I believe in developing responsible, passionate, and committed human beings through the arts [...] rather than in developing great theatre actors, producers, and technicians only. For example, I might set up a forum theatre exercise in which I ask the kids [to improvise] and practice [...] asking for a raise from an employer. I might then ask that student to step out of the drama and be replaced by a different student who might have strategies to combat an unyielding boss. Thus, the original student has practice looking subjectively and objectively at the world around a confrontational situation.

I believe that the teacher must create an environment in which social interactions of all kinds are able to flourish and through which theatre serves as a catalyst for these interactions. [...] As the students group and re-group, they talk, laugh, and discover similarities and differences. [...] [S]tudents must learn to work with everyone, whether they like them or not. (Perlowski 2011c)

What calls me to this work is having the opportunity to offer young people the chance to self-actualize through the activities and structures of drama [...] to allow people to practice the subjective and objective, [the] convergent and divergent thinking that must necessarily happen to anyone who is called to create in any field. Moving in and out of drama, improvising by saying "yes," making your partner look good, walking through a situation and then stepping back to analyze it – what other art form offers this? [...] [to] find a way to think more critically, to make more positive decisions. I [am] awed by the window into power dynamics that the tools in this field allow me to see. [...] I want to be able to offer this life raft to others [...] even if it is for just one hour a day for ten weeks. I want to help people in this way. (Perlowski 2011b)

EXAMPLES OF SOCIALLY RESPONSIBLE LESSONS AND PRODUCTIONS

Conflict with Authority – Steve Bogart

Steve Bogart teaches near Boston at Lexington High School. He is also a playwright and director. Socially responsible theatre education characterizes the program he and his co-teacher, Sandy DiMartino, have built at the school. In addition to their Drama of Social Issues class, they address social change and issues of interest to students in all of their classes. "Conflict with Authority" is a unit they use in their improvisation classes (Bogart 2003).

The Lesson

- Journal Assignment

Write about a conflict you have had with an authority figure. Describe the situation, the setting, the background, and exactly what happened. Write about something that you would be willing to share with the class.

- Partner up and share your stories. Pick one story to work on first. If it is person A's story, B must play A. You must play the authority figure, you may not play yourself.
- Show scenes. Remember to look at what is behind the villain's "attitude." What happened to make him feel this way? Change the scenes to [another] way they might have worked out, either fantastical or realistic. (Note: consider doing three or four scenes before feedback.)
- Discuss the possible motivation for the authority figure and the child to respond the way that they did. Is the motivation based on something that happened in the past (internal) or is it an external motivation? ("I've got work to do.") External motivations come from without. A character's reaction to them is a character choice under pressure. Internal motivations come from within: needs, desires, hopes, wishes, dreams.
- List external motivations kids might have: your parents, for example, have threatened to cut off your allowance if you don't have a B+ in English; fire alarm goes off for real fire; friends pressure you not to hang out with new kid, etc.
- Now list possible external motivations for adults: a really bad toothache; you lose your eyesight; your spouse leaves you and the kids; your child is kidnapped.

We ask them why people react so strongly to things, why someone might yell at a child or a young adult. [...] We have them do a scene showing what happened in the authority figure's life that [explains why] he or she might have reacted that strongly. [...] In a couple of different cases, kids have come to me and said, "You know what, I never realized that when I came home drunk that night my mother was thinking about how she lost her best friend." [...] [A] student had a conflict with a guidance counselor and the guidance counselor came to me and said "Are you doing that [conflict] lesson? Because the student actually came to me and apologized and said 'I know why I made you angry and I know why I did it now.'" Sandy DiMartino

Figure 3.7: Students enact a conflict grounded in life experiences.

- List kids' internal motivations: I will go to school even though I'm sick because it's too hard to make up the work; you join a club to be closer to that cute guy/girl; working for money to buy a car; you give up a friend because you are not having fun with her anymore.
- List adults' internal motivations: you give up sleep to go have fun; you give up parts of your social life to advance in your career; you begin an exercise program to get in shape.
- Scene. Create a scene in which we see an external motivation come into play for one or all of the characters. The choice they make in that moment will give us insight into the character.
- Pre-scene. Choose one of the two authority figures (A's or B's) that you just worked with. Create a scene that shows what motivated your authority figure

to behave the way that he did in the scene that we just saw. Create an external motivation for the character.

- Consider the way people deal with external situations. Why do people make the choices that they make?

Drama with English Language Learners – Richard Silberg

Richard describes the context for a lesson he developed for his middle school English language learners (ELLs) drama class (see page 140).

> The class is composed of thirty students who are categorized as either Level 1 or Level 2 English language learners. Some are newcomers to the United States, some have been here a few years. Some have little, if any, formal training in English; others have had some academic or informal exposure in their home countries. In 2010 (the first year of the program), there were eleven different home languages in the class: Spanish, Portuguese (Brazil), Arabic, French, German, Russian, Nepalese, Mandarin, Japanese, Tagalog, and Tibetan.
>
> This class was formed through meetings with our English language learner coordinator and various site administrators [...] to better meet the needs of our English language learners. It seemed as if many of our kids were leaving our school and becoming lifelong English language learners at the high school, never fully moving into the mainstream. We were thinking of how, given our current schedule, we could increase the amount and intensity of language instruction.
>
> [...] We saw that the electives period opened up a possibility for another opportunity for focused, academic language instruction. We decided that drama would be the ideal place to create a new curriculum that built language competency and literacy in both conversational and academic ways. [I] [...] was certified and trained in ELL techniques and [...] had some experience already at adapting activities to suit [ELL students'] needs. [...] The difference [...] would be that the class would be specifically designed to meet the needs of ELL students. The important thing [was that] [...] we take a basic drama activity, common to many drama programs, and turn it into a language activity by simply changing our focus or lens. (Silberg 2011c)

Richard shares Statues, a lesson he did with his students.

Objectives

Journal Entry for both Beginning and Advanced ELL Students

Answer the following questions:
- Have you ever seen a statue?
- What was it? Describe.

Advanced – Answer the questions above plus:
- How do you think an actor could imitate that statue?

Vocabulary (to copy into journals)
- Freeze. In theatre it means a motionless pause in the action.

Drama Objectives (written on the board)
- To create interesting statues using only the actors' bodies to create a mood or a feeling in our viewers.
- To learn how to communicate the needs of a director to an actor using only words.

Language Objective (written on the board)
- To use verbs that give directions (put, lift, place).
- To create a speech using formal English that explains the meaning of our statues.

Activity

Activity (students work in pairs and use a Statue Worksheet to facilitate their participation)
- One student is the sculptor; the other the statue.
  1. Decide where your statue will be located like in a park, a theatre, a town hall, a city center, or on a boulevard of heroes.
  2. Decide who the statue represents, such as a famous scientist, an actor, a writer, a musician, a composer, a politician, a religious leader, a sports hero.
  3. Decide what the stature is made of (wood, metal, stone, etc.).

The only way you can communicate to your partner is by giving instructions on how to stand or sit, the position of legs and arms, the way the head is to be held or turned, the gestures of the hands, the facial expression, whether the eyes are open or closed, etc. There can be no physical contact, only words. Here are some directions you might use:
- Move your head to the right.
- Move your _____ to the _____.
- Lift up your left foot.
- Look like you are strong.

After you are satisfied with your sculpture, you will give a public speech to the whole class about the statue that you have created as an artist. Make it important. Use phrases like:

- What I have tried to do here is _____.
- Notice the magnificent way that _____.
- See how I have captured this moment of her victory _____.

Statue Worksheet

- The location of the statue is _____.
- The statue represents _____.
- The statue is made out of _____.

Words to use to "sculpt" your statue:
- put
- lift
- raise
- lower
- hold
- bend
- straighten
- take
- move

Examples of phrases to "sculpt" your statue:
- Move your head to the right.
- Lift your left foot off the ground.
- Bend your right elbow.
- Take your right hand and put it on your waist.

Examples of phrases to use in your speech:
- Notice the magnificent way I _____.
- What I have tried to do here is _____.
- See how I have captured the moment by _____.

Evaluation

Evaluation is based on how well students use the language modeled in their drama work. Note the academic versus conversational language when presenting the statue. This is essential, as it follows Kate Kinsella's[4] concepts that academic literacy, not conversational literacy, is the goal of ELL instruction (Silberg 2011c).

Devising Socially Engaged Performances – Jenny Lutringer

Jenny Lutringer has taught high school and middle school for a number of years. Integrating study of avant-garde theatre, journal writing, and discussions of current events and concerns in the students' lives, Jenny challenges students to use theatre as a catalyst for change and reflection (Lutringer 2003c). This unit is also learner-centered, as described in Chapter 2, and an example of Discipline Based Theatre Education, as described in Chapter 4.

Days One, Two and Three

Objectives

- Describe, analyze, and interpret the work of The Open Theatre.
- View and discuss an example of the type of performance we will be developing.

The Lesson

The Ideals of The Open Theatre

Explain that the next unit will be based on the work of this theatre company: "We are going to create our own play like The Open Theatre created their play, *The Serpent*. Over the next few days, keep your eyes open. Watch the news, read the newspaper, listen especially closely in history class. We are going to take our current events and respond to them through performance." (Students keep a journal and engage in reflections and discussions throughout the process.)

- Share several scenes from the videotape of *The Serpent* performed by The Open Theatre. After each scene, stop and ask questions:
  - What are the actors doing with their voices?
  - How do the actors manipulate their bodies?
  - What is this scene about?
  - How does this scene relate to the previous scene(s)?
  - What historical figures and events do you recognize?
  - How do you think we view this differently today than the audience back then viewed it?

- Read excerpts from the background materials packet about The Open Theatre.
- Discuss Joseph Chaikin and The Open Theatre process. Share language such as *representational* and *abstract* versus labels like *weird*.

Journal Questions

- What do you want to tell an audience about the world you are living in today?
- What current events have you found especially powerful lately? Why?
- What commentary do you have on them?

Activity

Ensemble Exercises: Fine tune skills students need to develop for this unit

After each exercise, tie it back to the ensemble nature of The Open Theatre. The following are a few sample games and exercises: the objective is to establish a basic vocabulary of levels and to show students the importance of level variation.

Levels 1–10

- Ask students to show physically what levels correspond to what number in their body, with Level 1 being when they are closest to the floor and Level 10 when they are highest on the floor.
- Play a game calling out numbers between 1 and 10 at which students move instantly to the level that corresponds with that number. Challenge them on specifics (e.g. What is the difference between a 2 and a 3? A 9 and a 10?).

As a result of this activity, we can easily create and evaluate a frozen statue and determine if it needs a low or high number and why.

- Form group statues in response to words like power, love, peace, despair. This is done silently. Each group member must be at a different level and they are not allowed to discuss how to achieve this.

Discussion

After playing these games and exercises, discuss:
- Why do we need this knowledge of levels?
- How is this way of creating frozen statues different from how we normally work? How does the rule that everyone must be a different level aid this process? How does this relate to the process of The Open Theatre? (*Variation:* Do the same exercise with movement and pace: 1 is slowest, 10 is fastest. Repeat with volume: 1 is softest, 10 is loudest.)

[Jenny then has students do a series of give-and-take exercises with their bodies, voices, or visual art materials. She follows each movement, speaking, or drawing exercise with questions and ties their work back to that of The Open Theatre.]

Days Three, Four and Five

Objectives

- Dissect newspaper articles and begin to realize the world around the article.
- Represent the events and people in the article through frozen statues, gestures, and phrases.
- Decide what issues are to be incorporated into their scenes.
- Establish an approach to scene work.

Discussion

Group Work: Students are divided into groups

One article on current events is given to the class or different articles are given to each group in the class to discuss. Articles are related to current events of interest in the lives of the students.

- Who are the characters involved in this story?
- Who is the victim? Perpetrator? Bystander?
- Who are the characters involved that we might not see in the story?
- What are the relationships between the people?
- What is the basic sequence of events?

Activity

Bringing Articles to Life

- Each person in your group assumes a different character from the situation suggested by the article and forms a statue. Different people (victim, perpetrator, bystander, etc.) should be represented. Ask students to keep the same character as we create frozen statues.
- Ask students to choose or create one statement or phrase that they think is central to their character. The phrase can be from the article.
- Ask students to create a gesture or movement to accompany the phrase. It might highlight the meaning or contrast ironically. (A mother who lost her son might cry out "My baby!" and either reach out for him or rock a child in her arms.)
- Ask students to stand in a circle and share their phrases and gestures, going around the circle without stopping. Sidecoach students to use their entire bodies

with their gestures and to use different levels. (*Variation*: Have everyone whisper their phrase, build to an intensity.)

- Ask students to break out of the circle and walk around the room freely. Tell them, "When I touch you on the shoulder, say your phrase and perform your gesture." Quicken the pace as it progresses, eventually allowing the students to say the phrases on their own. Sidecoach and work with students to get them to build to a climax of overlapping phrases and gestures until it explodes into either a freeze in their original statues or freeze created one person at a time.
- Ask students to create a frozen statue to show one occurrence that might have led up to this event, one occurrence that might happen years after this event, and one occurrence that happened at the climax of this event. Sidecoach students to use different levels to explore how they best can represent their characters physically and to show how the different characters relate to each other.
- Ask students to share their statues, one statue from each group. As you tap each character in the statue on the shoulder, they come alive and perform their gesture and line and return to their frozen position.
- As the class watches a group's statue become animated, they describe, analyze, and interpret the statue and identify the character playing each role (victim, perpetrator, bystander).
- For the last group that shares, invite them to experiment. Assign an order to the students in the statue. Have the students perform their gesture/phrase in that order four times in a row, building in volume and intensity from a whisper as they go.

Discussion

- Is this a performance?
- How is/is not this a performance?
- How is this different from "traditional" scene work?
- How does the lack of traditional dialogue affect the audience?
- How does the increase in volume affect the performance?

Jenny offers the following for establishing a classroom goal with students:

- Take time to establish a goal with students and to select the issue or topic. This is crucial to development of scene work and commitment to the project. Decide also on the approach. Will each class produce one class performance? Or will smaller groups within the class select their own topics and develop their own performances?
- Wait for a good time to talk about being socially responsible. I share the quote from *Spider-Man* that "With great power comes great responsibility." We talk about why we must be very careful when doing scenes based on real-life events,

which not only should we be serious about our message, but we should respect the memory of any victims involved. I compare it to September 11 and how it would be to make a mockery of that event.

- Tie in a discussion of responsibility and integrity. The work of The Open Theatre was based on avant-garde performance that was more abstract and representational than realistic. Sometimes students get caught in wanting to show the actual event onstage (e.g. shooting, killing, explosions). Many times I tie in responsibility/integrity. Talk about how tragic events have been effectively staged over the centuries. Encourage them to consider adding representational meaning to the event.
- Stress the ensemble nature of the performance. Discuss that one person, for example, can play several parts because they are a neutral actor. This does not change the events or facts; it is just open-minded casting.
- What do we want to say to the public?
- What issue or theme do we want to develop our performance around?
- Why is this article or issue important?
- What kind of scenes do we want to develop over this issue?
- How important is it to portray things accurately?
- Can we change the events? The people involved?
- Must a man play a man or might a woman play the role?
- How can we portray these events on stage? Must we do it realistically?
- Can we do it realistically?

Days Six through Ten

Objectives

- Develop a series of scenes to be combined into a final performance.
- Incorporate performance techniques employed by The Open Theatre.
- Work with the group in an ensemble fashion.

Discussion

Daily Questions

Pose a question to the class every day. The groups develop scenes to answer these questions. The same group(s) work with the same issue or event every day. Wait to create the next day's question until seeing the students' work at the end of the day. The questions are a way of making sure students cover different perspectives that they might miss otherwise. Purposely do not pose the questions in chronological order.

- What is a solution to this problem?
- What happened to cause this problem?

- What commentary do you want to share?
- What happened to the perpetrator to cause this event?
- How did this event affect the victim's family?
- How did the American public respond to this event?

Activity

Daily Scenes to Correspond to Daily Questions

Create a scene to address the question. Within each scene you must incorporate the following:
- Nontraditional movement (slow motion, breaking movement into steps, frozen statues, repetition, being a machine or animal).
- Nontraditional dialogue (songs, humming, making a noise, repetition, monotone, narration of a scene as it happens, speeches, headlines/quotes, numbering).
- Historical facts, figures, and events about real events and people.
- Repetition of a theme or imagery to connect all the scenes together (e.g. what it means to be proven guilty, patriotic songs underscoring different events, etc.).
- Breaking of the fourth wall and integration of the audience (e.g. dumping a barrel of apples into the audience and inviting them to eat; choosing audience members to serve as jury members in a scene; moving someone out of their seat; pointing at the audience and pronouncing them guilty; demanding the audience stand and recite the Pledge of Allegiance).
- Chorus section. Create a component that comments on this situation from an outside view.

Jenny offers an example of how this phase of her unit was developed by students:

> the class decided to choose one theme/idea [injustice] and have all groups combine into one large class performance. [...] Every day we would choose a new event. Each group would choose a different aspect of the event to portray, a different question to respond to over the same issue. One group was assigned [...] the chorus section [...] [which] is meant as a commentary versus a "scene." [...] The chorus [section is] performed several times and changed only slightly. This allowed the audience to really absorb their message. (Lutringer 2002a)

[One group Jenny worked with connected the Buddhists, who set themselves on fire because of religious persecution, to the Jews whose dead bodies were burned during the Holocaust. They then interjected Joan of Arc being burned at the stake. Underneath this all – connecting the different historical figures – was a girl reciting a poem about the fiery flames of injustice that attack those who are different.]

At the end of each day, we share, critique, and rework our scenes. This is a good time to work with any students who are hesitant to embrace the abstract nature of the work.

Discussion

- How do these scenes connect together?
- What things might we incorporate to strengthen this connection?
- How might you rework your scene to make it less realistic?
- What will this add to the meaning?
- What are the benefits of nontraditional performance like this?

Final Performance Preparations

Objectives

- Combine their previous scenes through transitions.
- Prepare for a final presentation/performance.
- Effectively use transitions to maintain the flow and intensity of their piece.

Activity

Putting the Scenes Together

Rehearse and share two scenes that will be performed back to back with transitions.

Discussion

- What happened at the end of each scene?
- What happened to the audience at that point?
- How can we keep both the actors engaged and the audience still interested? (Discuss the fact that once your performance starts, you are performing the entire time. There should not be a break in character.)
- How can performing transitions highlight your message? (Students offer examples.) All your scenes should be linked in this way.
- Students are given a day or two to work on transitions. As a class, establish an order or scenes and write it on the board. Revise as necessary.

Performance day

Objectives

- Perform final piece.
- Perform all scenes without breaking from the performance.
- Connect their work with the work of their peers.
- Describe, analyze, and interpret their work and the work of their peers.

NOTE: For the first full performance, I do not invite an audience. Many times the students are quite taken by the impact of their work and they need to debrief alone, as a class.

On the day of the performance, review with students the order of scenes they have established and allow a three to five-minute brush-up rehearsal. Set area for performance. Perform.

Discussion

Pre- and Post-performance Questions

- How might this performance impact an audience differently than a traditional performance? Than a documentary?
- How are you, the actor, impacted differently in this piece than from other types of work?
- What is the impact of combining this wide assortment of events from our past into one performance?
- What connects these events?
- What separates them?
- How does this type of work compare and contrast to a poem? A piece of literature? A history book? A movie? A song?

Throughout the process, students are encouraged to share their personal responses in their discussions and journals, and in conversations with each other and Jenny.

IDEAS FOR FURTHER REFLECTION

What Is, What Could Be, What Ought to Be, and *What Will Be* My Socially Responsible Practice?

Look at *What Is* and *What Could Be*

What is the current relationship of your theatre program to the people and activities in the rest of your school and community? Invite colleagues, parents, students, business leaders, or others into this conversation as appropriate.

- In what ways is my program representative of the students in my school? In what ways is it not?
- In what ways is my classroom and my program inviting and accessible to all of the students in the school?
- Is the material I teach and produce age appropriate? In what ways is it not? How does the material I teach and produce relate to the lives of my students? In what ways do I make that connection consciously and intentionally? How am I teaching to transfer ideas to students' lives?
- What are the obstacles I face to find appropriate material? How can I overcome these obstacles?
- How do I characterize my interactions and communications with students? With co-teachers? With parents and administrators? With others involved with my program? With those in the communities served by the school? Who might be other partners with me?
- How often do I interact with people who are not in my program?
- If I could make one positive change in my professional relationships, what would I do?
- What links are there between what I do in my program and the rest of the school, the community, and the world? What links would I like to have?
- How does my teaching philosophy reflect my views of socially responsible practice?
- What would a handbook for my program contain? Would new students reading it feel included and clear about how to be involved? How would they find out what the acceptable behaviors with peers and adults are?
- What is my district's censorship policy? Does it address issues that might arise in my program? Who might help me draft a policy regarding censorship?

Consider the kind of community you want to have in your theatre program. Refer to the lists you made at the end of Chapter 1 and revisit your vision of the theatre education community in which you most want to work.

- In what ways do we create a safe place to take risks and experiment in this program?
- How do people from different cultural backgrounds, races, genders, religions, sexual orientations, languages, ages, and abilities interact with one another?
- How do people express their individuality?
- How do we deal with "problem" individuals? (What is a "problem individual"?)
- How do we care for each other?
- How do we give each other feedback?
- How do we respond when we become aware of differences?

Take your vision of a socially responsible theatre program and think about examples from this chapter and from other teachers and artists you have seen or read about. Begin a plan of action to effect positive change in your program and school.

How Did I Come to Think This Way?

Jot down your response to the following questions. Think honestly and without judgment about how these experiences might have shaped your thinking and perspectives of yourself, colleagues, parents, and students. How do you see this thinking affecting your practice?
- What did your parents and other influential adults teach you about your race, religion, gender, sexual orientation, culture, heritage, language, abilities, socio-economic status? What did they teach you about people who were different from you in these or other ways?
- Are you proud to be a member of your race, gender, socio-economic status, etc.? Do you still practice customs and cultural events that are connected to these aspects of your identity?
- Has there ever been an incident in your family or a conflict because of one of these areas of difference?
- How many people who are different from you in terms of socio-economic status, race, language, religion, culture, gender, sexual orientation, or abilities/disabilities do you interact with regularly?
- What is the most difficult area of difference you face yourself? What areas of difference do you find difficult when interacting with students or other adults? How might this affect your practice?
- Whom can you go to with questions?

Make a plan to address your questions and to learn more about areas of difference represented in your program and community. Make a plan for deepening the socially engaged and socially responsible aspects of your classes, productions, and program. Move "onto the ice," as Roxanne Schroeder-Arce (2002a) said.

SELECTED RESOURCES

There are many excellent resources on topics addressed in this chapter. In addition to the works cited in the chapter, the following offer ideas for further reading and reflection.

Bailey, Sally. 2010. *Barrier-Free Theatre: Including Everyone in Theatre Arts – in Schools, Recreation and Arts Programs – Regardless of (Dis)Ability*. Enumclaw, WA: Idyll Arbor, Inc.

Cahnmann-Taylor, Melisa, and Mariana Souto-Manning. 2010. *Teachers Act Up!: Creating Multicultural Learning Communities Through Theatre*. New York: Teachers College Press.

Casanova, Ursula. 2010. *¡Sí Se Puede!: Learning from a High School That Beats the Odds*. New York: Teachers College Press.

Catterall, James S., Richard Chapleau, and John Iwanaga. 1999. "Involvement in the Arts and Human Development: General Involvement and Intensive Involvement in Music and Theatre Arts." *Champions of Change: The Impact of the Arts on Learning*. Washington, D.C.: Arts Education Partnership.

Darling-Hammond, Linda. 2010. *The Flat World and Education: How America's Commitment to Equity Will Determine Our Future*. New York: Teachers College Press.

Delpit, Lisa. 1995. *Other People's Children: Cultural Conflict in the Classroom*. New York: The New Press.

Donkin, Ellen, and Susan Clement, eds. 1993. *Upstaging Big Daddy: Directing Theater as if Gender and Race Matter*. Ann Arbor, MI: University of Michigan Press.

Drake, Brett, and Shanta Pande. 1996. "Understanding the relationship between neighborhood poverty and specific types of child maltreatment." *Child Abuse and Neglect: The Official Journal of the International Society for Prevention of Child Abuse and Neglect* 20 (11): 1003–018.

Garcia, Lorenzo. 2000. "Significant Theatre and Education on the U.S.-Mexican Border." *Stage of the Art* 12 (14).

Gay, Geneva. 2010. *Culturally Responsive Teaching: Theory, Research, and Practice*. 2nd ed. New York: Teachers College Press.

Howard, Tyrone C. 2010. *Why Race and Culture Matter in Schools: Closing the Achievement Gap in America's Classrooms*. New York: Teachers College Press.

Lanoux, Carol, and Elizabeth O'Hara. 1999. "Deconstructing Barbie: Using Creative Drama as a Tool for Image Making in Pre-Adolescent Girls." *Stage of the Art* 10 (3).

Lee, Enid, Deborah Menkart, and Margo Okazawa-Rey, ed. 1998. *Beyond Heroes and Holidays: A Practical Guide to K–12 Anti-Racist, Multicultural Education and Staff Development*. Washington, DC: Network of Educators on the Americas.

Noddings, Nell. 1984. *Caring, a Feminine Approach to Ethics and Moral Education*. Berkeley: University of California Press.

Noguera, Pedro, Aída Hurtado, Edward Fergus, eds. 2011. *Invisible No More: Understanding the Disenfranchisement of Latino Men and Boys*. New York: Routledge.

Noguera, Pedro. 2009. *The Trouble With Black Boys: ...And Other Reflections on Race, Equity, and the Future of Public Education*. San Francisco: Jossey-Bass.

Payne, Ruby. 1995. *Poverty: A Framework for Understanding and Working with Students and Adults from Poverty*. Baytown, TX: RFT Publishers.

Ressler, Paula. 2002. *Dramatic Changes: Talking about sexual orientation and gender identity with high school students through drama*. Portsmouth, NH: Heinemann.

Romo, Harriett D., and Toni Falbo. 1996. *Latino High School Graduation: Defying The Odds*. Austin, TX: University of Texas Press.

Saldana, Johnny. 1995. *Drama of Color: Improvisation with Multiethnic Folklore.* Portsmouth, NH: Heinemann.

Tatum, Beverly Daniel. 1999. *Why Are All the Black Kids Sitting Together in the Cafeteria? and Other Conversations About Race.* New York: Basic Books.

The Children's Defense Fund. 2011. *State of America's Children 2011.* http://www. childrensdefense.org/child-research-data-publications/state-of-americas-children-2011/ Washington, D.C.: The Children's Defense Fund.

NOTES

1. United for Human Rights (UHR) is an international, not-for-profit organization. Its purpose is to provide human rights educational resources and activities that inform, assist, and unite individuals, educators, organizations, and governmental bodies in the dissemination and adoption of the Universal Declaration of Human Rights at every level of society. See: http://www.humanrights.com/about-us/what-is-united-for-human-rights.html.

2. *From the Notebooks of Melanin Sun*, by Jacquelyn Woodson, won the Coretta Scott King Award when it was published in 1996.

3. U.S. Witness Theater (U.S. WT) is the American adaptation of the successful Israeli program developed by JDC-Eshel. It brings together Holocaust survivors and teens on a weekly basis to share life stories and ultimately create and participate in a performance piece based on their experiences.

4. Kate Kinsella, Ed.D. is a teacher educator in the Department of Secondary Education at San Francisco State University. She teaches coursework addressing academic language and literacy development in linguistically and culturally diverse classrooms. She publishes and provides consultancy and training nationally, focusing upon responsible instructional practices that provide second-language learners and less proficient readers in Grades 4–12 with the language and literacy skills vital to educational mobility. She has also received the California Department of Education's Award for Excellence for her contributions to improving the education of immigrant youth. She is coauthor of a 2010 publication by the California Department of Education on research-based English language development within secondary schools. Dr Kinsella serves as a guiding force on the National Advisory Board for the Consortium on Reading Excellence (CORE).

Chapter 4

Comprehensive Theatre Education

Theatre is everywhere in our society [...] except in the typical pre-K–12 curriculum. Relatively few comprehensive sequential theatre education programs exist in the United States. [...] If substantial programs are ever to exist, theatre must be perceived as an academic discipline relevant to all students rather than an extracurricular activity for a selected few. The teaching of theatrical knowledge and skills through the inherent processes of theatre can result in an appreciation of the complexity of the art form, recognition of its existence in all cultures throughout history, and understanding of its power and relevance in today's global society.

Kim Wheetley

Even to discuss the significance or meaning of the arts, we must enter into the contemporary discourse of virtually all discrete disciplines – historical and social concerns, gender, morality, geography, language – in short, to even start addressing the content of the arts we must address the entire human condition.

The College Board National Task Force on the Arts in Education

When my son was little, he regularly engaged in dramatic play. He moved easily in and out of the roles of director, performer, designer, playwright, critic, and audience. "OK, Mom, wear this hat and stand like this – over there by the fort (the sofa) – and when I take out my sword you flip on the light and say: 'Who goes there?'" He would then critique my character interpretation and help me understand my motivation, all the while revising my lines. Admittedly, his pre-school approach to theatre was more egocentric and dogmatic than learner-centered, but even now that he is older, he and his friends still think of theatre, and life for that matter, holistically. They do not see the world in which they live as fragmented into academic subjects and disciplines.

Powerful stories, vivid experiences, lively imaginings – drama – walks in the door with every child. Young people are inherently whole and integrated beings. It is our job is to see that truth and engage with them from that standpoint rather than educating in a piecemeal fashion where the whole is rarely discussed or acknowledged. "The world of adolescents is not divided into the neat subject distinctions that give us comfort, and it is their world – in fact, our real world – that should direct our effort" (Oddleifson 1992).

Cathy N. Davidson (2011), in her research in neuroscience, learning, and digital media, concurs and highlights how industrial age practices, testing, and centralizing and privileging selected subjects disenfranchises and disheartens so many learners.

> No one benefits from an *educational system* that defines learning so narrowly that whole swaths of human intelligence, skill, talent, creativity, imagination, and accomplishment do not count.
>
> By funneling all of the different ways we learn about the world into a very few subjects that count and are tested [...] we make education hell for so many kids, we undermine their skills and their knowledge.
>
> [...] Right now, they feel like failures. They are not. They are only "failures" if judged by the narrow hierarchy of values by which we currently construct educational success. As an educator, I want to change that hierarchy of values in order to support a more abundant form of education that honors the full range of intellectual possibility and potential for everyone. (Davidson 2011, original emphasis)

Neil Postman (1990) describes his view of learning that makes meaning of seemingly isolated bits of information.

> What children need is a curriculum that would have at its core the drama of knowledge; a curriculum that would allow children to create meaning from disparate and disconnected facts that fill the world [...] a curriculum that would convey the idea that all life is a drama – an improvisation, if you will – in which the point is not to make things happen but to make meaningful things happen. (Postman 1990, 6)

The American Alliance for Theatre and Education (AATE 1992) extends these ideas.

> The educational value of theatre is derived from each individual's inherent need to transcend personal limitations and to participate in the universal human experience. Its unique contribution to learning is that it provides a functional laboratory in which to experience human interaction. Education in theatre is important for individuals to perceive the world clearly, communicate expressively, and respond intelligently in the ever-changing drama of daily life. The collaborative art of theatre fosters balance between individual integrity and social cooperation. (AATE 1992)

This chapter explores models of theatre education that allow children to succeed, and to see and experience their world holistically, more abundantly, and in ways

Children learn best when they encounter whole ideas, events, and materials in purposeful contexts, not by studying subparts isolated from actual use. Zemelman, Daniels, and Hyde

I was a shy seventh grade student. [...] I preferred to be a director or on crew. [...] My experience as that shy child has helped me to bring out that kid from the corner. [...] I want them to feel like one unit, like a team, like a family [...] to strive to be their best and be supported by each other. Ann Batten Bishop, Teacher

that help all students flourish. Learning in theatre is best served when we foster in students a desire to inquire, experience, define, and reflect on the world fully and from multiple perspectives.

A couple of years ago I observed a preservice student teaching a vocal unit to a high school theatre class. She was having students echo her as she recited the lyrics from a Gilbert and Sullivan patter song. A few of the students were obediently parroting her, though many were distracted, distracting others, doing the exercise in a detached manner, or doing it without proper breath support or articulation. This appeared to be a classroom management problem. As I continued to watch, however, I found myself thinking that I, too, would be disinterested in this activity. Why were the students being asked to do this? They were not studying Gilbert and Sullivan, and there were no curricular or cultural links to the text. They were not being asked to think about or interact with the material or each other. They were not enjoying it and the vocal activities definitely were not even warming anyone up for class.

Both my student teacher and I learned something about best practice that day. I was reminded that at one time I led warm-ups and taught vocal and movement exercises that were not linked to what was being studied or rehearsed. There was little connection among activities within a lesson or across curricular units. I was teaching theatre in the same disconnected way I had been taught, which was the same way my teachers and their teachers had been taught. Not surprisingly, students were not transferring the knowledge and skills being taught to their work in class or onstage. I critically examined some of my teaching methods and discovered that disjointed, compartmentalized study of theatre actually thwarts many students in their growth as artists, thinkers, scholars, or citizens. Development, application, and transfer of knowledge need to be linked together and embedded in a comprehensive study of theatre. That approach fully engages students in learning. The results are not mere acquisition of information but *understanding* and the ability to *apply* that understanding in class and onstage.

Rather than separate instructional units about acting, play analysis, or lighting, what might a larger study of theatre look like? The teachers I spoke with engage students in learning theatre history, production, and criticism. Their students create original work and talk easily about the style, its historical roots, its meaning, and the art and craft necessary for its creation. In many schools, the arts teachers talk and work together, jointly developing cross-curricular explorations and projects. Some theatre teachers, independently or in collaboration with teachers from other academic departments, integrate content from across the curriculum. All totaled, this is *comprehensive theatre education*. It is an interwoven study and exploration of all aspects of theatre. It encompasses a core of holistic study of the theatre disciplines and then expands and intersects with work across other arts disciplines and academic areas (see Figure 4.1).

In my definition, comprehensive means all-inclusive. It also implies balance – of kinds of activities, experiential approaches, instructional methods, ranges of art forms, types of instructors, ethnicity, cultural values, and the like. Jane Remer, *Changing Schools Through the Arts: How to Build on the Power of an Idea*

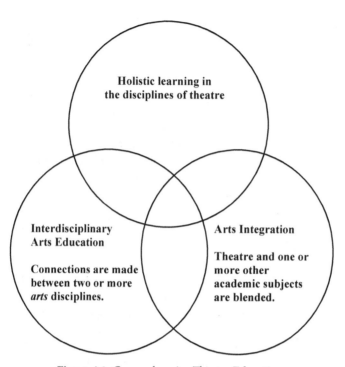

Figure 4.1: Comprehensive Theatre Education

DISCIPLINE-BASED THEATRE EDUCATION: A FRAMEWORK FOR LEARNING

Knowing that comprehensive theatre education is "an interwoven study and exploration of all aspects of theatre" is fine, but how is this interwoven study created and what does it look like in action? There are any number of ways to conceptualize comprehensive education in theatre.

Discipline-Based Theatre Education (DBTE)[1] is one example of a conceptual framework teachers use when developing curriculum and designing lessons. DBTE is a clear articulation of holistic education in theatre. It integrates many instructional approaches providing "a variety of strategies for experiencing, understanding, reflecting upon, and valuing works of theatre and the theatre process" (Wheetley and SCEA 1996).

The Discipline-Based Theatre Education framework is structured for students' active exploration of theatre through eight theatrical roles (see Figure 4.2) and four methods of inquiry through which students investigate these theatrical roles (see Figure 4.3). These explorations and investigations result in an interwoven theatre education (see Figure 4.4) that enables students to learn broadly and deeply about theatre from multiple perspectives.

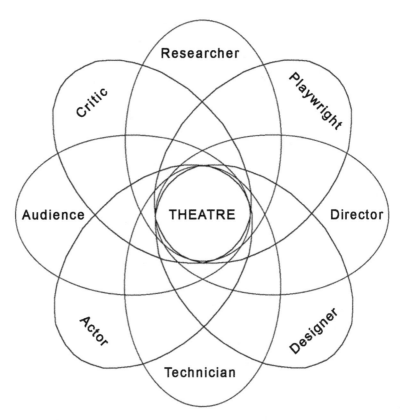

Students understand theatre holistically by connecting and blending
their experiences in the eight theatrical roles.

Figure 4.2: Discipline-Based Theatre Education Conceptual Framework.
Southeast Center for Education in the Arts (SCEA) (1996). Copyright reserved

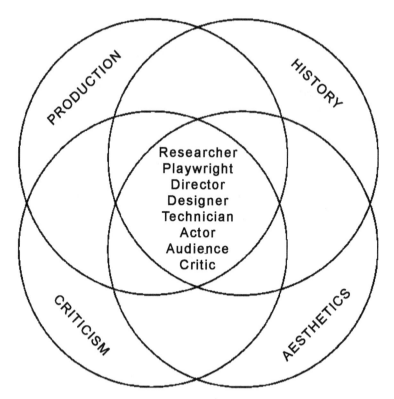

Work in production, history, criticism, and aesthetics unifies study and challenges students to make meaningful connections between the eight theatrical roles. Students

- create informal and formal theatre by researching, improvising, writing, designing, constructing, rehearsing, and performing (production);
- consider theatre in social, cultural, and historical contexts (history);
- reflect on the aesthetic qualities and characteristics of theatre (aesthetics);
- make informed judgments about the theatre they create and experience (criticism).

Figure 4.3: Learning Theatre through Methods of Inquiry.
Southeast Center for Education in the Arts (SCEA) (1996). Copyright reserved

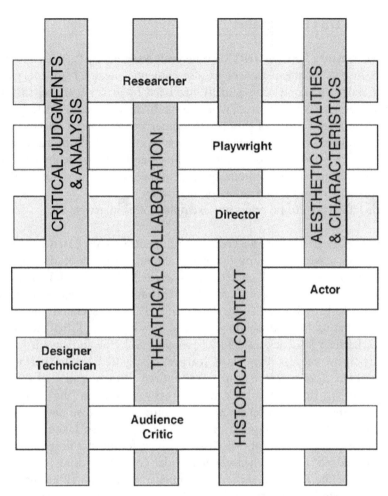

Given a program that incorporates a strong foundation of theatrical components, a balance of learning opportunities, and dynamic instruction, teachers and students can weave an exquisite and enduring discipline-based theatrical tapestry.

Figure 4.4: The Theatrical Weaving.
Southeast Center for Education in the Arts (SCEA) (1996). Copyright reserved

Students in DBTE Programs

As holistic theatre education, DBTE is inherently socially responsible and learner-centered. Instructional experiences are also *authentic*, meaning students gain the kinds of skills and knowledge actually practiced by artists working in various theatre professions. Students read, write, research, direct, design, create, perform, critique, and attend works of theatre. They interpret and derive meaning about their lives and the lives of people from worldwide cultures both past and present. In addition, they work across other disciplines and interact with professional artists at school and in the community. Student assessment and evaluation reflect the comprehensive and varied nature of their study.

Valerie Labonski (2011a) offers one example of this interweaving.

> In my Theatre III/IV class we create forum theatre scenes based on [research about] peer pressure or dating violence [...] [and] based off of Michael Rohd's [*Theatre for Community Conflict and Dialogue:*] *The Hope Is Vital Training Manual* [...] Students receive feedback through scene sharing and mock facilitations. [...] Student audience[s] watch [...] the scene[s] and [...] we discuss what useful feedback looks and sounds like. [...] [Then] we practice the Liz Lerman feedback model [...] [see page 81]. The audience is prepared to participate because they have [earlier] responded to the performance in a written format. Performances are entirely student run [...] [and] the student[s] [...] run the feedback model. I act as a guide to [the] process [...] [keeping] the discussion on track and encourag[ing] the students to engage in honest dialogue. During the performance, I have also taken notes, but I usually keep quiet during the discussion. I have found that nine times out of ten, the students, through the feedback model, cover everything I have written down. After the feedback session is complete, all of the written feedback is given to the student performers. The performers are then given an opportunity to review the feedback and ask further questions if necessary. During these feedback models, I am continually surprised by how respectful, insightful, and honest my students are in their responses to each other's work. I feel that it is my job as a teacher to create opportunities like these. If you empower students as artists and thinkers, they will rise to the occasion and exceed your expectations. (Labonski 2011a)

Autumn Samsula Casey (2003) uses the Discipline-Based Theatre Education framework for a unit in her advanced theatre class. Her high school students have an integrated experience in theatre history, research, text analysis, dance, acting, criticism, and costume design and construction. They learn about

If the theatre walls could be glass instead of concrete then people could see in and hear. And conversely the people inside could look out [so they are not] isolated and not just in their own black box, in their own created world and not anyone's reality.
Kim Wheetley

Figure 4.5: Students serve as dramaturgs for an upcoming production.

Elizabethan history while exploring themes from one of Shakespeare's plays that Autumn correlates with events in their lives. In later lessons, students learn about Elizabethan culture, see how clothing of the period was made, and experience how the clothes enhance or constrict movement while learning the Allemande. They conduct research, do text work, and use costumes to rehearse and perform scenes from the play. Criticism and aesthetics are integrated throughout (Casey 2003).

Two of my former students chose a DBTE approach when they taught costume design and technology as part of their preservice education. Using a process drama structure, the teachers introduced a crime for which the only clues were articles of clothing. Acting as detectives, students looked at each article of clothing for clues about suspects. They researched period costumes, drew sketches, wore the clothing, took on the roles of characters suggested through their research, and enacted the events leading up to the crime and arrests.

When Deb Alexander (1999) learned of the DBTE framework, she became intrigued by the thought of using it as a springboard for a middle school theatre curriculum. As discussed in Chapter 2, Deb adapted the framework by using *The Diary of Anne Frank* (Goodrich and Hackett 1958) as the core through which the four methods of inquiry and eight theatrical roles would all intersect. Students explored the themes, events, and ideas of the play in a sequenced, interactive, and holistic semester-long class. Detailed excerpts from Deb's curriculum are included at the end of this chapter (see page 240).

Jenny Lutringer's (2002a; 2003a) unit in Chapter 3 on The Open Theatre is another example of effective holistic theatre education – a learner-centered and socially engaged unit (see page 207).

Although many teachers are the only theatre professional in their building offering comprehensive theatre education for students, when there are two or more theatre teachers in a school, there is the opportunity to blend classes, team teach, or co-teach. Diane Stewart (2002) and another theatre teacher in her school, joined their two ninth grade theatre classes to address Shakespeare, Elizabethan history, culture and voice. Other teachers regularly integrate curriculums, exchange classes, co-teach, or co-direct. Modeling the collaborative nature of theatre, they are sharing their individual and collective strengths and knowledge with all of the students.

The American Alliance for Theatre and Education (1992) notes that a comprehensive theatre curriculum is also a collaborative effort between educators and administrators.

> A balanced curriculum in which students develop internal and external personal resources, create drama/theatre through artistic collaboration, relate drama/theatre to its social context, and form aesthetic judgments must be developed by teachers of theatre and administrators who work in tandem. (AATE 1992)

I am at my best when "students are comfortable leading and being led and can switch roles quickly and with great facility. A student who is assistant director might have been a chorus member in a previous show, a lead in another, and a techie in another. It's all about the overall production and the team." Marissa Meek, Teacher

INTERDISCIPLINARY ARTS EDUCATION

Disciplinary integration in art is educationally desirable not only because it represents the actual ways in which artists and arts-related professionals experience art, but because it is an effective way to underscore and reinforce what is important. Stephen Mark Dobbs

Interdisciplinary curriculum should be an expansion of, not a substitute for, a sequential comprehensive curriculum in each subject discipline. Connecticut Guide to Interdisciplinary Curriculum Development

Professional artists have long challenged boundaries among arts disciplines. It is important to students' comprehensive study of theatre that they too have opportunities to challenge and experience the similarities, differences, and authentic intersections between art forms. Comprehensive theatre education includes meaningful curricular and co-curricular experiences in which theatre is integrated with one or more of the other arts disciplines. Teachers incorporate work from different art forms in specific units of study in their classrooms, work in a cross-disciplinary fashion in productions, or develop special interdisciplinary projects in the school or community.

Mandy Whitlock (2010) collaborated with an art teacher and her advanced art students. Together they created a cross curricular production called "Windows to the Soul."

My advanced [theatre] class was in the playwriting unit and I had them write original scenes and monologues based on [their] credos [...] about what they felt and thought about life. Those pieces were then given to the art class where [...] students picked the piece that spoke to them. [...] Using an antique window frame as the basis of their art piece, they created a visual art representation [...] [for a] performance art piece created by the actor. We brought the visual and performance artists together for a dress rehearsal where the actors saw the art for the first time and worked with the artists to incorporate the art and artist into the performance. The night of the show, the actors performed with the artists, and art as a backdrop and a gallery was created for patrons.

[...] This [...] year, I created another opportunity for collaboration with art called "Take a Walk in My Shoes." [...] Student actors were given shoes as the inspiration for an original scene or monologue and then the shoes and original pieces were given to the art students to create art sculptures, paintings, etchings, etc. [...] We received a grant to take the artwork and performance pieces to a gallery in the city [...] [where] a video of the performances [...] [was] on display for a month.

Figure 4.6: Theatre and art teachers work together with students on an interdisciplinary project.

[…] The students learn so much about the collaborative process and how different art forms are used to express human emotions, thoughts, and objectives. The students met different students that they may not have known before the project and writing, planning, collaboration, artistic, and performance skill mastery was demonstrated. (Whitlock 2010)

Some theatre teachers also teach English classes and regularly integrate the disciplines of literature and theatre. Jo Beth Gonzalez (2002b) teaches *Julius Caesar* to her sophomore English classes. In a single lesson, she draws correlations between the play, Greek history, current events, and students' lives. She then integrates exploration of the text with exploration of acting styles, enactment of scenes, and a discussion of the work from critical and feminist perspectives. Misty Valenta (2002) created a drama lesson in which she drew on music, movement, and drama to engage students in exploration of events and themes from the novel *Watership Down*.

I believe in the use of theatre structures across the curriculum [...] as tools upon which to hang other kinds of learning. Theatre provides wonderful learning opportunities for making text visual and exploring history. Julia Perlowski, Teacher

Carol Cain teaches at West Side School, a grades 3–8 arts magnet program in LaGrange, Georgia. The school uses a Discipline-Based Interdisciplinary Arts Education approach. Carol feels there are enormous benefits that come from working with other arts educators who teach through and across the arts.

The beauty of where I work is that I gain total inspiration from the visual art and the music teacher who I work with. And that [...] is a strong part of what I feel is [...] our success. That's been probably the best part of this job for me [...] working with [my arts colleagues] and many of the plans that we've developed [...] together. (Cain 2003)

She describes how integrating theatre into her middle school English classes has benefitted her students.

We were going over [...] two hundred vocabulary words we'd learned during the semester [...].When I'd call out a word [...] they'd kind of stumble around until somebody said "Oh yeah, it means blah blah blah." [...] I got to this one set of words, and I called them and they knew every single one of them. "How do you all know those words so well?" "Oh, Miss Cain, don't you remember? Those are the ones we did the drama scenes with." I went "Oh, yeah!" [...] They had written and, of course, performed their own scenes using the vocabulary words, and obviously they remembered them. (Cain 2002)

In addition to interdisciplinary instructional units, teachers collaborate on productions with colleagues in art, music, and dance. Bradford High School in Kenosha, Wisconsin, is an example of a program in which the arts faculty members jointly develop interdisciplinary curriculums and performances. In addition to regular classes offered in each arts discipline, the productions are mounted through Theatre Practicum classes for which students register and receive credit. Practicum classes are held after school or in the evening to allow as many students as possible to participate. Holly Stanfield (2002) heads the performing arts program in the school. When the program started Holly was employed two-thirds of the time teaching one theatre class and one television class. The curriculum and the program grew with student interest and support from the principal and school board. She now collaborates with six other colleagues in music, theatre, English, and television. All of them teach classes and direct. They teach the Theatre Practicum together, modeling and encouraging students to explore connections across the arts.

Most of the teachers who teach across the arts do so alone, within their own classrooms or productions. There are now national initiatives urging interdisciplinary arts education and collaboration among teacher-artists from different disciplines.[2] Teachers doing interdisciplinary arts co-design curriculum, co-plan lessons, or team teach with other arts colleagues. Intentional planning to ensure that projects expand (versus substitute for) a sequential curriculum in each arts discipline is an essential. Some theatre teachers also serve as guests and specialists in other classes or as a resource to arts colleagues in other fields. Regardless of the form, interdisciplinary arts projects more authentically reflect students' lived arts experiences in the twenty-first century.

To fully engage ideas, construct meaning, and remember information, students must regularly employ the whole range of communicative media – speech, writing, drawing, poetry, dance, drama, music, movement, and visual arts. Zemelman, Daniels, and Hyde

ARTS INTEGRATION

We may learn much about human behavior through social studies, literature, and science, but drama requires that we feel our way into the situations of others. [...] Many educators do not seem to understand that drama is a way of knowing – and often a more stimulating way than that offered through the distanced learning provided in a purely intellectual approach. Oscar G. Brockett

Most of my kids aren't going to go into theatre as majors. Most of them [...] are going into something else, but [...] [the] kids [who] come out of my theatre program will have an advantage over others [...] because they can interact and [...] think on their feet and they [...] can present themselves in a manner that makes people want to listen and follow. C. Gary Cooper, Teacher

Integrating the curriculum with other school subjects makes learning more engaging for those already attracted to theatre. It also makes theatre more accessible to a wider range of students and enables the development of life skills.

The Partnership for 21st Century Skills advocates integration of the arts to advance students' learning across core academic subjects and so develop readiness for success in the twenty-first century. (Partnership for the 21st Century 2010, 1)

> As a whole [...] the arts are uniquely situated to provide links from school-based learning to themes that are essential to every child's understanding of the modern world. This is because the arts, which thrive on the free expression of the imagination and the creative instinct common in all human beings, have enabled us to explore the changing nature of our existence and to understand how that nature has both evolved and remained constant over time, culture, and place. The arts inculcate key lessons for participation in a democracy, as they balance the preservation of ideas with the challenging of old ways and the development of new visions. (Partnership for the 21st Century 2010, 16)

Infusion is but one approach to integrating the arts with non-arts disciplines. There may be as many variations on arts integration as there are teachers engaged in its practice. The President's Commission on the Arts and the Humanities' report, *Reinvesting in Arts Education* (2011), states:

> Arts integration is the practice of using arts strategies to build skills and teach classroom subjects across different disciplines, including reading, math, science, and social studies. In recent years, it has formed the basis for several successful school reform initiatives, and has generated a lot of enthusiasm from classroom teachers, school administrators, and policy researchers for its ability to increase student engagement and overall learning. (President's Commission on the Arts and the Humanities 2011, 10)

Kim Wheetley (2009) speaks of curriculum integration and describes it as

> an instructional approach that enables teachers and students to identify and explore concepts and issues without regard to artificial subject-area boundaries. [...] Applying knowledge and skills learned in one subject to another subject area complements and deepens understanding in both.

Kim goes on to say

> Unfortunately, when integrating the arts into multi-disciplinary experiences, there is a tendency to use them as a vehicle for learning in other subjects rather than as part of holistic instruction. Having students listen to music while they write may provide atmosphere and inspiration, but they are learning nothing

about music. Teachers need to build their knowledge, skills, and practices so that integration of the arts is essential not peripheral. (Wheetley 2009)

Teacher-artists can integrate theatre with the broader school curriculum to effectively reach and teach students across the school population.

In their book *Dramatic Literacy*, J. Lea Smith and J. Daniel Herring (2001) describe potential intersections in the middle school curriculum between theatre and literature, science, mathematics, and second language learning. They illustrate the benefits of integrated learning across the curriculum for middle school students.

Drama creates a setting where a person is able to explore and experiment with content through self-perception, social interaction, movement, and language – reading, writing, speaking, and listening. Integrating drama into content studies provides the middle-level learner with a learning environment which supports their developmental needs for voice and ownership in the learning process. (Smith and Herring 2001, xi–xii)

Other teachers collaborate with colleagues and develop units of study that they co-teach in some fashion. Becky Schlomann (2004) designed a pilot unit that integrates theatre with the mentorship program Peer Assistance and Leadership (PALs).[3] The centerpiece of the unit is development of a Theatre-in-Education (TIE) piece through which students achieve the objectives of both the theatre and PALs curriculums. Becky first looked at each subject to see if there were correlations in terms of curricular goals and objectives. She then looked at her teaching style and methodologies and those of the PALs teacher. She built lesson plans and evaluation strategies based on ways in which their styles complemented and overlapped with each other.

There are also sturdy pioneers who have brought about positive change by placing the arts at the center of the curriculum in some of our nation's most challenging schools.

When New York's Educational Priorities Panel (Connell 1996) studied a group of struggling inner-city elementary schools that raised their standardized test scores dramatically and got off the city's academic "probation" list, panel researchers made a surprising discovery. Even though probation status focused urgent attention on the "basic" reading and math content appearing on achievement tests, many of the schools that got off the list had actually *increased* their arts programming. "These successful schools," the report said, "were distinguished by a strong arts program that was infused through the

instructional program and that included most of the students in the school."
(Zemelman, Daniels, and Hyde 2005, 161–62, original emphasis)

In *Third Space*, Deasy and Stevenson (2005) present compelling stories of how
the arts transformed schools in ten of the most economically disadvantaged
communities in the U.S. They echo the need for ownership and excellence while
highlighting the importance of a shared vision among students, teachers, and the
community.

The authors of the Partnership for the 21st Century's *Arts Skills Map* speak to
the logic of integrating the arts throughout the education of every child "because
the arts [...] have enabled us to explore the changing nature of our existence and
to understand how that nature has both evolved and remained constant over time,
culture, and place" (2010).

Teachers wishing to learn how to teach theatre while also addressing the increasing
need to improve learning in other subjects now have a number of professional
development models around the country to consider. Katie Dawson (2011a) directs
Drama for Schools (DFS) at The University of Texas at Austin through which
arts integration programs are tailored to the needs of a school community. DFS
projects bring UT and school districts into long-term partnerships through onsite
mentorship and distance learning support so teachers build knowledge, skills, and
practices to integrate drama and theatre in their classrooms. DFS graduate students
and professional teaching artists collaborate with K–12 teachers and curriculum
specialists to design and implement "drama-based instruction to increase teacher
efficacy and student engagement across the curriculum." A teacher might learn to
present a history lesson about the battle of the Alamo in which

> students might join together to write and produce a play about the event. This
> activity would go beyond merely reading a textbook and would engage the students
> in group research, practice of their English and writing skills, memorizing lines
> that included historical facts and dates, and teaching them social and disciplinary
> skills required for working within a team. (Dawson 2011a)

Programs like this are growing as districts scramble to raise achievement scores and
to keep students in school. Teachers in a district where 95 percent of students are
considered as "underachieving" found that within two years of a DFS partnership
state test scores improved by 43 percent. Other schools facing bullying issues as
well as low academic achievement find that their teachers who have participated in
these arts integration programs have helped change the school culture while also
raising test scores (Dawson 2011a).

In another model, professors from American University in Washington, D.C.,
team with professional teaching artists from Imagination Stage theatre. Together

they teach K–12 teachers how to integrate the arts to help students at risk of academic failure become "successful learners" (Mardirosian 2009).

Katie Dawson (2011b), drawing from work on authentic learning contexts by Newmann and Wehlage (1995), reminds us that integrating drama and theatre into the curriculum with a learner-centered focus encourages teachers to incorporate strategies that facilitate higher order thinking, articulate multiple perspectives, connect knowledge to the world outside the classroom, and provide social support to deepen student learning. An authentic learning context implies that activities that are rooted in a student's cultural and personal context will be more meaningful and thus more productive than those removed from the student's life (Newmann and Wehlage 1995).

SUCCESSFULLY COLLABORATING WITH COLLEAGUES

Working with other teachers and artists in a quality comprehensive theatre program means negotiating territory, resources, boundaries, work styles, and work ethics. In summarizing the need for dialogue in any program of excellence, Steve Seidel and his colleagues conclude

> a misalignment of ideas among decision makers about what constitutes quality often complicates a program's pursuit of it. Alignment is easy to ignore, and achieving alignment among decision makers at all levels often requires far more basic investigation, dialogue, and negotiation than is given. (Seidel et al. 2009)

My most rewarding and my most troublesome teaching and artmaking experiences can be linked directly to the unique demands of collaboration. Whether in joyful or agonizingly difficult projects, the joy or trouble almost always stemmed from what happened, or did not happen, *before* the project began. How much preparation, communication, negotiation, shared understanding, and investment were in place before we started had a direct impact on how well the project went. These outcomes can also be linked to how willing everyone was to relinquish some control and to let others share leadership. With each new endeavor, I learn more about dealing with change graciously. I am learning that different is not always bad and that new can be exciting. I am also learning that harboring unspoken expectations is a luxury I cannot afford when young people are involved. I have to communicate with colleagues clearly, early, and often. I need to explain what my students need, what our boundaries are, what I can give to the project, and what I cannot. I must be willing also to listen to what my colleagues are saying. We will then best serve our students.

When working on projects with other teachers and teaching artists, it is in everyone's best interest to be in agreement about the approach, scope, and details of the project *before* beginning to work with students.

- Initiate conversations with colleagues in theatre, music, art, dance, and other disciplines. Get to know them and their interests.
- Find common ground. Look for ways in which you and your colleagues might share

  - an interest in collaborating;
  - a vision for the school;
  - respect for and commitment to students;
  - common curricular objectives or methodologies.

- Seek out and work with people who are open to problem solving and who tolerate divergent thinking.
- Develop a willingness to change how things have been done in the past, how schedules are arranged, how subjects are taught and by whom.
- Devote time for collaborative planning. Remember to plan assessments and evaluations that reflect objectives in each discipline as well as integrated knowledge and skills.
- Be honest about how much time you can invest.
- If possible, start small. Do pilot or short-term projects with clear beginnings and endings.
- Do not expect to have all of the answers or the best answers all of the time.
- Expect to make mistakes. Learn from everyone's mistakes.
- Prepare students. Tell them what you anticipate will happen in collaborations with other teachers or guest artists. Assure them that some things will change, that there will be surprises, and that you are looking out for their best interest. (Be sure that you are.) Let students know they can come to you with questions, concerns, and discoveries.
- Hindsight is 20/20. Take what you learn in each project, especially what worked well, and let that propel you into the next project. Focusing on what did not work does not foster progress.
- Be patient. Find and cherish the small successes and build on them.

Figure 4.7: Tips for Successful Collaborations

Suggestions for designing successful collaborative projects were gleaned from many conversations with teachers and artists (see Figure 4.7). While by no means a complete list, these suggestions are a valuable resource on your journey toward best practice.

AN EXAMPLE OF COMPREHENSIVE THEATRE EDUCATION

Drama-Based Interdisciplinary Unit – Deb Alexander

As discussed in Chapter 2 (page 57), Deb Alexander's curriculum model engages students in learner-centered and holistic theatre education. While developed for middle school students, the lessons and structure easily lend themselves to work with high school students. Deb explains her adaptation of the DBTE model and uses *The Diary of Anne Frank,* originally adapted by Frances Goodrich and Albert Hackett, to demonstrate her model. "Model A is based on the [...] [SCEA] model. At the center [...] however, is a play from which the different theatrical roles stem and interconnect" (Goodrich and Hackett 1999, 7) (see Figure 4.8). Model B illustrates how students in the six roles explore the play. As shown in Figure 4.9, "the first four steps are a process through which students learn tools and build the foundation necessary to create a final product in Step Five" (8).

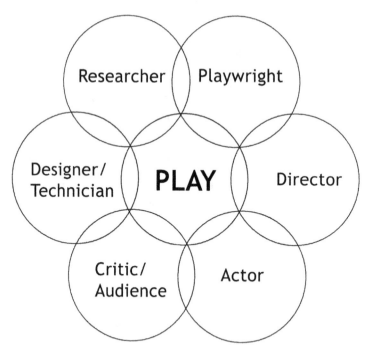

In this design, the teacher has placed a play at the core of the curriculum, The play serves as a link between the Methods of Inquiry and the Perspectives. Copyright Alexander (1999).

Figure 4.8: Model A: A Drama-Based Interdisciplinary Model

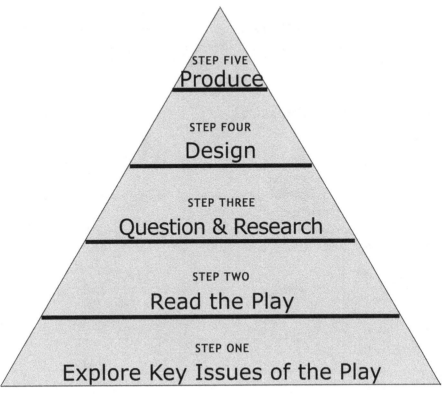

Students move through the curriculum sequentially, building on knowledge, skills, and understanding acquired in preceding steps. Copyright Alexander (1999).

Figure 4.9: Model B: Curriculum Sequence

For the first six weeks, students are introduced to the core material by exploring key issues in the play and reading and analyzing the script using various drama techniques. The next two weeks are designed to help students ask questions and to learn alternative means of research through the exploration of oral histories, internet sites, visual art works, and other library resources. The next four weeks are dedicated to the design process as students transform the classroom into a workshop to explore scenic, costume, lighting, and sound design. The final six weeks are reserved for students to produce specific scenes from the script. They [...] create a theatre company and share their work with an invited audience at the end of the term. [...] The primary focus is on student development and learning leading to a production of selected scenes versus a production of a play as the primary objective. (Alexander 1999, 9–10)

Not wanting to dilute the history presented in *The Diary of Anne Frank* by covering too much material, Deb selected three themes or issues to explore: oppression, survival, and hope. The following selected lessons combine the steps in Model B with those themes through the semester long class.

Step One: Exploring the Issues

Lesson 1: Oppression

Objectives
Identify and define what a stereotype is.
- Explore the consequences of stereotyping by playing the roles of the victim, perpetrator, and bystander.
- Debate in two groups the fate of one victim by examining the pros and cons of their personal choice.

Methodology:
- Group discussion
- Theatre games
- Role drama
- Debate

Focus:
- What is stereotyping and how does it affect our everyday lives?

Materials:
- Soup can without a label
- *National Geographic On Assignment: USA*
- Star of David
- Holocaust photo
- Butcher paper
- Tape
- Markers

Discussion

- Show students the can without the label.
- What could be in this can?
- How are we able to identify its contents?
- What other kinds of labels exist (e.g. clothing)?
- What do labels say about a person?

- How do we label people in our lives?
- How do we label ourselves?

Share photos of everyday people:
- Describe this person in one word.
- How can one word describe someone?

Write the word "stereotype" up on the board:
- How do we stereotype in our everyday lives and why?
- What are the consequences?
- How are teenagers stereotyped by adults?
- Why are they stereotyped?
- What is the result?

Activity

Create a Community

Everyone walk around the room in your own space as yourself. Change directions. Head for open space. Create a community of people who are like you according to the specific instructions that the leader calls out. Example: "Create a community of people who are like you from the knees down." All students who are wearing sandals might create a group while those who are wearing running shoes might create another group.

Create a community of people who are like you
- neck up
- ankles down
- neck down
- waist up

What is the name of your community? Break up and walk around. Create a community of people who are like you. (Continue for at least three times.)

Variation

Ask students to find people who are like them in invisible versus physical characteristics. (Examples: favorite movie, music, number or gender of siblings.)

Discussion

- What is a community?
- How do you choose who is in your community and who is not?

- In this exercise, when did things get difficult in figuring out who was in your community and who was not?
- In your school or neighborhood, who is in your community?
- What happens when someone does not belong to a community?
- How does stereotyping play into creating a community?
- What are the dangers of stereotyping?

Activity

Rumor Mill

There is a new kid at school who is not like you. In pairs, talk about this new student that you just saw. They are not like you. How are they different? Move into groups of four and share the information that you have heard so far about the new student.

Discussion

- How does stereotyping play into spreading rumors?
- What are the dangers of spreading rumors?

Activity

Child/Parent Role Play

Divide the class into pairs. Each pair will improvise a situation that the new student might experience. Share selected short scenes with the class and discuss.

Situation One:

Child: You want to go outside and play in your new neighborhood.
Parent: You don't want your child to go out – try to keep them safe.

Situation Two:

Child: You don't want to go to school especially after the events that occurred due to the rumor mill.
Parent: Try to convince your child why it's so important that they go to school.

Discussion

- Should the student continue going to this school or transfer? List pros and cons.

Activity

Labels

Show the picture of the Star of David and other "labels" that the Nazis used to define their prisoners. "For the next several weeks, we will be exploring a period of history called the Holocaust in which stereotyping played a major role in the death and destruction of several races of people due to the discrimination of a select few who thought themselves [...] superior to everyone else."

Discussion

- How do you define stereotyping?
- How does stereotyping lead to discrimination?
- How can we fight discrimination?

Lesson 2: Survival

Objectives

- Create a hierarchy of needs similar to Maslow's hierarchy of needs.
- Examine the chronology of decrees which revoked the rights of the Jewish population. Discuss the impact of these laws on the individual based on their needs (social, emotional, physical).
- Create individual and group tableaux of what makes them happy and images of when that happiness is taken away.

Methodology:
- Frozen statues, tableaux and images
- Group discussion

Focus:
- What do humans need to exist happily?

Material:
- Handout
- Chalkboard
- Chalk
- Chronology worksheet

Discussion

- Distribute "Rights and Freedoms Worksheet" for students to complete independently (see Figure 4.10). Have students work in small groups to discuss their decisions. Each group works to come to consensus and ranks the rights as a group. Small group responses and their rationales are shared and discussed.
- Laws that revoked the rights of individuals during the time period of the play. (*Frederich* by Hans Peter Richter [1987], is an excellent reference with a complete chronology of the period.)

Think of the freedom that the following rights afford you and your family. Think of the ways you and your family would be affected if these rights were revoked. Remember, if these rights were revoked, this would mean giving up things you already have. Rank these rights from 1 to 6 – 1 being MOST important to you.

The right to

- own or use a telephone
- date/marry whomever you choose
- own an MP3 player, TV, or computer
- own a pet
- go to a movie or rock concert
- leave your house whenever you choose (You would still be able to leave the house, but there would be strict limitations on when you could go out.)

Figure 4.10: Rights and Freedoms Worksheet

Activity

Frozen Statues and Images

Discuss the ways an individual would be affected through the revoking of rights and freedoms. Students work in pairs using their bodies to describe their thoughts and feelings.

- One student is the sculptor and the other is the clay. The sculptor molds the clay into a frozen statue of an activity that makes them happy. (Examples: playing baseball, talking on the phone.)
- Next, the sculptor molds the clay into an image of a feeling they have when the activity they enjoy is taken away. (Examples: frustration, anger.)
- Have the statues start out and slowly transform to the image with an eight count.
- Have the sculptors sit down in the audience and observe the transformation.

Choose specific statues and images that stand out for the students to discuss.
- o Literally, what do you see?
- o How does the image change?
- o What does this image say about this person?

- The sculptor and clay switch roles. Repeat steps one through four.

Variation

If students are uncomfortable touching each other, have the sculptor model while the clay mirrors them.

Activity

Create group tableaux

- In groups of four to six, create two tableaux similar to the ideas discussed in the above exercise.
- Create a tableaux of an activity that a group of people would enjoy.
- Create a tableaux of those people when that activity is taken away.
- Show the two tableaux in sequence starting with the first and moving to the second in an eight count.
- Share and compare and contrast the tableaux with the class.

Variation

Have students devise a group image for the word "freedom" and a second image for "oppression," or "freedom taken away."

Discussion

- What do students need to survive?
- How do students survive day to day in middle school?
- When things get really bad, how [do] you keep your head up?
- What do humans need to survive?
- Name one thing that no one can take away from you.

Lesson 3: Hope

Objectives

- Create tableaux representing a series of responses to a natural disaster.
- Define the different roles of a rescuer through role play.

- Work as an ensemble in role to explore the fate of three families and state the consequences of their decisions.

Methodology:
- Role drama
- Tableaux
- Group discussion
- Partner and group debate

Focus:
- How many people are at risk and how are we going to rescue them?

Materials:
- Photos of natural disasters
- World War II photos of American and Russian soldiers freeing Holocaust victims

Discussion

- Share pictures of natural disasters.
- Discuss as a class:
  - What is a natural disaster?
  - Why do people rebuild their homes and communities in the same place after they are destroyed?
  - Who helps these people rebuild their community?
  - Who rescues these people?
  - What qualities does a rescuer possess?
  - How much are you willing to risk to save someone's life?

Activity

Create a day in the life of a natural disaster

Break into groups of 4–5 students. Choose a natural disaster and create three tableaux to represent a day in the life of a community.
- Beginning – what people were doing before the disaster
- Middle – the disaster hits
- End – after the disaster/picking up the pieces

Discussion

- Describe what you see.
- How are they dealing with the aftermath?

Activity

Teacher in Role

The teacher is an editor of the big newspaper in town. She has called upon her fellow reporters (students) to interview the survivors of a recent hurricane.

Editor: "Greetings fellow reporters! I'm so glad that all of you could make it today despite the nasty weather. As you know, our town has been hit by one of the largest hurricanes this year. I understand there are many people who have lost their homes and maybe some who lost their lives. It is up to you to go find the survivors and get their story. Please be as sensitive as possible. This is a very fragile situation. Are there any questions?"

- Break into teams of two.
- Label each other A or B.
- Person A is the reporter who interviews person B.
- Person B shares their story of how they survived the hurricane. Some questions to consider:
  - Who rescued you?
  - How did you hold on when things got really bad?
  - What words of advice do you have for people who have never experienced a hurricane?
- Switch places.
- Person A is now a rescuer who tells their story of their rescue mission while person B interviews them.

Activity

Town Meeting – Group Decision

"We are all huddled in a group shelter together. We are past capacity and there is no room to lie down on the floor. Food is running out and the end of the storm is not in sight. There are three families who want to enter our already overcrowded shelter. What should we do?"

- Divide the students into pairs to argue the pros and cons of letting more people into the shelter.
- As a group, discuss the consequences of letting three more families into our overcrowded shelter or leaving them out in the storm.
  - What are the pros and cons?
  - How do these weigh on our conscience?

Discussion

Share photos of American and Russian soldiers and Danish citizens rescuing Jews from concentration camps.

- What does it take to make a hero?
- How are these rescue missions different/the same as saving someone from a natural disaster?

Step Two: Learning the Play

Deb used a staged reading activity to introduce the play. The reading was then integrated with interactive drama work as illustrated in the following lesson. Other methods she used to explore the scenes were teacher-in-role, discussion, role play, frozen images, story as a springboard, library research, questioning and inquiry, and student journal writing. Throughout the reading of the script, the students actively question the play, filling up a question box located in a visible spot in the classroom (Alexander 1999, 33).

Objectives

- Design the Annex

Focus:
- What memories does the Annex hold for Otto?

Materials:
- Personal item from home

Discussion

- Act I.1 – Otto Frank returns to the Annex for the first time since the war ended.
  - How does Otto Frank first discover the Annex when he returns from the concentration camp?
  - How do you show the personalities of people who might have lived there at one time?
  - What do the walls look like?
  - What is on the floor?
  - What kind of furniture is there?
  - What is the state of condition of everything?
  - How do specific props represent character or story?

Activity

Personal Prop

Students bring an item from home that they think they might see lying on the Annex floor and which Otto Frank might find. Create a demonstration for the students by bringing in four or five personal props of your own. Use an open space for the demonstration. Turn over a couple pieces of furniture, such as a desk or chair, and place your props in very specific areas in relation to the furniture. Once the props are placed, pick one prop up and tell a story from Otto Frank's point of view. "I remember this pink sweater. I gave this to my wife for her birthday. I'm surprised she kept it this long. Oh look [...] there's a stain from where she spilled her coffee when Anne was chasing Peter around the table." Next, ask each student, one at a time, to place their prop in the space and to tell their story. By the end of the exercise the classroom should be transformed into the Annex.

Discussion

• What kind of memories does your prop bring back for Otto Frank?

Journal Writing:

• Otto's first thoughts when he discovers your personal prop:
  ○ Whom did it belong to?
  ○ How was it used?
  ○ Why didn't the Nazi's confiscate it?

Step Three: Questions and Research

Deb offers an overview of her approach to research and dramaturgy.

> It should be stressed with the students that research is about asking questions and not necessarily finding all of the answers. If the play is well written, the issues are complex and there is rarely a simple solution to the characters' problems.
>
> The hardest step of the research is already done for the students since [...] the students [...] [have been] filling up [the] question box [...] in the classroom as they read the play. Students select one question that intrigues them to start their research. [...] They use the library, computer, internet access, and interviewing as their tools to find out more information.
>
> Check out several books ahead of time relating to the topic from the public library to use as a resource in the classroom. [...] Specific websites are great starting points students can explore for further information. [...] Use alternative

methods of research such as listening to music, research collages, artwork, and interviews. (Alexander 1999, 59–60)

Activity

Workstations

Create small teams of students and several workstations in the classroom, each requiring a different method of research. The teams can rotate to each workstation as they begin their research. There should only be one team per work station.
- Workstation one: juvenile literature and children's books.
- Workstation two: music from the time period.
- Workstation three: artwork from the time period.
- Workstation four: computer access.
- Workstation five: interview center – how to create a simple interview.
- Workstation six: the school library – periodicals and abstracts.
- Workstation Seven: history books and world atlas.

Activity

Timeline

Have teams create a historical timeline on the bulletin board. Put the characters from the play in the timeline to see how history affected the action of the play.

Step Four: Design

Objectives

Transform the classroom into the world of the play by moving classroom [or rehearsal] furniture around.
- Place furniture in proscenium, thrust, and arena settings.
- Choose one character from the play and design their room with paper and pencil.

Exploration of design and technology served as a powerful tool for students to address their questions about aspects of the play. The following are excerpts from a larger unit that considered scenic, sound, lighting, and costume elements for the play.

Focus:
- How do we create the world of the Annex?

Materials:
- Classroom furniture
- Paper
- Rulers
- No. 2 pencils
- Colored pencils

Discussion

- Give the students a variety of classroom or rehearsal furniture. Their task is to transform the classroom or a designated space into the world of the play. Example: Create the four rooms in the Annex: Anne's and Mr. Dussel's room, Van Daan's attic, Peter's room, and the main living area with a sink and stove.
- What is missing?
- How do we personalize these rooms to show who occupies them?
- How do these rooms reflect the personality of the characters and the conflict of the play?

Activity

Different Theatrical Spaces

Discussion

- How do we adapt this world we have created for the stage?
- What are the three different kinds of stages?
  - Proscenium: audience on one side
  - Thrust: audience on three sides
  - Arena: audience on four sides (in the round)
- How would we adjust the set for each of these stages?
- What considerations do we have to take in? Discuss:
  - Sightlines
  - Levels
  - Planes
  - Diagonals
  - Stage pictures
  - Audience
- What furniture/set pieces can we do without?
- What kinds of props can we use to dress the set?

- Describe the walls.
- Where is the furniture placed onstage?

Students choose one of the configurations of the set either in proscenium, thrust, or arena. Based on what they designed above, they draw a ground plan that they could give to the director for rehearsal purposes.

- What do you need to inform the director about?
- What challenges do you face with this set?
- What are you willing to change? Why?
- What do you want to stay the same? Why?

Choose one character and design your room on paper. Example: How does Anne decorate her side of the room versus Mr. Dussel? How do their decorations reflect their personalities? Why is set dressing so important?

Step Five: Costume

Objectives

Explore line, shape, and color through pinning different pieces of fabric to their bodies.
- Replicate a 1940s fashion with the bag of scraps and one model.
- Start to draw a costume rendering of a specific character from the play.

Methodology:
- Design activities
- Group discussion

Focus:
- How do costumes help define character?

Materials:
- 8–10 bags full of scraps of fabric and/or hangers with various costume pieces
- 8–10 boxes of safety pins
- Picture from the 1940s (male and female)
- Paper
- Colored pencils
- No. 2 pencils

Discussion

- Break students into groups of four or five. Give each group a bag of scraps or costume pieces. Have them explore the many different ways to use their costume pieces. They can pin their scraps on in any way they want. See what each group comes up with and share.

Activity

Designing Costumes

Show students a picture of a costume from the time period of the play you are reading. Have them choose one person in their group to be the model and the other three the designers. Their task is to recreate the costume to the best of their abilities using their bag of scraps and safety pins. Girls and boys can work separately for the draping portion of this lesson.

Discussion

- How does the placement of fabric on the body change the shape of the garment?
- What choices of fabric do you use to show character?

Activity

Costume Rendering

Each student selects one character from the play and creates a costume rendering on paper. They can use swatches from the scraps of fabric to pin to their rendering to show the color and texture of the costume.

Discussion

- How do the costumes reflect that they have been hiding for two years?
- How do the costumes change to reflect a passage of time?
- How do we show the characters have lost weight?

Step Six: Create a Theatre Company

With the help of the teacher, students assign themselves to specific roles within one of three theatre companies. The final class project/production consists of
- a dramaturgical display on a bulletin board.
- a student resource packet.
- a short performance by each company of one long scene or several shorter scenes.

The performances are shared with the school or selected classes.

Please read the job descriptions and then answer the questions below to the best of your ability. Your opinion does matter. Take your time with these considerations. Feel free to discuss your thoughts with me.

Name: _____ Period: _____

JOB DESCRIPTIONS

Job #1 – The Director
Directors need to be leaders. They are responsible for helping create a unified vision for your scene. They must be able to work well with many people including the actors, designers, and technicians. They will stage and block a short scene, meet with the designers on a regular basis, and help create a ground plan for your scene. They will keep a director's book.

Job #2 – The Stage Manager
Stage Managers must be extraordinarily organized. They must have excellent "people skills" because they are responsible for keeping the lines of communication open between the director, actors, designers, dramaturgs, and front of house. They are at rehearsals every day and are responsible for overseeing set-up and strike. They will run the technical rehearsals and call the cues for the show during performance. They are responsible for overseeing props, sets, costumes, and other technical needs. They will keep a prompt book and help people who request specific information.

Job #3 and #4 – Actors
Actors must always be ready for rehearsals by warming up ahead of time and being on task. They will work closely with the director and stage manager. They are to help with technical duties when asked by the stage manager, and they are responsible for helping set up and strike after rehearsal.

Job #5 and #6 – Designers
Designers are responsible for designing the sets, costumes, lights, and sound. They will work closely with the director and stage manager to make sure the vision of the scene is realized. They will also work closely with the dramaturgs to let them know if there is any research material that they need so they can make a specific decision. They will be required to help build the technical elements and oversee crews during the process. Designers will be required to document their process by drawing renderings, building scale models, and justifying color choices.

Job #7 – Assistant Stage Manager (ASM)/Technical Support
ASM's will work directly with the stage manager. They are responsible for helping meet the director's and actors' needs. They will help set up and strike for each rehearsal. When they are not needed in rehearsal, they will assist the designers, front of house, or dramaturgs depending on the need. They will work backstage for the performance.

Job #8 – Front of House/Box Office/Marketing
This is a good position for students who excel in math and visual arts. Front of House/ Box Office/Marketing people are responsible for organizing the audience. They decide where the audience sits and they set up the seats. They will be responsible for overseeing the ushers on the day of performance. They are responsible for creating a ticketing system and deciding how to sell the tickets. They are also responsible for letting the school know about the performance through announcements, posters, flyers, and any other marketing technique they want to use.

Job #9 and #10 – Dramaturgs
Dramaturgs need to be computer literate. They are responsible for setting up the dramaturgy board with specific information about the show. They should select the best work done by the students during our study of this play and be creative in how they display the work. They are also responsible for helping to create the layout for the student resource packet and for collecting the program information to publish for the performance.

NOTE: Students with certain job titles (Front of House/Box Office/Marketing or Dramaturg) work with all of the Companies.

QUESTIONS TO ANSWER:
1. List your first, second, and third choices.
2. For EACH choice, answer the following questions:

   • Why do you want this job?
   • What strengths do you bring to this job?
   • What role do you NOT want? Why?

Figure 4.11: Theatre Company Job Descriptions

Activity

Which Role Best Fits You? Joining a Theatre Company

• A good theatre company is only as good as its members. How can this project be a team effort?
• Identify protocols and procedures for working together.

Students read the Theatre Company Job Descriptions handout in Figure 4.11 and answer the questions.

After the students are divided into the three companies, they meet as a group with the teacher and check in with each other about their progress at least once a week. They make decisions together about how to help each other meet deadlines.

Activity

Dramaturgical Display

The dramaturgs create a bulletin board to display all of the research the class has done in steps one through four of Model B. The intention is to help the audience better understand the play. The dramaturgy board should include but is not limited to:

- Historical facts
- Historical timeline
- Design information
- Costume renderings
- Scenic design
- Photos from the process
- Description of roles in theatre company
- Student responses about roles and process
- Themes and issues

Activity

Student Resource Packet

The "Student Resource Packet" is a program that will be handed out to every audience member in order to prepare them for what they are about to see. The student resource packet is produced by the dramaturgs and is similar to the bulletin board except it is in the form of a small booklet. For this activity the emphasis is on layout versus writing endless pages of information. The Student Resource Packet sums up steps one through four of Model B. Resource packets should include:

- Table of contents
- Names of everyone involved in the process and their roles
- Background information (historical data)
- Plot of the play
- Themes and issues
- Design page
- Director's notes
- Games and activities
- Special thanks
- Bibliography or where to get more information

In The Diary of Anne Frank, there are not any two-person scenes that last very long so each group can produce two to three scenes. I suggest [using] the following scenes:

Act I.2: pp. 17–18 – Anne and Peter
Anne and Peter meet for the first time. Anne is admiring his cat Moushi.
Anne: "What's your cat's name?"

Act I.3: p. 32 – Mr. and Mrs. Van Daan
Mr. and Mrs. Van Daan are arguing about Mr. Van Daan's smoking.
Mrs. Van Daan: "Isn't it bad enough here without your sprawling all over the place?"

Act I.3: pp. 43–45 – Anne and Mr. Dussel
Anne and Mr. Dussel discover that they are sharing a room together.
Anne: "You're going to share my room with me."

Act II.1: pp. 75–76 – Anne and Peter
Peter takes Anne her cake after she has had a fight with her family and abruptly leaves the room. This is the first time where Anne and Peter really have a conversation. They discover they are not as alone as they first thought they were.
Peter: "You left this."

Act II.2: pp. 81–84 – Anne and Peter
Anne and Peter's first date
Anne: "Aren't they awful?"

Variation: Students can create their own scenes based on what is not in the script to help answer some of their questions about the characters. For example, one could write a scene from Mrs. Frank's point of view about how she is unable to communicate with Anne or a scene where Mrs. Van Daan is grilling Peter about his date up in the attic. Students can create their own modern day version of Anne Frank by exploring a parallel situation of what might be going on in the world, community, or school right now.

Figure 4.12: Suggested Scenes from *The Diary of Anne Frank.*

Activity

Performance of Scenes

Select one to three strong scenes from the script that involve two to three actors. Each scene is no longer than fifteen minutes. (See Figure 4.12 for suggestions.) Each company is responsible for directing, acting, and creating the production elements for their scene(s).

The performance includes a brief description from each company of the process that they went through to get to this point. The post-show discussion is facilitated by a teacher or student. Reflections about the process take place through group discussion, self-evaluation, and journal writing.

IDEAS FOR FURTHER REFLECTION

Revisiting Appreciative Inquiry

Another Look at *What* Is

Ask yourself these questions about your current program:
- What is the relationship of my theatre curriculum and my program to that of the rest of the school?
- What is the balance between instruction, reflection, production, aesthetics, history, and criticism in my theatre program? What is the relationship between curricular and co-curricular activities? Does this balance offer comprehensive education in theatre?

Another Look at *What Could Be*

Let yourself imagine what is possible. Ask yourself:
- If the next time I went to my school I had a new, comprehensive theatre program, what would it look like? How is the whole program balanced and interconnected? What is my emphasis, and how do I allocate time and resources? What collegial relationships do I have?
- How does the content and practice in this program relate to content and practice in the other art disciplines and the other academic subjects students study?
- What challenges and obstacles were faced and overcome to bring about this change? Who helped me, and what resources and support did we garner in this process of change?

Another Look at *What Will Be*? Re-envisioning a Secondary School Theatre Program

- What opportunities for change do the answers to the previous questions point to? As you reflect about best practice and have conversations with your colleagues and mentors, ponder these additional questions. Think about them in light of your core values and beliefs, your vision for your theatre education program, and your day-to-day teaching and production practices.

- What should students know about theatre and be able to do in theatre and drama by the end of thirteen years of public education?
    How can this be true for all students in your school?
    How do your curriculum and production choices speak to this intent?

- What is at the *core* of your *practice*?
    What is it about *theatre* that drives and inspires you?
    What is it about *teaching* that drives and inspires you?
    Does your attraction to theatre and attraction to teaching work in harmony or conflict with each other?
    Can these/should these attractions be at the core of your school *program*? Your *curriculum*?

- What should be *studied* in K–12 theatre education?
    Taught?
    Experienced?
    Produced?
    What content should be included in your *curriculum* and what content in your *productions*?
    How do you envision your classroom work intersecting and overlapping with your production work?

- What roles do seeing, making, critiquing, and writing about theatre have in your curriculum?
    In your production program?

- Whose history will you study and/or produce?
    What dramatic literature?
    Whose aesthetics?

- In what ways and by what means (learning styles and modalities) will learning take place in your curriculum?
    How are your program and curriculum learner centered?

- How is socially responsible and socially engaged theatre education evident in your curriculum?
    Your program?

- How can this be accomplished in a comprehensive, holistic (DBTE), and integrated fashion as you address local, state, and national standards?
    How is your curriculum more expansive than just "covering the required standards?"

How does your program reflect the presence of media in our lives?

How does your curriculum and program actively engage *students* in the *use* of technology?

How do *you* use technology in your teaching?

Production work?

SELECTED RESOURCES

In addition to the works cited in this chapter, the following sources offer ideas for further reading and reflection.

Annenberg Media. "Connecting with the Arts: A Workshop for Middle Grades Teachers." www.learner.org/resources/series199.html.

Black, Katie Lebhar, and John W. White. 2011. "Deedle Deedle Everyone: How One Theatre Program Created a School-wide Curriculum Based on *Fiddler on the Roof*." *Teaching Theatre* 21 (12): 12–20.

Journal for Learning through the Arts. Scholarship: University of California. ISSN: 1932–7528. http://escholarship.org/uc/clta_lta.

Newmann, Fred, and Gary Wehlage. 1995. *Successful School Restructuring: A Report to the Public and Educators by the Center on Organization and Restructuring of Schools.* Alexandria, VA: Association for Supervision and Curriculum Development.

Pink, Daniel H. 2006. *A Whole New Mind: Why Right-Brainers will Rule the Future.* New York: Penguin.

NOTES

1. Discipline-Based Theatre Education was developed by Kim Wheetley for the Southeast Center for Education in the Arts (SCEA), a nationally recognized center for professional development located at the University of Tennessee at Chattanooga. SCEA was prompted in this move by development of Discipline-Based Art Education (DBAE) initiated in 1985 by The Getty Center for Education in the Arts. DBAE is an effort to make art education more comprehensive and on an equal footing with other academic subjects taught in the schools. Believing that the arts are marginalized because of narrow focus on art production, DBAE advocates sought to expand art education through inclusion of aesthetics, art history, and art criticism. Inherent in all Discipline-Based initiatives are interactions between arts specialists and classroom teachers that foster study of other disciplines in arts classrooms and inclusion of the arts in other subjects.

2. There are a number of national projects and initiatives intended to foster and support arts integration and interdisciplinary arts education. The National Standards for Arts Education (1994), for example, included dance, music, theatre, and visual arts standards addressed at connections and relationships between art forms. The National Coalition for Core Arts Standards (NCCAS) began a National Arts

Standards Revision in 2011. In 2002, the Consortium of National Arts Education Associations published *Authentic Connections: Interdisciplinary Work in the Arts* to assist arts educators in teaching the arts with integrity through these national standards. The Interstate New Teacher Assessment and Support Consortium Committee (InTASC), a program of the Council of Chief State School Officers, has developed *Model Standards for Licensing Classroom Teachers and Specialists in the Arts* (2002). This document presents principles "to clarify how the common core of teacher knowledge and skills play out for both classroom teachers and arts specialists in the context of teaching the arts" (InTASC 2002). The Annenberg Foundation and the J. Paul Getty Trust have jointly initiated integrated arts education in schools. The Annenberg/Corporation for Public Broadcasting has developed a series of professional development videotapes and related websites.

3. Peer Assistance and Leadership, or PALs, is a national peer mentorship program that prepares high school students to work as mentors to elementary and middle school students.

Chapter 5

Theatre Education Outside the Box

It seems clear to me that there is a deep connection between children and artists: they both want to discover the truth, to imagine the impossible, to delight in the now, and to name what is beautiful. As we listen to the news and struggle with our own families, careers, and communities, there is an urgent need for our children and our artists to take these journeys of discovery together.

Abigail Adams

In high school, I was in theatre arts and did not have very good teachers [...] I put myself in community theatre so that I could get a better experience, and it truly changed my life. [...] I saw with my own eyes what theatre could do [for] those that love it.

Rebecca Podsednik

This book would not be complete without acknowledging that a lot of theatre education for secondary school students is taking place *outside* of school and traditional school structures. These programs provide powerful examples of best practice for both school-based and community-based theatre teachers.

Youth theatres, community theatres, professional theatres, and a host of community-based agencies and organizations offer learning opportunities in theatre for large numbers of young people. Some students attend schools with no theatre programs; others turn to community-based programs as refugees fleeing theatre programs where their voices are not heard or their presence noticed. They seek a place where they are welcomed and where they can find diverse, high-calibre theatre experiences. They find value working with artists who share their interests and passions and who appreciate their unique talents.

Peter Brosius, director of the Children's Theatre Company (CTC) in Minneapolis, highlights the role, as theatre educators, that professional theatre organizations are playing as they reach out to underserved youth. CTC commissioned a play exploring tensions between African American and Somali immigrant youth in the neighborhood around the theatre. They also staged *Antigone* promenade style (no seats) so actors could mingle with audience members. In this staging, a soldier could push audience members aside or "Creon might grab you and dance with you" (Peter Brosius, cited in Lamb 2003). He calls this a "very vivid, muscular theatrical presentation" and noted that young people in the audience had "eyes as big as saucers." He wants to say to adolescents, "You think you know what theatre is? We're going to surprise you" (Lamb 2003). The theatre also offers secondary students interested in playwriting, directing, acting, or theatre design and technology onsite lab programs with industry professionals.

Professional artists can surprise, intrigue, and challenge adolescents in any number of ways. Allison Manville Metz (2002) wondered if watching and creating avant-garde theatre might be an engaging vehicle for self-expression for disenfranchised youth. She developed a project bringing together students from the public schools and artists at Salvage Vanguard, an avant-garde theatre in Austin.

Metz raised a provocative question and suggests new avenues for theatre teacher-artists to explore.

> The importance of alternative education, as well as arts education, has been documented, but what about alternative arts education? Not only do I believe that avant-garde theatre has a lot to offer young people, I believe the world of avant-garde theatre has much to learn from youth on the margins of society. If theatre educators, artists, and marginalized youth can begin to appreciate the potential of a reciprocal relationship between the theatre form and the young population, there is no telling how the future of art and the future of young lives can be enhanced. (Metz 2002, 98)

For many of our nation's children, a touring production, a one-day residency with an artist, or a community theatre class will be the only theatre education they receive. Community-based theatre programs and teaching artists embodying best practice recognize, however, that plunking children into the seats of a theatre or leading one-day "drive-by dramas" is not theatre education and is far from best practice.

School doesn't teach me. It oppresses me. High School Student, New York City

COMMUNITY-BASED THEATRE EDUCATION

This chapter offers a brief look at artists and arts organizations that offer learner-centered, socially responsible, and comprehensive theatre experiences to middle and high school students. Whether in their own venues or through partnerships with schools, artists who embrace principles of best practice provide rich perspectives about theatre and theatre making. They offer a glimpse of a much broader range of forward-looking practice and activity.

ALBANY PARK THEATER PROJECT

The Albany Park Theater Project (APTP) is "a multiethnic, youth theater ensemble that inspires people to envision a more just and beautiful world" (APTP 2011a). The theatre is situated in "one of three of the most diverse neighborhoods in the U.S." (Feiner 2011). David Feiner and Laura Wiley founded APTP in 1997 to be a place that

> shares the untold stories of urban youth, immigrants, and working-class Americans, humanizes issues that impact real people. [...] prepares teens for purposeful lives as adventurous dreamers and accomplished achievers, and enriches the cultural vitality of Chicago. [...] APTP's plays have told the stories of people whose lives are impacted by immigration policy, globalization, war, inequalities in public education, poverty, child abuse and neglect, addiction, domestic violence, gang violence, the criminal justice system, prejudice and intolerance, gentrification, and more. (APTP 2011a)

APTP combines music, dance, and theatre in intricate storytelling that grabs the heart and pulls audiences into worlds they may not know exist. Wiley passionately described the impact she hoped for APTP.

> This is what I hope my theater work does for people: it takes them inside worlds they're curious about but have no real access to; it bears witness to truths that many folks – both government leaders and lay people – try aggressively to distort or to ignore; it makes beauty and meaning out of sometimes ugly, sometimes confusing strands of human experience; it is a creative act that, while often standing in for a memory, can actually become a new memory, can become a new truth – that, while telling one story, can actually become a new story and inspire the creation of yet other stories. (Wiley 2011)

The level and range of APTP's artistic storytelling, coupled with strong, socially engaged activity is impressive. From the gathering, polishing, and winnowing of powerful personal stories, to the artistic heights the company strives for – and achieves – to their tutoring program, to summer and year-round performing arts workshops, to the free ticket program to introduce college theatre majors to "art that changes the world," to their initiative to start a community garden in the neighborhood – one cannot help but be inspired by APTP. Whether seeing a performance or visiting their impressive website, it is clear that this is not only a theatre, but a caring community for some of Chicago's most often overlooked young people. As David Feiner has said, "Love is not a word we shy away from at APTP" (Feiner 2011).

APTP is free and open to any teen who lives or attends school in Albany Park. Ensemble members engage in months of preparation for each production. Story collection and analysis, and development and refinement of scripts and performance skills all interface seamlessly as this diverse group develops as young people and gifted performers. Through this ongoing process, ensemble members take the stage and move audiences as powerful, confident, and daring collaborative artists.

Beyond receiving rave reviews for their work, this youth theatre truly does change lives. "APTP teens have a 72 percent better high school graduation rate, 42 percent higher college matriculation rate, and a 600 percent higher college graduation rate than the average for students in Chicago's public schools" (APTP 2011b). Most are the first in their families to graduate from high school, and more than 90 percent are the first in their families to go to college. Many return to APTP to work or volunteer (APTP 2011a). These teens have struggled with life's darkest issues and, through APTP's full-bodied theatre work, they become more fully themselves. This truly is theatre-making that is far-reaching, life-changing, and an embodiment of best practice.

PEOPLE'S LIGHT AND THEATRE

Like the Albany Park Theater Project, artists in the resident professional company at People's Light and Theatre (PLT) are actively engaged in the life of children from Malvern, Pennsylvania, and its surrounding communities. "Theatre rooted in service to the community" was part of PLT's mission from the theatre's inception. It means "being engaged in the community – living here, being a soccer coach as well as an actor [...] so [...] you're not removed from the community" (Adams 2002). Staff link professional productions and educational programs to best serve audiences and youth participants "resulting in a unified commitment to excellence throughout the organization" (PLT 2011).

On a visit to the theatre located forty-five minutes from Philadelphia, I was struck by the easy place young people occupy in many of the activities of this theatre organization. Artistic Director Abigail Adams explained PLT's connection to young people.

> I work with kids because I like to be in their company. [...] And I think that makes it a genuine experience and [...] a more equitable power structure [...]. Yes, it's a led collaboration, but there are times [...] with all of us who deal with kids [...] where the adults are in a collegial set-up with the kids. [...] Everything I do with the kids is reflected in everything I do with the resident company or the national circle of artists that we're working with. There's absolutely no difference to me in what I'm learning or working on. (Adams 2002)

PLT makes long-term commitments to area children. Years ago they began "The New Voices Ensemble," an interactive program at the theatre for young people from Chester, a city about forty-five miles from PLT. Chester has struggling schools and a severely depressed economy. PLT realized that if these children were going to work with the theatre in Malvern, they were going to have to provide transportation – so PLT got a van. PLT teaching artists eat meals with the kids, teach them, act in season productions with them, and help them with their homework and college applications. The first New Voices group began as sixth graders, and PLT staff made a commitment to learn and work with them until most graduated from high school. It was not easy in the early years, but ultimately New Voices became a rich learning experience for all involved and has now expanded to include youth from nearby suburban communities, thus further diversifying the Ensemble. Some members of the original group have now gone on to work at the theatre.

In addition to New Voices, PLT offers classes year round for youth and adults and professional development workshops for teachers and students. Community service programs include extended residencies by PLT teaching artists to over 30,000 young people a year, and Project Discovery High School, a program that builds long-term interactive relationships with area schools and provides them with free tickets to PLT shows.

PLT is a living, breathing organism, responsive and connected to the world beyond the theatre's parking lot. They are neighbors and fellow citizens in their community, partners who continue to grow, change, and serve with innovation and impact. Abigail Adams understands that their connection to youth is central to the vitality of the theatre.

> There are minutes at a time when one or another of these children is so transformed by the work that he or she becomes the embodiment of the best that is possible in theatre. No senior artist in the company can match the truth, the imagination, and vitality of these children when they are fully engaged with one another in a play. Their work is how I measure excellence: our need of them is just as urgent as their need for us. (PLT 2011)

FULTON YOUTHEATRE

Fulton Theatre, also located in Pennsylvania, is a professional regional theatre offering the community a fairly typical fare of performances and education programs. What is not typical and what draws a diverse group of teens to this historic Lancaster theatre, is the award-winning Fulton Youtheatre, a performance ensemble that embraces the youth of the community with commitment and compassion.

Fulton Youtheatre is a project dedicated to teens with various physical or emotionally disabling conditions and youth deemed to be "at-risk" or "disadvantaged." The Youtheatre program is guided by teaching artists Barry Kornhauser, an award winning playwright and director, and Adele Ulrich, a choreographer and movement therapist (Kornhauser 2011b). The Youtheatre's intent is to challenge its teen participants "to create and perform original dramas that address topics of pertinence to their lives or that of their peers around the globe." Meeting year round with a core summer intensive, ensemble members are provided a safe place to grow artistically, emotionally, educationally, and socially. Youtheatre members also receive a weekly stipend for their work (Kornhauser 2011a).

In 2004, the Youtheatre was one of only ten arts companies in the United States (out of an applicant pool of more than 800) to be selected by the NEA (National Endowment for the Arts) as a national model for arts education. [...] Since then, the NEA has refunded the company through its "Learning in the Arts For Children and Youth" program. [...] [In 2008, Youtheatre] received its highest honor, the "Coming Up Taller" Award of the President's Committee on the Arts and Humanities.

[...] The teens are referred to [Youtheatre staff] from a wide variety of social welfare agencies, the juvenile justice system, psychiatric institutions, rehabilitation centers, [and] school guidance counselors. [...] The teens have been convicted of crimes ranging from drug dealing to armed robbery; others have been victims of physical, emotional, and/or sexual abuse; and there are those who live with fetal alcohol syndrome, clinical depression, post-traumatic stress, bipolar disorder, anorexia, and addiction. Some are homeless. Clinicians, therapists, social workers, and juvenile probation officers who serve these youth attend periodic rehearsals and are available as needed. All rehearsals and performances are [American Sign Language] interpreted, and sign language lessons are a part of each day. When children of migrant families joined the ensemble, [English language learning] lessons also occurred daily. With the recent addition of immigrant and refugee teens into the ensemble, Spanish, Nepali, and other languages are [...] spoken in the productions. (Kornhauser 2011a)

Youtheatre often partners with national service organizations. For their original production, *Chain Reaction*, which exposed modern-day human trafficking and slavery, they worked with Free the Slaves, an organization in Washington, D.C. With *The Heart Knows Something Different*, a piece that presented images and stories of youth in the foster care system, they partnered with New York City-based Youth Communication.

The company has performed as the keynote presentation at national conferences and in the Pennsylvania state legislature. Responses to Youtheatre

This experience makes me feel open and confident. I'm still a little shy inside of me. I feel safe to tell anything in this group I trust. This is the only place I could find where I feel safe [...] This program is in my heart. Jo

Jo, Youtheatre Company Member

Figure 5.1: *Chain Reaction* at Fulton Youtheatre, directed by Barry Kornhauser and Adele Ulrich.

performances show immediate and far-reaching impact. Personnel with the Pennsylvania Department of Public Welfare, arts in education specialists, and state representatives commend the group "for touching the lives of many at-risk youth and empowering them to have a voice on the harsh realities they face." The Youtheatre is seen as creating "powerful, original dramatic works of the highest artistic calibre" (Kornhauser 2011c).

All local Youtheatre performances are free and typically attended by teens from area youth organizations. "Good will" donations are collected at each performance and all proceeds are given to local organizations that company members select. For *The Heart Knows Something Different,* donations were given to a local agency that provides advocates for young people in the foster care system. For their play about new immigrants in the United States, *For We Were Strangers in the Land,* donations went to two local refugee services groups (Kornhauser 2011a).

This program brings many principles of best practice to the young people they serve. Assessment by the NEA shows that Youtheatre's members show consistent growth in "artistic knowledge, performance skills, and social and emotional development" (Kornhauser 2011b). Reaching young people often not served by school-based theatre programs, "the Youtheatre is dedicated to creating art that reaches out to others with a message of hope and in celebration of the human spirit" (Kornhauser 2011a).

FLINT YOUTH THEATRE

Flint, Michigan, is the birthplace of General Motors and the United Auto Workers. Since the 1970s when the American automotive empire began to falter, Flint's economy has steadily declined, and its unemployment rate soared to twice the national average. Flint is also the home of the Flint Youth Theatre (FYT). This nationally recognized program has long offered innovative and diverse programming in partnership with the Flint schools and cultural and civic groups. In addition to a season of their own productions, FYT offers year-round classes, hosts professional touring productions for young audiences, and explores and develops new work with and for young people and adults to bring about social change. Among other topics, they have devised original pieces dealing with violence, growing up female, and displaced persons.

One FYT project in particular, which united the community against school violence, illustrates how the practice of theatre education at a professional theatre continues to evolve in service to young people and their community (Lazarus 2001).

As history unfolded in Flint, it became clear both to then FYT Executive Director Sue Wood (2001) and Artistic Director Bill Ward (2001a) that FYT's mission to produce challenging theatre of the highest quality would best be served by a close and active relationship with the Flint community and public schools. In a 1995 study by the Flint schools, it was determined that Flint ninth graders were 70 percent more likely to have engaged in group fighting at school than the national norm, and 400 percent more likely to have used a gun or other weapon to get something from a person (Flint Youth Theatre 2001, 52). After the shootings at Columbine High School, Flint area schools reported a rash of bomb scares, gun threats, and gang attacks in elementary, middle, and high schools. Flint was thrown into the national spotlight when five-year-old Kayla Rolland was fatally shot by a classmate at her school (Flint Youth Theatre 2001). Bill reflects that

> suddenly Columbine is here. [...] It's not just something happening over there and something I'm just responding to because I've seen it televised. I am here in it. [...] [Our] work is an attempt [...] to respond to that particular incident and all the other incidents like it. (Ward 2001a)

Bill's response to school violence in Flint took shape through a special project focused on stimulating civic dialogue. FYT was selected as one of sixteen projects in the country supported by the Animating Democracy Lab component of the Animating Democracy Initiative (ADI), which is coordinated by Americans for the Arts and funded by the Ford Foundation. Pam Korza (2001), speaking for Americans for the Arts, said "We have observed that the arts can play a role by providing a compelling and alternative point of entry and by serving as convener, offering safe places for difficult dialogue."

For their lab project, Sue enlisted the support and active participation of a range of community and grassroots partners. In conjunction with FYT's drama work exploring school violence, each partner organized activities designed to stimulate civic dialogue: study circles, a university symposium, a mini-grants program for schools and community organizations, a student conference, and a video documentary of the project.

The centerpiece of the FYT Lab Project was an original performance piece entitled ... *My Soul to Take*. The production itself represented public discourse as it confronted, surprised, and challenged school and public audiences to think critically and discuss this complex issue. In an interlacing of light, sound, movement, music, and language, FYT youth artists captured the swirl of reactions and opinions surrounding a school shooting. More than a play, this multi-layered performance collage juxtaposed time and space and was deliberately non-prescriptive as it shed light on the multiple and conflicting issues influencing school shootings. We heard the easy rhetoric of politicians and the pleas of parents as causes were sought and blame placed. A chorus of plaintive voices asked what everyone in the audience was thinking: "Can't somebody do something?" We met the mother of a slain

Figure 5.2: ... *My Soul to Take* flier.

child in a moving series of monologues each of which began "After the shooting, it seemed like there was always someone from the media coming up to me and asking me 'how it felt.'" We first learn about her son as a youngster full of love and imagination and later as a precocious, increasingly private adolescent filled with a passion for music. It is only toward the end of this eclectic montage that we again see this mother and come to realize her son was not a victim of the shooting, but the shooter himself, a victim of another kind of violence. And all the while, ever present, just left of center stage, stood a high-powered rifle propped vertically in a tall Plexiglas case. Audiences had come to ignore its presence, only to be haunted by that indifference by the play's conclusion.

In the spirit of shared ownership, the piece began not with Bill as playwright alone at his computer, but with him as an observer to children and community members' explorations of school violence through drama. British theatre artist and teacher Gillian Eaton led a series of process drama sessions with middle and high school students (Eaton 2001). As Bill observed these sessions from the side of the room, students improvised and discussed artwork, stories, and events that would reveal their feelings about rage, fear, and its impact on them. Groups of adults also participated with Eaton in process dramas in which they created improvisations and explored the Pied Piper story and the issue of "lost" children. Inspired by this work, Bill wove a stylized version of the Pied Piper through ... My Soul to Take and so presented a timeless metaphor of a Piper who lures children away after government leaders fail to keep their promises. Based on the authentic perceptions of the Flint children and the adults who participated in the process dramas, the parallels of the story to today's society were profound. From these improvisations, his imagination, and extensive dialogue with Eaton as ad hoc dramaturg, Bill created ... My Soul to Take.

Four thousand people saw ... My Soul to Take. It was estimated that more than four hundred students and adults participated in process dramas before and after the performances. More than thirteen hundred people participated in study circles, a community symposium, and/or a student conference FYT organized as part of the project.

FYT's Lab Project serves as an example of the interlacing questions, concerns, rewards, and risks facing any arts organization doing community-based theatre work with and for young people. The work at FYT has been successful in large part because Bill and Sue shared common concerns about their community and its children. They chose to be an active partner with the schools and other agencies willing to address community concerns. These factors cannot be underestimated as one considers the challenges and rewards of working with young people in socially engaged theatre projects in school or in the community (Lazarus 2001).

This work doesn't offer any kind of prescriptions. It doesn't pretend to do that. But it [...] serves as a way to illuminate issues and to cause people to think. [...] Maybe the work actually causes people to either have dialogue, or in the most wonderful of cases, causes people to become activists themselves and do something in their community.
Bill Ward

CREATIVE ARTS TEAM

Since the work of the Creative Arts Team (CAT) began in the 1970s, this New York City-based professional theatre has exploded the boundaries of theatre education. Based at City University of New York (C.U.N.Y.), and drawing on models of theatre-in-education and other applied theatre forms, CAT teaching artists work in classrooms and with parents, community leaders, and policy makers to confront issues facing New York City's young people. Their work is learner-centered, intentionally socially engaged, and socially responsible.

In the years since CAT began offering its own brand of theatre education, it has emerged as an international pioneer, disrupting assumptions about both the quality and nature of theatre work with and for youth. CAT's professional teaching artists work in schools and community sites engaging participants and facilitating their examination of social issues, such as violence in intimate relationships, teen pregnancy, parent-child relationships, gun violence, and violation of civil liberties. CAT teaching artists work with organizations around the world, from South Africa where they teamed with universities developing an AIDS outreach project for adolescents, to the Middle East where they worked with actors from different countries to create a piece for young people about tolerance.

Artistic Director Chris Vine (2000) regularly questions CAT's pedagogy and methodologies. He spoke about working with CAT teaching artists to critically examine their own theatre techniques and practice.

> "Student-centered" [is] a phrase that everybody uses, but what does it actually mean in terms of the relationship between you the artist, the selection of the material that *you're* making, the curriculum students are having, [which is] cooked up [by the] schools, [and] the methodology [...] we use that we say [...] empowers them, gives them voice. [...] And what are we trying to be student centered about and for? How do we recognize it is happening?
>
> We deal with social issues, but [...] [we do so] when the young people decide that they want to put them in their work or they come up with an issue [they've] discussed in their group. [Issues are] not coming in because I'm bringing in a curricular list saying, "All right, we're going to look at race for the moment or we're going to look at violence or we're going to look at whatever." (Vine 2000)

One of CAT's programs is the CAT Youth Theatre. Free to middle and high school students from the five boroughs of New York, young people gather weekly with Youth Theatre teaching artists to devise original theatre pieces that are performed throughout the year. The adolescents meet with Youth Theatre Director, Helen White, Chris, and CAT artistic staff as a community of artists. Youth and adults negotiate shared understandings about how they will work together as co-learners

Figure 5.3: Community-based youth theatre programs allow students to grow as artists while they explore topics about the world that deeply touch their lives.

and human beings. Exploring multifaceted topics and themes offered by the young people, company members devise and craft their productions.

> The CAT Youth Theatre does not begin with a list of extant objectives: there is no agenda of theatre skills to be taught, nor a list of social issues to be addressed, nor developmental outcomes to be achieved. The starting point is the young people themselves and an agreement to work in the medium of theatre. (White and Vine 2001, 9)

With the help of the Paul A. Kaplan Center and C.U.N.Y., CAT is able to offer professional development classes to new generations of teachers, college students, and teaching artists. Working with Chris, Helen, and youth theatre members in a sort of laboratory, college students and working theatre educators investigate practices for devising high quality theatre with high school students.

Helen talks about why she chose to work in youth theatre.

> I think [...] youth theatre [...] brought together all the things I love most passionately in [the] most [...] satisfying way. [...] We create original theatre – the quality of the theatre has become increasingly higher and higher and higher. We're creating community with the young people that keeps expanding as the youth theatre has a longer [and] longer history [...] I've got Youth Theatre members who [...] [want] some support and [...] ideas for how they're going [to start] their own youth theatres. So the work is [...] fulfilling and that community [keeps growing]. (White 2000)

Nurtured by their shared passion for theatre, CAT artists of all ages are helping the Creative Arts Team and CAT Youth Theatre continue its impressive work.

IMAGINATION STAGE

Imagination Stage is located in Bethesda, Maryland, a stone's throw from the nation's capital. Built on the belief that the arts should be "inclusive and accessible to all children, regardless of their physical, cognitive, or financial status," Imagination Stage offers professional productions, classes and camps for young people ages one through eighteen, after school programs, school residencies, early childhood classes and performances, film-making, and professional development programs in arts integration for teachers, students, parents, and families (Imagination Stage 2011).

Programs at Imagination Stage clearly represent an environment that welcomes all who wish to participate in the theatre's services, regardless of ability. Access and inclusion activities go far beyond offering occasional signed performances or special seating. Their motto "At Imagination Stage: Everybody Plays!" is realized as they provide classes and programs specifically designed to meet "the needs of students with cognitive, language, gross motor, or developmental disabilities" and to meet the needs of students who are deaf and hard of hearing. They also offer "inclusion support" for all children and work with students and caregivers to find the best environment for each student, whether in "inclusive settings alongside typically developing peers," in specifically designed classes, or in the Pegasus Ensemble, which offers students with disabilities the opportunity to engage in text, movement, and improvisation work that culminates in fully staged productions (Imagination Stage 2010; 2011).

There are many other community-based theatre programs throughout the country of varying quality and with diverse core values and practices. Those that embody characteristics and elements of best practice create sites outside of school where young people feel welcome, safe, and valued as creative thinkers and artists. These are programs that are learner-centered, socially responsible and offer comprehensive theatre opportunities.

TEACHING ARTISTS AND ARTISTS IN RESIDENCE

At one point I was doing [some professional work as a playwright] and [...] I had to be away [from my middle school students] for several days. [...] [When I came back the students] were wondering "Well, why don't you just do that? [...] You should be doing something else than just teaching [...] because you [can] do something else." I said, "Why not have the [...] strong artist in a teaching position?" [...] [Playwriting] is the "something else" that I do. [Teaching] is what I do. Gloria Bond Clunie, Teacher and Playwright

In parts of this country, many schools hire local artists to direct plays with high school or middle school students. This can sometimes be problematic for the youth involved. If the director-for-hire does not know the students, their needs, or interests, students can be caught in awkward hierarchical or dogmatic interactions. If the director is not informed about learner-centered, socially responsible, and discipline-based practices, what are the students learning about the art and craft of theatre?

There are, fortunately, wonderful exceptions. Independent, freelance teaching artists and theatre companies committed to principles of best practice have a significant impact on young people.

John Heinemann (2002) teaches in Nebraska at Lincoln High School with Patsy Koch. Their theatre program has partnered with Illusion Theatre in Minneapolis in a program called TRUST: Teaching Reaching Using Students of Theatre. Illusion is a professional theatre that performs theatre pieces to stimulate dialogue, reflection, and social change, and they have developed a number of interactive performance pieces around topics of importance to young people. Lincoln High students involved in the program tour performances and facilitate discussions around pieces such as *TOUCH* (1978), a collection of vignettes about physical abuse.

> The school contributed by giving two periods to work with a small number of kids. [...] The District pays a stipend [for a] community member who does the Health and Human Services aspect of performances and moderates [the] shows.
>
> We're doing so much more educating outside of the classroom. It's been an amazing, powerful tool, not only for the students who we perform for [...] but [...] [it's] an incredible experience for the actors. [...] It changes your life when a ten-year-old child comes up to you and says "My mom's boyfriend does that to me, and I don't like it, and I want it to stop." [...] This high school student has the power to get them to a [professional who will find a] place where they're safe and real change can happen. (Heinemann 2002)

April Gentry Sutterfield (2011) is a teaching artist from Little Rock, Arkansas. She was a middle school theatre teacher before returning to graduate school where she explored drama and theatre for youth and communities, playwriting, devised work, youth theatre, and solo performance. As a teaching artist and director, April engages in a broad range of professional, community-based projects as a teacher, writer, director, and co-creator of socially engaged original work.

> Both art and education serve as mirrors and windows in society – awakening our souls to inequities and injustice while opening our eyes to unrealized hope and possibilities. I hope my teaching and directing provide the window through which students understand that civil discussion will prevail over polarizing debate, that careful reflection will replace unquestioned action, and that service for "other" will trump comfort for self. Finally, I hope my students leave the class and rehearsal process with a greater capacity to accept the beauty and improve the flaws they see. [...] If so, I have fulfilled my potential as a teacher and director. (Sutterfield 2011)

Many secondary school theatre educators build partnerships bridging schools to teaching artists, theatres, community centers, museums, universities, or other agencies and organizations. The result is a rich collaboration for the artists, teachers, and young people involved. The examples throughout this chapter illustrate the potential for theatre educators and artists to be co-learners and co-teachers of our young people. As secondary school teachers and professional community-based artists work and learn together, the box of twentieth century theatre education can be recycled, discarded, or rebuilt.

Voices from the field
COMMUNITY BASED THEATRE EDUCATION

CREATIVE SPACES: ARTS INTEGRATION WITH A SOCIAL JUSTICE FOCUS – GILLIAN McNALLY

Gillian McNally and colleague Connie Bethards developed a precollege summer arts program for middle and high school students to address "relevant social issues in their community." Creative Spaces is a program for middle and high school students that embodies elements of interdisciplinary arts education and arts integration "outside the box" of the public schools.

The University of Northern Colorado (UNC) is situated in Greeley, Colorado, a town with a meat packing plant and a racially segregated community. Schools in Greeley are predominately Latino and low income, or white and middle class. There are very few opportunities for students from the racially split town to come together. Could an arts program be a place where students with completely different life experiences meet to collaborate on the creation of original art and to dialogue about issues important to them?

In the summers of 2007 to 2011, Connie Bethards, a visual arts educator, and I inaugurated a program at UNC to bring the diverse Greeley community together through meaningful artmaking. We created an integrated arts program for teens to explore relevant social issues in their community through visual and theatre arts.

The program had four goals:
1. To expose young people to professional artists and college professors.
2. To use the arts and socially relevant pedagogy to instigate discussion and awareness of issues facing teens in their local, national, and international community.
3. To recruit top-level students to the theatre and visual arts program at UNC.
4. To provide scholarships for students who are from low-income/first generation families.

Creative Spaces was inspired by the term "Third Space" in the book of the same title by Richard J. Deasy and Lauren M. Stevenson (2005) of the Arts Education Partnership. Steve Seidel, director of Project Zero, in the introduction to *Third Space: When Learning Matters*, describes the idea behind the book's title:

> "[T]hird space" [...] is the "space between" teachers and learners, between the various individuals in a learning group, and between the learners, teachers, and works of art. This is the space in which meaning that has been negotiated and constructed by the members of a group emerges. When students, teachers, and others gather around a work of art created by an artist or a student [...] and they strive to understand that work – what they see, what it means to each of them, what it makes them feel – they not only make sense of the work, they build community and understanding among themselves. (Steve Seidel, cited in Deasy and Stevenson 2005, vii)

In the spirit of this idea, we wanted to create the safe space where young people, professional artists, and teachers could come together to co-create art in a nurturing, challenging environment. In our sacred Creative Space, traditional hierarchies of student/teacher were challenged. Teachers were facilitators/ guides, creating art side by side *with* the students. We embraced what Lazarus (2004) calls "socially responsible practice." Our goals reflected Lazarus' notion that "[S]tudents learn in, through, and about theatre as members of society and citizens of the school and the world" (Lazarus 2004, 9).

We often used the term "unschool" in Creative Spaces. What we meant by this was that we broke away from the concept that there is a definite right and wrong. In Creative Spaces, open-ended questions pushed students to consider how their creative work could be clearer, more imaginative, and more meaningful. We feel that this philosophy set up a trusting arts community where students felt open to take risks, grow, and create art to their true potential. In a final evaluation of the program, a student reflected, "In school I am excluded, but here I am included."

Connie and I collaborated with students to investigate socially relevant topics through arts-based activities. Each morning, theatre and visual arts students explored themes such as diversity, human rights, scarcity and abundance, the media, and immigration. In 2011, students created a beautiful text and image-based informal performance based on the theme "America then and now: 1911–2011." Through visual and drama-based activities, we explored thought-provoking questions such as, "What does it mean to belong in America?" "Why do people leave their home country?" "What happens on the journey to a new place?" "What challenges do immigrants face when they arrive in America?"

From the beginning, we wanted to fight against a trend in arts education to create performances filled with stereotypical characters or poorly written "cute" scripts. When you involve young people in challenging material from which they create original art, the results are thoughtful, insightful, and imaginative.

Each summer we were amazed at the level of insight and the amount of critical thinking the students brought to the themes. They began to create bridges in their lives between self, community, and artmaking. A first-generation, seventeen year-old Latina student clearly made this connection when she wrote her artist statement.

> I believe the arts have the power to change the way people think and the way people see the world. As an artist, I want to become a part of something beautiful. The arts are essential to my community because it gives people like me an opportunity, a chance to show everybody what we've got. That we're not just a bunch of kids going nowhere. Without the arts, we blend into the crowd. We choose to give up our creativity and become black and white. As an artist, I firmly believe that we're going to change the world and open up the minds of those who choose to blind themselves. (Creative Spaces participant 2011)

As a result of being in Creative Spaces, students saw that concerns about the world could be fruitful material to create meaningful art within a trusting community. During the summer of 2009, one of the Latino visual arts students created a large sculpture of a black-and-white skeleton resembling Day of the Dead icons. In one hand, the figure carried a photo of the recent protests in Greeley over the large immigrant deportation raid at the local meat packing plant. In the other hand, the figure carried a large sign that read, "I'm just like you." The huge 2007 deportation raids of Greeley (some of the largest in U.S. history) shook the Latino community to its very core. The creation of this sculpture created dialogue in the visual art studio and in the gallery for the final presentation. As teachers, Connie and I were both impressed by the level of sophistication and maturity of this student. As an undocumented citizen, he used his time at Creative Spaces to express his social and political opinions through his artmaking. Not only did this student create a strong political statement, but his strong artistic choices served to lead other students in the class to make bold choices as well.

If we are to develop the leaders of the twenty-first century, theatre arts teachers must protect these "creative spaces" in their own classrooms by embracing socially relevant pedagogy. Theatre classrooms are the perfect laboratories where engaged citizenship can be practiced, interrogated, challenged and, eventually, rewarded. (McNally 2011)

A detailed lesson plan from an earlier project Gillian designed is included at the end of this chapter.

Voices from the field

A TEACHING ARTIST'S REFLECTIONS – SUSAN DIRENDE

Susan diRende's approach to artmaking with secondary school students is an inspiring example of the practices of many teaching artists. Susan is a Renaissance woman. She is skilled as a movement artist and vocal coach. She is a playwright, screenwriter, performer, and director currently living in Los Angeles. Susan also has a palpable love of teaching. She has worked with English language learners and high school students in community-based programs and directed a number of shows at the high school level. As she teaches and interacts with students, she nurtures them, challenges them, and fosters in them a conviction in their ability to make wonderful theatre together (diRende 2002). Susan draws her inspiration from many sources.

Each act of theatre is a breath in the life of human culture. How important is one breath to life?
Susan diRende

Otto Rank wrote once, "You cannot go to school to be an artist, you can only go to school as an artist." Whenever I work, whether with professionals or beginners, I am always clear that we are all equally artists. All I may have is greater skill or more knowledge, but we can only make art if we are all artists.

For me one of the challenges [...] [is] to encapsulate the essence of fostering artistry into a process [for] [...] people who have little contact or experience with theatre.

I heard someone define humans as meaning-making machines [...] and I do believe that each act of theatre is an act of making meaning. [...] Once humans collaborate and perform together in front [of] others, they create a communal experience of value and meaning, the impact of which lingers and expands through the culture. Each act of theatre is a breath in the life of human culture. How important is one breath to life?

I also think theatre fosters understanding of difference. To effectively write or portray a character, you have to get inside their head to come to terms with the good and bad in a range of types with a host of life experiences and perspectives. [...] And difference becomes attenuated by realizing how alike people's motives, fears, and dreams can be. [...] And this is not in the name of some abstract philosophy of compassion and tolerance but the visceral experience of identifying with a character.

I had college students who struggled a whole semester with the idea of objectives in acting – that the character's actions are guided by what he or she wants from the other characters. It seemed they resisted knowing this about the characters in the play because they resisted knowing this about themselves. Then I realized their education had [...] [separated] them from a true knowledge of their desires, their wishes, their goals. The education system in the United States, it has been written, was designed to develop 10 percent leaders, 15 percent bourgeoisie, and the rest as laborers. I don't know how true that is, but [...] some relation to their own motivations had been stripped from them. [...] If alienation from the knowledge of one's motivations can produce followers, then it seems reconnecting people with their ability to see [their motivations] strikes me as a first step to developing leaders. (diRende 1996)

AN EXAMPLE OF THEATRE EDUCATION OUTSIDE THE BOX

Empowering Ophelia – Gillian McNally

Gillian McNally (2002a) is a professor at the University of Northern Colorado. She has worked as a professional actor, director, and teaching artist at the Denver Theatre Center and People's Light and Theatre Company. Earlier in her career, she formed The Ophelia Project Ensemble and led the group as a director-teacher. This ensemble of middle school girls was drawn together to develop an original adaptation of *The Light Princess* (MacDonald 1969). Named for the ideas forwarded in *Reviving Ophelia* (Piper 1994), Gillian's goal in starting the ensemble was "to create a safe place where lost adolescent female voices could be heard" (McNally 2002a, 5). The following rehearsal plan is part of a learner-centered rehearsal process in which the girls could share their voices and deconstruct assumptions about gender (McNally 2002b).

We want to bring art to children in its full-strength formulas: robust, powerful, idiosyncratic, critical, and more than a little bit dangerous. If we have to leave these attributes outside the classroom door, we would do better to leave art out of the curriculum altogether.
Zemelman, Daniels, and Hyde

Lesson Plan: Ophelia Project Ensemble

Objectives

Teacher Objectives

Create a sense of safety in playing characters of the opposite gender.
- Discuss and examine the girls' perspectives on female gender roles.
- Generate interesting material for the script of *The Light Princess*.

Student Objectives

- Engage in two activities to help focus their energy.
- Discuss their perceptions of gender characteristics.
- Physically enact the agreed-upon gender characteristics.
- Apply discussion of gender to three scenes from The Light Princess.

Focus:
- Gender

Materials:
- Large piece of paper
- Marker

Activity

What's on top of your pile?

- Find a partner that is not in the same grade as you. Sit across from them.
- Decide roles: one partner is "A" one is "1."
- "As, talk to partner 1s about your day for two minutes nonstop. Talk about things that could keep you from focusing on our work today." (Sidecoaching: Keep talking! Go further into detail about one particular event.)
- Reverse roles.

Zip, Zap, Zop

- Stand in a circle.
- Everyone say "Zip, Zap, Zop." (Repeat four or five times.)
- First person starts with the word "Zip." As they say the word they point to another person across the circle, paying special attention to making eye contact with that person.
- This person says the word "Zap" and points to a third person.
- Third person passes "Zop" to a fourth person.
- Fourth person starts the series again by passing "Zip."
- Keep the cycle going. Once members get the rhythm of the game, encourage them to go faster.

Transition

As you know, each day we explore a different skill to add to our creation of *The Light Princess*. Since we have roles like the King and the Prince in *The Light Princess*, many of you will need to play male characters. We are going to look at how we view and represent masculine and feminine behaviors.

Activity

Gender Continuum Exercise[1]

1. On a large piece of paper, draw a line across it with *one* at the left end, *five* in the middle, and *ten* on the right end of the line. One is hyper masculine, ten hyper feminine, according to stereotypes.
2. Decide who they know who is a representative of *ten*, *one*, and *five*. (Make lists.) Why do they fit these categories? Where does Michael Jackson belong and why? Gay men and gay women? Suggest other names for their consideration.
3. Discuss the behaviors they associate with each category one to ten.

Figure 5.4: Teaching artists enliven students' understanding of theatre.

4. Have students walk around as themselves. Ask them to think about what number they are, but not to say it out loud.
5. Ask them to go to *one*. Keep sidecoaching them to go further as *one*: "You're only at a *three*! Push yourself to go to a *one* – get extreme!"
6. Go to *ten*. Keep sidecoaching and encouraging. Dare them to over exaggerate it.
7. Have them do various activities in different number types such as: sitting, standing, and posing for a photographer.

Discussion

- What did you notice as you did this exercise? Describe your experience.
- What surprised, challenged, delighted, or troubled you?
- Which activity or number did you feel most comfortable doing and why?
- What did you notice about how the group acted in *one* versus *ten*?
- Why do you think that is?

Activity

Scene Work

- Break students into three groups.
- Assign scenes five, six, and seven from the story *The Light Princess*.
- Ask students to choose roles, decide what their "gender number" is for their character, and to be prepared to improvise their scene in ten minutes.

Share Scenes

- Each group shares their prepared scene.
- Ask those not in the scene "What number do you think _____ was playing?" Ask actor if we are correct.
- Re-do scenes asking the actors to change their "gender number."
- Ask those watching
- How did the number changing alter their performance?
- How did it change the scene?
- Any ideas on how we could incorporate this into telling the story of *The Light Princess* in our play?

Closing

Sit in a circle. One by one, go around the circle and say a short phrase that comes to mind about the rehearsal today.

IDEAS FOR FURTHER REFLECTION

Explore Partnerships

Take an inventory of potential partners in your community and how many you know or are in contact with on a regular basis. Initiate conversations about ways in which you could work together for children in your community.

Go to the Theatre

Seek out theatre organizations in your community whose work you admire or have never seen. Attend a representative sampling of their work including classes, workshops, and residencies. What can you learn from them about the craft of theatre making, relationships with the community, or new play development? What about their work might be of value to your students? Invite friends and colleagues who may be unfamiliar with the theatre to go with you. Generate dialogue about the works you see. Reach out to these people as partners in your theatre education program.

SELECTED RESOURCES

In addition to the works cited in this chapter, the following offer interesting sources of ideas for further reading and reflection.

American Alliance for Theatre and Education
http://www.aate.com

Arts Connection
www.artsconnection.org

Arts Education Partnership
www.aep-arts.org

Arts For Learning
www.arts4learning.org/

Association of Teaching Artists (ATA)
www.teachingartists.com/

Chicago Arts Partners in Education
www.capeweb.org
Education programs for the Kennedy Center
http://artsedge.kennedy-center.org/

Lincoln Center Institute
http://www.lcinstitute.org

Performing Arts Workshop
www.performingartsworkshop.org

NOTE

1. Adapted in 2002 from an exercise developed by Stacy Wolf, The University of Texas at Austin.

Chapter 6

Breaking the Mold: Best Practice in Theatre Teacher Education

Former high school students testified that their teachers' positive qualities of "lifelong humanity" (e.g., lifelong nurturance and relationships) and "lifelong endurance" (e.g., lifelong passion and resilience) played critical roles during their adolescent experiences and development. Teacher educators should not assume these personal attributes are automatically hardwired into all future high school theatre and speech teachers. They must be actively taught as essential traits for the profession and periodically assessed throughout preservice educators' course work and field experiences. We must not only produce outstanding artists but outstanding people to work in the secondary schools.

Laura McCammon and Johnny Saldaña

The students watch us, all the time. We must honestly ponder what they see, and what we want them to learn from it.

Ted and Nancy Sizer

The notion of "best practice" raises questions and is a call to action in many facets of our field. Teachers and artists talk about needed change on the local, state, and national levels. The following steps are often suggested as catalysts for change:

- Develop opportunities through school districts and professional associations to see best practice in action, to observe and interact with colleagues in classrooms and rehearsals, and to participate in mentorship programs and exchanges.
- Generate dialogue and pursue and strengthen partnerships between educators, artists, the university theatre faculty, education faculty, and government, civic, and cultural agencies and organizations at the local, state, regional, and national levels.
- Create opportunities for critical analysis of our work.
- Conduct research about comprehensive, learner-centered, socially responsible, comprehensive secondary school theatre education and publish findings broadly.
- Engage in advocacy within and outside of our field at the grassroots and national levels.

The *most frequently* cited arena for change, however, is
• Revision of theatre teacher education to better correlate with best practice principles.

Bringing about needed changes in secondary theatre education must include an honest, clear-sighted view of what is the present state of education for preservice theatre teachers. Despite strides in select undergraduate theatre teacher education programs, budget cuts, lack of genuine administrative support, and little shared ownership of teacher education leave gaps in preservice education that impact our future teachers and their future students. College curricular offerings and content in courses for preservice teachers often are not aligned with best practice. On many campuses, theatre departments and colleges of education rarely work together to develop best practice programs for theatre education majors. What new teachers find in schools is also often out of step with best practice because it can be difficult in many communities to find numbers of secondary school theatre teachers who are modeling best practice principles. This leaves preservice teachers few places to see best practice in action with students.

University and college theatre education faculty, who might bridge these gaps, are asked to carry heavy teaching loads and meet publication expectations and service responsibilities at their colleges, while also needing to supervise sometimes large numbers of student teachers in the field. Some theatre education faculty members are still teaching theatre education as it was practiced fifty years ago. They are isolated from colleagues in education and theatre education and they themselves may never have taught in a secondary school. Fieldwork and student teaching, which should "close the loop" on a complete preservice education, are sometimes limited or poorly supervised, leaving students during this most important facet of teacher education without careful mentoring or knowledgeable supervision. Without changes in these areas, preservice teachers are left to flounder or to replicate old models and outmoded practices.

RETHINKING THEATRE TEACHER EDUCATION: WHAT COULD BE

I knew as a high school student that I wanted to do something service oriented [...] to [...] give back. [...] It went from "Should I go into the medical industry where I can give back by serving people in need?" [...] and [...] because I had such an outstanding theatre teacher [who] really changed my life and a number of kids' [lives] in that school, [...] I thought, "I could teach and I could use [...] how she taught me to help students achieve [...] because in theatre I could teach kids how to think, create, and [...] get up in front of people and not be afraid." [...] C. Gary Cooper, Teacher

Forty years from now many of today's theatre education majors will still be teaching in our schools. During that time the tides of social and political change will wash over those schools many times, removing traces of today's reform efforts and leaving new landmarks, new buzz words and trends, newly revised standards and curricula, and reconfigured requirements. What are the tools necessary for a novice teacher to prepare for a voyage of this kind?

To help teachers navigate the currents and eddies of these changes, to respond to the challenges they will face, to teach and to reach all of the children they will encounter, there must be shifts in the way teachers are educated. New theatre teachers themselves must have a comprehensive theatre education, one that seeks connections between ideas, methods, and techniques in theatre and other fields. The education of teachers must include consideration of various social, cultural, and historical contexts and not be merely the accumulation of discrete skills, activities, and facts. Synthesis of often conflicting and ambiguous information, critical thinking, and a willingness to experiment and find one's own voice and style as an educator and artist is essential.

Those who prepare teachers for this sort of educational journey must assume a role of partner in the learning process, someone who learns *with* students, one who guides, mentors, challenges, nurtures, questions, and supports, one who models a cross section of instructional strategies and methods of inquiry and practice while modeling passion for the field and compassion for learners. In this learning environment, students are encouraged to carefully consider material presented, to sift and winnow, to find meaning, and to develop a fundamental understanding of what they are to teach and why.

Rather than offering quantities of prescribed games, activities, and lesson plans, or a single method or approach, those preparing others to teach for a lifetime must afford them opportunities to skillfully use the many resources and timeless tools of their craft and be able to discern when to use them, with whom, and why. This understanding empowers future teachers with a confidence and ability to separate the essential from the nonessential, to develop unique instruction for each circumstance, to improvise, to encourage diverse perspectives, and most importantly, to teach their students rather than their lesson plans.

A teacher of teachers assumes that each student can succeed and perseveres in demonstrating the pedagogical skills that encourage that success. Acting as an advocate rather than adversary, master teachers leading preservice teacher programs set high standards, challenge assumptions, take risks, reflect, admit mistakes, adjust, and demonstrate the importance of lifelong learning, while also having the courage to advise those away from teaching who have little propensity for the practice.

Teaching, at its best, inspires, invigorates, and challenges. When a class moves from an awkward group of strangers to a community of individuals united by a commitment to the importance and integrity of teaching, then one knows why teaching is called a noble profession. Those who teach theatre are twice blessed. They have the privilege of being artists in a dynamic art form and the joy of sharing the rich history, power, and significance of that art form with the next generation of audiences and artists. This can happen only as we prepare our theatre teachers to be thinkers and nurturers of the human spirit as well as artists and educators.

NEW DIRECTIONS IN THEATRE TEACHER EDUCATION

There are theatre teacher education programs around the country that strive to embody the characteristics and elements of best practice. They are, as Laura McCammon encourages, nourishing the hearts of future teachers (see page 306).

Bob Colby, Bethany Nelson, and Christina Marin teach in the theatre education program at Emerson College in Boston. Bob spoke about partnerships with K–12 schools and how the faculty have woven theory, practice, and field experiences into a teacher education program that enables students to learn and apply best practice principles.

From the very [...] first day of class, [we] immerse [students] in some of the strategies they weren't likely to have encountered and that we think are the basis of good practice. [...] [For example,] they'll be immersed in [...] play-making experiences as a series of ongoing, in-class activities and [...] we send them out to observe practicing teachers in the area doing [similar activities] with their students. [...] We've woven in stories of cultures really strongly from day one. We ask them to [always] think about that in terms of their practice. [...] And they have pre-practicum experiences that are done in schools [...] with students of color. [...] We can point a student to a particular school to see a certain kind of high-level, experienced teacher doing something that they can be invited to model and be comfortable modeling. Those teachers also come in and teach seminars [...] within some of the other coursework that we offer. [...] We try to keep that partnership between the practice sites and the college as close as we can.

By the end of the first year [students] realize all of the different possible ways in which the work can proceed and challenge the sort of orthodoxy of many of their own experiences. [...] [We] help them see that the constructivist approach to education is going to help them as they shape theatre pieces [and] listen to the understandings of a group of people and build from there. [...] We try to make explicit those links between what best practices in education in general are and how that actually actively translates to the theatre classroom. [...] [When students say] "Well, I'm teaching acting. I don't know what this idea about modeling or

Figure 6.1: A teacher and her students each share stories about their heritage and culture.

coaching or facilitating that I read about in education is," we [...] [deal with and] talk about [that]. We have an opportunity to effect considerable change in what's happening in the New England states. (Colby 2002)

The philosophy of teacher education at Emerson resonates with other teacher educators who participated in national think tanks on theatre teacher education[1]. Sandy Zielinski (2002) is Director of Theatre Education at Illinois State University (ISU). ISU graduates are employed in schools throughout Illinois. Like Bob and Bethany, she and her colleague, Cindee Brown, have developed a program that places preservice teachers in the schools from their first year in the program. In this way they immediately apply theory to practice.

> When they're freshmen they hear about student-centered practice and performance-based assessment. [...] They have to be attuned to the students from the very beginning. [...] [They learn that] although at times they can lecture, that's one method out of a hundred [they] can choose. [...] So they have to problem solve. [...] It's never static. [...] They have to attend to each student's problems, they have to attend to secondary teachers' problems, professional problems, and listen and respond from that point of view versus "This is what I want to do." (Zielenski 2002)

Laura McCammon taught in the public schools in Tennessee for eighteen years prior to moving to Arizona for graduate work. Now, as head of the theatre education program at the University of Arizona, she talks about a shift in her own practice.

> I used to say "Before you go into your field placement, these are the things you need to find out." [Now I] [...] ask [...] "What do you need to know before you can teach this class?" [...] I want to see [...] about getting them to establish their own parameters [so] [...] they'll see it as something they've created themselves. (McCammon 2002c)

> I compare a good theatre program [...] to ice skating because a good ice skater has to have good technique [...] to do the jumps. [...] You've got to have those things in place, but you can still be artistic about it. [...] [Championship figure skaters have] an awful lot of joy in what [they do], and that's one of the things that distinguishes [them from] the mediocre skaters and the really wonderful skaters. [...] [That] brings so much joy, [it] just draws the audience in. I think that's kind of the way teaching is. There's a lot of technique – and you've got to have the technique – but you also have to figure out how to have joy in your work. (McCammon 2002b)

At my own institution, The University of Texas at Austin, I too have thoughts about how to help students find the joy, passion, compassion, and strength for this work. I wonder how best to position primarily eighteen through twenty-two-year-olds – still adolescents themselves – for their work as professional theatre educators. College students who were part of the testing culture in their K–12 education often ask for definitive or "right" answers to the messy questions of education. Encouraging and nurturing them as they struggle, discover, practice, and evolve their own answers and their own teacher identity is essential to their success (Beijaard, Paulien, and Verloop 2004; Gee 2000/2001; Travers 2000). Sharing multiple perspectives on the practice and using multiple approaches to their own comprehensive theatre education encourages them to learn, apply, reflect, and develop their unique practice. Through class and fieldwork we engage these preservice students in an investigation of practices that are learner-centered and socially responsible. Best practice principles are embedded in field experiences and coursework in drama-in-education, directing young performers, theatre for young audiences, improvisation, and other teaching methods. We continue to explore new models for early placement of students in the field and more extensive correlation between classroom experiences and interactions with professional theatre artists and educators. Community-based learning opportunities and partnerships that foster ongoing dialogue among preservice teachers and with excellent K–12 theatre educators, as well as ways to have preservice students explore their "teacher's heart," as Laura McCammon describes it, are areas for growth we continue to develop.

As our field continues to expand and explore the variety of methods for teaching theatre in high school, collaborative partnerships should be considered as one piece of preservice training and professional development.

THE RELATIONSHIP BETWEEN LIFELONG LEARNING AND BEST PRACTICE

So many teachers in the field have a desire to learn more. Many have an "I would do better if I knew better" attitude and are hungry for opportunities to learn more (Cooper 2011; Chuter 2011a; Gribbons 2011b; Harvey 2010). In a study Amy Jensen and I conducted with Texas and Utah teachers (2011), we found that teachers who engage in best practice often are those who pursue continuing education through graduate study, professional development programs, classes, and/or workshops (Lazarus 2011; Lazarus and Jensen 2011). Year-round, summer, online, and distance-learning programs, as well as active involvement in state and national professional theatre education organizations, play an enormous role in expanding the practice of many teacher-artists (Labonski 2011c; Perlowski 2011a; Silberg 2011a; Kelley 2011; Chuter 2011b; Whitlock 2010).

Valerie Labonski (2011), who received a Master's degree in a summer program, frequently references the impact on her present practice of that graduate study and her ongoing interactions with colleagues from that experience (Labonski 2011a; 2011c; 2002). When Julia Perlowski went to a resident graduate program to learn about educational theatre, she was planning to study children's theatre and knew only to replicate traditional models of theatre practice she had seen. She took a Theatre of the Oppressed class with Chris Vine and a youth theatre class with Helen White. "My whole life changed after that. [...] I had never seen or participated in anything in education like what they were offering. [...] My debt to them is enormous." Julia also realized in graduate school that the practices she was learning were helping her develop both professionally and personally. "They taught me how to make not just a living [...] but a life" (Perlowski 2011b).

Distance and online programs with onsite summer components can expand teachers' knowledge of best practice. The University of Northern Colorado (UNC) helps working teachers continue their education while keeping their teaching positions in a similar blended program.

UNC has developed an online Master's program with face-to-face intensives for two summers. This approach allows theatre educators to learn throughout the year with colleagues from around the country while also being able to apply that learning with students in their own classrooms. This program is

> an academically rigorous program examining the philosophical, theoretical, and practical implications in the field of theatre education. In this program, students [...] reflect on the bigger challenges that constantly face theatre educators in the classroom – and more broadly in the country. (University of Northern Colorado 2011)

Other teachers find that offering innovative professional development programs to colleagues reinforces their own continuous learning and extends best practices into a wider arena. For example, Spencer Sutterfield (2007) developed The Dyslexia Project, "a performance-based professional development model for improving teacher efficacy with students who have dyslexia." Sutterfield used professional development structures, "ethnodrama/documentary theater, and theatre-in-education" and found that "performance is an ideal medium for inspiring empathy and understanding in teachers and [...] improving the educational experiences of students with dyslexia." Mandy Whitlock frequently leads sessions for teachers in her school or district. Most teachers engaged in lifelong learning are also regular presenters at local, state, regional, or national professional conferences.

CHALLENGES TO CHANGE IN THEATRE TEACHER EDUCATION

There are challenges that must be overcome for best practice to become the norm in theatre teacher education. Some states only require students to take six hours in theatre prior to certification. Other states do not offer certification of theatre teachers at all. Many college and university theatre departments do not have full theatre education curriculums or have programs that are understaffed, underfunded, or marginalized. While efforts have been made at the national level to develop standards and to promote quality theatre teacher education (InTASC 2002; AATE 1992), change must be enacted at the state and local level. As those closest to theatre teacher education – professors of education, theatre, and theatre education – partner and become advocates at the state and local level for quality theatre education, as they model best practice and work to share best practices with those secondary school teachers who supervise future educators, preservice teachers will be enabled to use best practices with students in the field. In this way will we see the change we hope to bring about. Figure 6.2 is an open letter to inspire and challenge the next generations of theatre educators to be agents of change on their professional journey.

Dear Future Theatre Educator,

Your role as a theatre educator is to live in the intersection between art and education. It is not always an easy place to be. You are embarking on a journey of exploration, study, and production of theatre with students in your school community. This is a shared adventure, one in which students collaboratively discover relationships between their lives and the lives of those who have preceded them and those who follow them. This journey so powerfully captures aspects of the human experience that it can enable learners to better understand themselves, their fellow human beings, and their world.

But this requires a teacher. Someone who will navigate between learning and artmaking, someone who recognizes that production of plays with young people is also about development of new understandings, that art is only art when it can stir in us an understanding of beauty or the contemplation of ideas beyond mere words. This shift in understanding should cause our hearts to care about the strangers who people the world of a play and who people the world in which we live. That is the gift of theatre and to teach less is to deprive our students of a powerful tool through which they can grow. It must be used skillfully, responsibly and with a clear sense of purpose.

The impact of theatre on your students may not be visible to you, but you must trust that, if taught with integrity and clarity, theatre education will enrich those whom you serve and enlarge their humanity.

You are about to enter a noble profession. You have the privilege of working in a dynamic art form and the joy of sharing the rich history, power and significance of that art form with the next generation of artists and audiences. This will happen as you yourself continue to grow as an artist, a thinker, educator, and a deeply caring human being.

Sincerely,
Your Future Colleagues

Figure 6.2: A Letter to Future Theatre Teachers

Voices from the field

NEW DIRECTIONS IN THEATRE TEACHER EDUCATION

THE HEART OF A TEACHER – LAURA MCCAMMON

Laura McCammon (2011) taught high school for many years and now heads the theatre education program at the University of Arizona in Tucson. Her thoughts here and at the end of the chapter illumine the qualities that enliven theatre teachers engaged in best practice.

> *[Theatre teaching] is only one half skill*
> *the other half is something else... something bigger!*
> *You gotta have heart!*

This slight paraphrase of the Adler and Ross lyric from *Damn Yankees* (1955) speaks to the core of good teaching. We know that good theatre teachers are masters of what Sam Intrator (2007) describes as the ways of teaching: the way of the subject, the way of the method, and the way of understanding students. These are the skills of teaching. But they are also masters of "something bigger" – the way of the heart. According to Intrator,

> Available, energized, and soulful teachers provide opportunities for our children and colleagues to thrive because – as teachers – our moral energy matters, our idealism matters, our capacity to be fully present for students and colleagues matters. In other words – who we are matters. (Intrator 2007, 326)

What are the characteristics of a teacher's heart? Here are a few I have noticed during my thirty-plus years in theatre education, first as a teacher and now as a teacher educator:

First and foremost, a teacher must have *passion*. A love for theatre and the desire to make a difference in the lives of kids are what brought most of us to teaching in the first place. Passion compels a forty-year-old man to leave his job and, at great financial sacrifice for his family, return to school to become a teacher. Passion drives and sustains career teachers year after year. As a former high school student said, "[Teaching theatre] must be a labor of love." (McCammon et al. 2011, 65)

Within every teacher's heart is an element of *courage*. Teaching and doing theatre requires everyday acts of courage: to admit when you are wrong, to risk trying something new in the classroom, or to speak to the school board about the efficacy of arts programming. Courage is also what leads a new teacher to seek out a teaching position in a barrio neighborhood, a rural school, or a "failing" school. It takes courage to push the field beyond the safety of the typical high school play and to produce a controversial or challenging play.

Teachers with heart have a sense of *commitment* – to their students, to their art, to their school, to their families, and to themselves. Because they believe in theatre education, they are willing to work long hours for little pay. They will give students second, third, and fourth chances. They will dedicate time to building sets and in the summer to reading new scripts, planning new challenges, and revising curriculum.

A teacher with a strong heart has *resiliency*. She continues to find a way to create theatre even in the face of budget cuts, program cutbacks, and administrative changes. He learns to pace himself and ensure his own health and happiness. These hardy teachers realize that there are ebbs and flows in student growth, in an academic term, and in a career, and they develop the resiliency to rebound from those periods of stress and distress.

Would it not be nice if along with courses in theatre content, adolescent development, and teaching methods we had another sort of course: we might call it "Heart 401" and describe it this way: "Focuses on the passion, courage, commitment , and resiliency needed for classroom teaching."

Reading Intrator's essay transformed my approach to teacher education. Now I endeavor to embed into all my classes and student meetings opportunities for my students to reflect and sometimes to remember their "teacher heart" – the passion, courage, commitment, and resiliency that inspired them to become theatre teachers. It is important for them to realize how much stronger they become semester by semester. Furthermore, it is important for preservice students to reflect in the company of collegial peers and a caring mentor. These acts could very well sustain a teacher when she begins her career and far beyond.

In the end, teachers with heart will change lives and ignite passion, courage, commitment and resiliency in their students:

> You may never know just *how* much you may affect and inspire a student to do what he/she loves and teach them to embrace their passions and differences. You could be the one to inspire a person to be brave enough to follow his/her dreams. (McCammon et al. 2011, 66)

"Inspired, memorable teaching irretrievably depends on the condition of a teacher's heart (Intrator 2007, 329)" (McCammon 2011).

Voices from the field

METHODS FOR TEACHING THEATRE: PREPARATION THROUGH COLLABORATIVE PARTNERSHIPS – JENNIFER CHAPMAN

Jennifer Chapman (2011) is a faculty member and director of the theatre education program at the University of Wisconsin-Eau Claire (UW-Eau Claire). Jen reflects on her experiences teaching pedagogy and methods through a partnership with a local school.

An exciting characteristic of a university theatre education program is its ability to foster collaborative community partnerships that are mutually beneficial. In a recent collaboration with a high school teacher from my community, I discovered that education students greatly benefit from early and frequent contact with high school students and teachers long before their student teaching experience. By partnering with Lucas Risinger, a teacher from North High School, I was able to bring a depth of understanding to my theatre education students' experience that they would not have had otherwise.

UW-Eau Claire offers a Theatre Education major and minor toward K–12 theatre certification, currently one of only two Wisconsin state universities that do so. Students must complete a class called Teaching Theatre Methods. The purpose of this class is to prepare them with a clear pedagogy for their future teaching. Most of my students plan on teaching high school theatre, and Wisconsin has an excellent set of published standards for theatre arts, grades 9–12. In addition to the standards, I use books written by high school theatre teachers that offer critical reflections on their practice, a textbook intended for high school theatre students, and a practical book of drama lesson plans.

After a couple of semesters of teaching the class, I felt that our discussions of ideas from these resources and theoretical applications were insufficient for fully understanding the depth and complexity of the field. Methods for high school theatre teaching are not a static collection of plans and delivery techniques.

They are a set of tools for effectively responding to changing circumstances and a collection of skills that preservice and inservice teachers develop as they learn to negotiate the multiple, and sometimes conflicting, needs of students, administrators, parents, and community members.

I contacted Mr. Risinger for help [...] [and] discovered we were both directing Jim Leonard's *Anatomy of Gray* that semester. [...] We hatched a plan for an exchange that would include bringing his students into my university rehearsals and taking my methods students to observe his work at the high school. I also requested that my methods students be allowed [to observe] his Theatre I class. I offered to teach two workshops in this class so that the exchange could expand his curriculum as well as provide my students with an observation opportunity. In our early planning stages, I was sensitive to the potential of community partnerships to be imbalanced in their investment and return, which can lead to feelings of "burnout" and resentment. My goal was to construct an experience that would genuinely benefit everyone involved.

Mr. Risinger brought his cast to the university and we paired each high school actor with the college actor playing the same role. My theatre education students who weren't cast in the show were invited to his rehearsals to lead warm-up games and help facilitate discussions. Students described feeling responsible for modeling good technique, language, and professional behavior. In my class, methods students wrote about and discussed the high school students' progress as they worked on scenes with the college students; just a little information about objectives, obstacles, and tactics seemed to shape their character work immensely.

Observation visits to the high school allowed my students to see how time constraints, as well as students' varying abilities and maturity levels, create a very different theatre environment than in college. In methods class, students commented how forty-five-minute high school class periods strongly define the depth and flow of a theatre lesson plan. They observed how varying levels of student engagement create a complex teaching and learning environment in both the classroom and in rehearsal. Additionally, they drew strong connections to our reading material. With just a few observation experiences, the college students were able to understand tensions between appropriate material and the social and cultural expectations of teenagers in a public school space.

In addition to deepening our students' experiences with theatre, Mr. Risinger and I also benefitted from our collaboration. Mr. Risinger, who does not have formal theatre training but has actively sought out professional development in theatre, expressed appreciation for giving him and his students some basic building blocks for character development that could be used in future rehearsals. His production of *Anatomy of Gray* went on to compete and win awards at the regional and state level as part of the Wisconsin High School

Forensics Association Theatre Festival. At the university and at the high school, I was given the opportunity to observe my university students' work, which helps me continue to revise the curriculum to best meet their needs. I also was given the opportunity to reconnect with high school students, a population I prepare preservice students to teach, but rarely now have the chance to spend time with in a classroom.

Our rehearsal exchange and visits to North High School were an invaluable part of the methods class and our collaboration affirmed my belief that theatre education works best when it is a partnership between universities and local schools. Our collaboration was effective because (1) my community has a high school theatre teacher interested in a partnership, (2) North High School is within driving distance of UW-Eau Claire, and (3) all of the stakeholders involved in the collaboration benefited. (Chapman 2011)

Voices from the field

BREAKING THE CYCLE IN TEACHER EDUCATION – ROXANNE SCHROEDER-ARCE

Roxanne Schroeder-Arce discusses inclusion and representation in preservice theatre education programs and links these ideas to her earlier essay on page 194.

As theatre education faculty, those who work very closely with future teachers, we must not underestimate what students are gleaning – or not gleaning – from work with colleagues in our departments. The dramatic literature and textbooks used in all courses, from acting to design to theatre history, are critical elements in the education of preservice theatre teachers.

Sadly, college and university programs nationwide offer limited opportunities for theatre students to experience plays about or by people of color. Theatre teachers are most likely to select and direct plays they have participated in or seen and most of the productions preservice teachers have seen and participated in are from their own high school or college experiences. The absence of diversity in what they see and study in their own education thwarts opportunities preservice teachers have to become confident to offer diverse works when they are teachers. This is a cyclical phenomenon and, therefore, the same plays are produced over and over and the canon remains starkly white.

Although representation and inclusion are the responsibility of the entire theatre department where a preservice teacher studies, until the responsibility is recognized and taken seriously, theatre education faculty must fill the void. Offering students more resources, such as diverse dramatic literature and exercises to prepare preservice teachers with culturally responsible education theory and resources, will help them meet the needs of students in their programs. Only as college theatre departments broaden the study and production of plays to include diverse cultural perspectives, and as theatre teachers – most of whom are white – become comfortable learning from students in the area of culture, will our field be able to get out of this cycle. (Schroeder-Arce 2011)

IDEAS FOR FURTHER REFLECTION

Develop a Teaching Philosophy for Best Practice

Read "A Letter to Future Theatre Teachers" (Figure 6.2) and jot down some notes about what you value about theatre and about education. What can you, and the art form you practice, offer all of the different young people in a school community? How do you see your role in the lives of these young people and how does theatre empower you as an educator and your students as learners, artists, and citizens?

Think about who your audience is for your teaching philosophy. It may be read by a principal or personnel director unfamiliar with theatre and theatre education. It might be seen by a future theatre colleague or director of fine arts for the school or district. How can you express your vision of theatre education in such a way that these people will understand your vision and feel your passion? Write several drafts and invite colleagues or other teachers to read them and give you feedback. Continue to revise your philosophy as you grow as a theatre education pioneer.

Rethinking a College or University Theatre Teacher Education Program

Revisit the ideas explored in Chapters 1–5 and consider to what extent your college or university program models the principles of best practice. In what ways can you change your curriculum, your program of study, and your relationships with colleagues on campus and in the community to bring more of these principles into the curriculum for your theatre education majors? Reach out to state and national professional theatre education organizations and individual faculty members and teachers in your area to help you realize your vision for your program. Develop a plan of action and invite others to join you on this journey of change.

SELECTED RESOURCES

There are multitudes of resources that examine different aspects of the education of teachers. In addition to works cited in this chapter, the following are additional resources for further reading and reflection.

Bennett, Jeff. 2001. *Secondary Stages: Revitalizing High School Theatre*. Portsmouth, NH: Heinemann.

Cahnmann-Taylor, Melisa, and Mariana Souto-Manning. 2010. *Teachers Act Up!: Creating Multicultural Learning Communities Through Theatre*. New York: Teachers College Press.

Dooley, Cindy. 1998. "Teaching as a Two-Way Street: Discontinuities among Metaphors, Images, and Classroom Realities." *Journal of Teacher Education* 49 (2): 97–107.

Garcia, Lorenzo. 2002. "Uncovering Hidden Stories: Pre-service Teachers Explore Cultural Connections." *Stage of the Art* 14 (4): 5–9.

Garcia, Lorenzo. 2000. "Placing 'Diverse Voices' at the Center of Teacher Education: A pre-Service Teacher's Conception of 'Education' and Appeal to Caring." *Youth Theatre Journal* (14): 85–100.

Gonzalez, Jo Beth. 2006. *Temporary Stages: Departing from Tradition in High School Theatre Education*. Portsmouth, NH: Heinemann.

Interstate New Teacher Assessment and Support Consortium Arts Education Committee (InTASC). 2011. *Interstate Teacher Assessment and Support Consortium (InTASC) Model Core Teaching Standards: A Resource for State Dialogue*. Washington, DC: Council of Chief State School Officers. Accessed 10 November, 2011. http://www.ccsso.org/Resources/Publications/InTASC_Model_Core_Teaching_Standards_A_Resource_for_State_Dialogue_(April_2011).html.

Lemov, Doug. 2010. *Teach Like a Champion: The 49 Techniques That Put Students on the Path to College*. San Francisco: Jossey-Bass.

Norris, Joe, Laura A. McCammon, and Carole S. Miller. 2000. *Learning to Teach Drama: A Case Narrative Approach*. Portsmouth, NH: Heinemann.

Palmer, Parker. 2007. *The Courage to Teach*. San Francisco: Jossey-Bass.

Prince, Nancy, and Jeannie Jackson. 2005. *Exploring Theatre*. 2nd ed. Columbus, OH: Glencoe McGraw-Hill.

Schonmann, Shifra, ed. 2010. *Key Concepts in Theatre/Drama Education*. Rotterdam, Netherlands: Sense Publishers.

Scherer, Marge. "Improving the Quality of the Teaching Force: A Conversation with David C. Berliner." *Educational Leadership* 58 (8): 6–10.

Taylor, Robert D., and Robert D. Strickland. 2008. *Theatre: Art in Action*. 2nd ed. New Jersey: Glencoe/McGraw-Hill.

Rohd, Michael. *Theatre for Community, Conflict, and Dialogue: The Hope is Vital Training Manual*. Portsmouth, NH: Heinemann, 1998.

NOTE

1. At the American Alliance for Theatre and Education (AATE) National Conference in 1998, the Higher Education and High School Networks received funds from AATE for a gathering of those concerned with theatre teacher education. The Planning Committee, co-chaired by the author, Jo Beth Gonzalez, and Kim Wheetley, determined that, rather than a single event, this think tank would be ongoing gatherings of diverse groups of thinkers and practitioners. The intent was to probe important issues, move the field to "a new level of thinking," and, hopefully, effect change in individual and collective practice of teacher education. Think tanks and forums continue to be held in individual states and at national conferences (Lazarus 2002).

Chapter 7

On the Frontier of Change

When we share a piece of our vision of the world with others, we are better able to see ourselves, to interact with others, and to make our own choices.

Robert Alexander

Be the change you want to see in the world.

Mahatma Ghandi

I began this book with my childhood desire to change the whole world. I know today that I cannot do that. But *I* can change. My thinking and my practice can change. I can embody alternatives to Industrial Age beliefs and practices and, in small and large ways, make a difference in the world.

This book has gathered together and shed light on teachers whose practices are examples of such possibilities. As Dee Hock (1999, 78) wrote, "When those possibilities engage enough minds, new patterns will emerge and we will find ourselves on the frontier of institutional alternatives ripe with hope and rich with possibilities." These teacher-artists are on the frontier of change. They have explored new patterns of practice and are pioneers in theatre education today. They have changed the world for the students and communities they serve and they have made the path less difficult for those of us who follow.

As a field, however, we are just on the verge of change, still at that crossroads with traditional practice, barely glimpsing these other possibilities. To change *what is*, we must continue to look at the best of *what could be*, engage in dialogue about our practice with those in the field and beyond, and intentionally shape *what will be*, a future for our field "ripe with hope and rich with possibilities" (Hock 1999, 78).

Over the last several years I have had the opportunity to read the work of and chat with some remarkable people about the future of education and theatre education. I find their ideas challenging, provocative, and inspiring. Individually and collectively, their thoughts reinforce and enlarge the characteristics and elements – the essence – of best practice.

A number of different visions, desires, and hopes for furthering the positive changes in our field are shared in this chapter. I begin with a handful of thinkers and writers who share their thoughts about education, our practice, and our future. The chapter concludes with the voices of teachers-artists who, as they work day to day with secondary school students, are the true shapers of change.

A WIDER VIEW OF CHANGE

Parker Palmer

Parker Palmer (2007) is a thought-provoking educator and writer whose ideas resonate with Dee Hock's call to leave Industrial Age thinking and embrace "alternatives ripe with hope and rich with possibilities." In *The Courage to Teach*, Palmer says this will happen as teachers live an "undivided life," as we choose to change and embody a courageous teaching practice in the face of and as an antidote to Industrial Age practices.

> To live divided no more is to find a new center for one's life, a center external to the institution and its demands. [...] It is a deeply personal decision, made for the sake of one's own identity and integrity. (Palmer 2007, 174)
>
> I call this the Rosa Parks decision, for she is our most vivid icon of the undivided life. [...] Rosa Parks decided to live divided no more – decided that she could no longer act as if she were less than a full human being, the way institutional racism had defined her. [...] She did a simple thing: she sat down toward the front of a segregated bus and refused to yield her seat to a white man. (174–75)
>
> [...] The decision she made was rooted in the only sure place we have: [...] the deep inwardness of an integrity that tells us we must do this thing. [...] She was simply tired, tired in her heart and in her soul, tired not only of racism but of her own complicity in the diminishing effects of racism, tired of all the times she had yielded her seat to whites, tired of the self-inflicted suffering her collaboration had brought on. (176)
>
> [...] What does all of this have to do with educational reform? As I have understood the nature of movements more clearly, I have realized that I meet teachers around the country who remind me of Rosa Parks: they love education too much to let it sink to its lowest form, and – whether they know it or not – they are sparking a movement for educational reform by deciding to live divided no more. [...] These teachers remember the passions that led them to become academics, and they do not want to lose the primal energy of their

Your vocation, your life work, is "where your deep gladness meets the world's deep need." Frederick Buechner

vocation. They affirm their deep caring for the lives of students, and they do not want to disconnect from the young. [...] What these teachers do is often as simple as refusing to yield their seat on the bus: they teach each day in ways that honor their own deepest values. (177)

[...] With that insight comes the ability to open cell doors that were never locked in the first place and to walk into new possibilities that honor the claims of one's heart. (178)

Ben Cameron

Ben Cameron (2000) is a scholar, artist, and arts activist with a long history of commitment to theatre education and honoring the claims of one's heart. Ben served as executive director of the Theatre Communications Group (TCG), worked at the National Endowment for the Arts as director of theatre programs, and has been an associate artistic director, literary manager, and freelance artist at professional theatres around the country. He has taught at several universities and served on the nominating committee for the Tony Awards. Ben currently heads the arts granting programs for the Doris Duke Foundation.

Ben talked about how he was introduced to theatre and how theatre participation is a powerful tool for enlarging the social development of young people. He speaks passionately about the value of theatre and theatre education to our children and our country.

> You're going to find a fierce commitment [to theatre education], especially from people who grew up in nonurban areas, who wouldn't have encountered theatre in any other context. [...] Had there not been the Junior League coming in and doing a sort of hands-on arts program with us, I would have gone through the gamut without ever knowing what theatre was. [...] For a lot of us [...] that [...] was the way we got introduced to theatre and we're appreciative of that.
>
> There's [...] one study that demonstrates that kids that work in theatre – not in the arts, but in theatre specifically – are forty percent [...] less likely to tolerate racist behavior than kids who are not participating in theatre. And the kids that participated in theatre – *participated* in theatre – not as witness [...] work better across racial lines than any other group. [...] The role for us is [to value] the inherent social dimensions [...] that [...] creative hands-on experience offers us.
>
> [...] When Kennedy stood up in the early sixties and said: "Everybody's going to have to take a sport and gym's going to be compulsory for everybody" [...] the argument was for your physical well being and the long-term sake of the country. You had to engage in this activity [...] no ifs, ands, or buts. It seems to me we're at that nascent point where we need to be able to say, for the spiritual

It is critical that we not abandon this fight. Ben Cameron

health of this country, "You will engage in the arts, no ifs, ands [...] or buts." (Cameron 2000, original emphasis)

Ben consistently stresses the importance of talking in a "listener-targeted way" about the value of what we do and of being a part of the change in our midst. Speaking in several different venues over a number of years, Ben raises critical questions and offers inspiring perspectives for taking charge of our future.

> For your local board of education, the value of the arts is that kids who work in the arts perform eighty points higher on the SATs than kids who don't. [...] And we have the tests to prove it. For the principals in your school systems, the value of the arts is that kids who work in after school arts programs show fewer disciplinary infractions than kids who don't. For parents, it is the reams of studies [...] that prove that kids who work in the arts have a greater complexity in thinking, greater tolerance for ambiguity, greater self-esteem, greater sense of self. . [...] For people concerned about community building, [...] the reason the arts and theatre are important is because high school seniors who work in theatre are 40 percent less likely to tolerate racist behavior than kids who never created a piece of theatre. Clarity on our values is essential to our survival. (Cameron 2001, 22)

> Just as effective education is increasingly shifting from the vertical to the lateral – just as students increasingly rely on one another for information, for guidance, and for instruction, a shift that brings the opportunity to emphasize collaboration, team work, and more – the arts have shifted as well. We are indeed arguably living in a golden age of arts education, but it is the lateral education rather than the vertical that now holds sway. Who among us does not see young people making movies, writing songs, writing rap, leading rich fictive lives on Second Life, and more? If we can look at the world through this lens of abundance, what endless possibilities might we not find? [...] Can we make this shift? [...] Regardless of the stress of the present, regardless of the uncertainties, how can we – individually and as a community – shift from the reactive to the proactive? (Cameron 2008)

> In looking to the future, I find inspiration in the words of two different thinkers. Our nineteenth-century American President, Abraham Lincoln, who in his second inaugural address said, "The dogmas of the quiet past are inadequate to the stormy present. As our case is new, so must we think anew and act anew." [...] [A]nd Wayne Gretzky, the Canadian ice hockey player, who when asked to account for his greatness said simply, "I skate to where the puck will be." (Cameron 2010)

I believe the arts invite us to access, not the easiest or most facile parts of ourselves, but the best parts. [...] In the arts, we not only ask for more, we demand more – more of one another, more of ourselves. Ben Cameron

How can we skate, as it were, to where the puck will be? Many of us did not choose this work; it chose us. But when we choose to answer that call, what we really do is, we honor the past, we commemorate the present, we shape and we change the future in a way that does honor to all and violence to none. I don't care how much opponents may try to shame us from that path. For those of us who are spiritually inclined, it is God's work we do. (Cameron 2008)

Maxine Greene

Maxine Greene (2000), a professor of education and philosophy (emeritus) at Columbia University, founded the Center for the Arts, Social Imagination, and Education, taught at the Lincoln Center for the Arts, and spoke at conferences and events throughout the country. She has written extensively on the arts, aesthetic education, and social change. I had the privilege of chatting with Maxine in her home as she spoke about her work and issues in arts education she was pondering. Like so many teachers engaged in best practice, Maxine's desire is to make her work as a teacher inviting and inclusive. "When I teach [...] I want to say, 'Come in. It's exciting.' [...] I don't want to say, 'I'm transmitting this. You have to have it if you're going to make it.' I want to say, 'This is an exciting life.'"

Noting how we inadvertently alienate young people in school by making assumptions about them she told the story of

> [An organization that] hired a group from the Ivory Coast [...] [to perform] for the kids in Buffalo. I said "What [...] do black kids in Buffalo know about the Ivory Coast [...] just because [they're] the same color? I don't want to have Jewish literature [just because I come from a Jewish tradition]." (Greene 2000)

Maxine stressed that it is essential to the future or our field that students are engaged in learning that keeps them "alive" in school. The arts are central to realizing that goal.

> Children are in search of meaning. They're not empty. [...] I [...] talk a lot about being alive because the schools don't do anything about that. [...] Sometimes the schools are for forgetting [...] the perceived world, the imagined world. [...] I write about wide awakeness. I want to think about classrooms that are dialogues. It's very important for teachers to know how many voices are silenced and what you [can] do to [not let that happen]. [...] [They have] to [...] understand [...] what's happening in the culture [and] about the relation between popular culture and what we're doing in the arts. [...] How do I attend to the students' world and communicate what I think is valuable? And how do I say, "What do you love?" I think, like Marcuse said, "Art doesn't change the world. It can change the people who might change the world." (Greene 2000)

In her book, *Releasing the Imagination* (1995), Maxine pushes us to move beyond the traditions of American education and to explore with children the possibilities of our collective human experience.

> To help the diverse students we know articulate their stories isn't only to help them pursue the meaning of their lives – to find out *how* things are happening and to keep posing questions about the why. It is to move them [...] to reach out for the proficiencies and capacities, the craft required to be fully participant in this society, and to do so without losing the consciousness of who they are. (Greene 1995, 165, original emphasis)

David O'Fallon

David O'Fallon, like Parker Palmer, knows that teachers and artists are stewards of "the inner wilderness. We need to nurture [the] inner wilderness. [...] and take time to do that" (O'Fallon 2002). To that end, David urges professional development programs for teachers and school personnel that build community and foster imagination, that promote deep thinking and meaningful connections with students. His wish for teachers would be

> working across multiple forms and thinking [about] connections and relationships. [...] Committing [...] to a community [...] so that other people hold us accountable in healthy ways for what we do. There's still a little bit of, "we're artists, and you should understand us" rather than [...] "I'm committing myself to building community."

There are people in this world who feel they don't have anything to look forward to each day. [As theatre teachers,] we have two things that we love to do each day. We love to make theatre and we love to teach.
Don Doyle

David's closing thought is a wish for teacher-artists to receive "continual affirmation and support for what they do, because it is not only so valuable now, but increasingly valuable" (O'Fallon 2002).

When I think about the value of theatre education, as evidenced by the work described in this book, I forget where the rest of our field is for a moment and really believe best practice is widespread. In reality, best practice in theatre education today is merely a glimpse of *what could be*. This practice exists as fireflies in the night, visible only in small, elusive glimmers.

This book has gathered some "fireflies" to illumine our thinking and light our paths. I have written for the pioneer, the one who, as Margaret Wheatley (1994) says, is calling "Land ho!" on desire, faith, and intuition. Those already on their journey have found in these pages reassurance that what they are doing with students is effective, though not always visible or valued. Others, hopefully, have found courage and encouragement to embrace change and embark on a new or enlarged path. I hope this book will create a positive epidemic of change and spread it to other pioneers for the benefit of our children, our schools, and communities.

Voices from the field

TEACHERS, CHANGE MAKERS, AND PIONEERS ON THE VERGE OF CHANGE

I leave you with the wishes, hopes, reflections, and advice of our most precious resource, our theatre teachers, teaching artists, and future teachers. In their day-to-day work with secondary school students, they are moving our future in powerful new directions. Their work reveals the signs of change for which our hearts are yearning.

Individually and collectively we are indeed "on the verge" as pioneers, change makers, and teacher-artists. I look forward to meeting you on this path as together we journey on.

> *One of the most exciting parts about teaching theatre is that there's always a passion there. In every semester there'll be a new group of kids [...] who see theatre not as "I'm going to do this the rest of my life," but "I understand what theatre is, and it will always be a part of what I want [...] I will go to the theatre or be in community theatre or do theatre [...] because it is so important in our culture – in our lives – and it's important [as] a place for our stories to be told." [...] [That's] when a student really begins to discover their talent and ability to contribute to a larger community, a larger theatre community.* John Heinemann, Teacher

> *I remember sitting in a professional development class and the teacher was talking about who he considered our "customers" to be. He said that he considered the parents to be the customers. The kids did not always know what was best for them, but the parents were the ones who were entrusting us with the most important thing in their life. After years of thinking about that, I've come to the conclusion that my "customer" is the twenty-two-year-old that the student will become. To that person, what I am doing makes all the difference.* Brendan Kelley, Teacher

[T]ouch each kid on a heart level and really have them know what [...] [you] see in them and [...] that [you] like them. [...] I am the adult and responsible and they know that [...] [yet] the child part of me can meet the child part of them and they see that and are drawn to that. [Meet] them in the heart space [...] [even] when [...] crawling on the floor [with them]. [...] [E]njoy them. Laurel Serleth, Teacher

I believe that students are drawn to my class because it is fun. I think that fun is an important component of the learning process. I also try to know every student personally and value what they have to say [...] to believe [in] and love every kid that comes through my program. Lena Paulauskas, Teacher

I constantly remind myself that if the students aren't listening, it doesn't matter what I say. Roxanne Schroeder-Arce, Teacher

A wish [...] would be that [teachers and students] could be involved in a production where they can see love dissolving difference or they can see what they've done has built a bond or [...] an understanding. [...] That it opened the door to somebody else. A door to possibilities. Tara Affolter, Teacher

I think that's my job as a teacher [...] to find [my] voice and [...] to use it. [...] [to] be all I can be to the world. Julia Perlowski, Teacher

I am learning that learning is never over – that embracing my ignorance as a challenge to learn more will benefit not only me but my students. Preservice Teacher

Number one is love and believe in the kids. And really sincerely, not patronizingly, not condescendingly, but actually really care about them and be with them. That's the first thing. [...] Number two: Create a safe environment before any work can be handled. Number three: [...] Really be an artist, because then you can create the art. If you know the techniques, but you can't catch the [dramatic] moment [...] you're not going to get them, because it's just not strong enough work. Betsy Quinn, Teacher

I really believe as educators you need to take time to [...] [take a] class. [...] You have to service your artistic soul. If all you're doing is being the director and producer of your theatre company, you're not getting to service your own artistic needs [...] [that] [...] inspire you. [...] If I have any [legacy] [...] it [would be] trying to create a network, a family of theatre teachers, bringing theatre teachers together so they don't feel so isolated in their field. Susan Morrell, Teacher

Invite people into your drama process to see [it]. [...] If the math teacher is not sure of what drama is and it is a foreign concept, then when cuts come and when [...] the opportunity to expand the program comes, you may not have those voices to [help you]. Everybody has been in somebody's math class, probably. Everybody has probably been in somebody's reading class. But throughout the country, everybody has not always been in a drama class – not the play experience – but a drama class. So it's hard for other people to value what they don't necessarily understand. Gloria Bond Clunie, Teacher and Playwright

I wish someone would have told me that this job would be not only the best I've ever had, but also the most challenging [...] often in one day! Preservice Teacher

All new teachers must remember that they are usually following in someone else's footsteps. That [former teacher] may have been brilliant, or they may have been awful, but those kids are in the program, at least in part, because of who was there last year. [...] You will not win them all over the first, or even the second year. [...] The time will come when you are recognized for who you are and what you bring and not for who you aren't and what is missing. Sarah Kent, Teacher

I think the fact that we [...] have the National Standards [...] is a really good sign. We [...] need to address implementation. Jeffrey Leptak-Moreau, Educational Theatre Association

A wish for a novice teacher. [...] Be aware that you're going be faced with reality. [...] You'll be idealistic [...] you have to stay that way and it will help you get through the reality of [...] budget and curriculum and buildings and things like that. [A wish for] a veteran teacher [...] look back and find why you were idealistic in the first place, as a new teacher. Kent Sorensen, Teacher

Each day brings new surprises, whether it be an unscheduled pep rally that your administration forgot to tell you about or a student that enters your rehearsal in tears because her family is having problems. Your show dates don't change, but your rehearsal schedule is in constant motion. Compromise and flexibility are vital qualities for a teacher. Bobby Malone, Teacher

Seek out people who are doing it differently [than you]. [...] Look at your own work and [ask], "What's really strong about it? What's weak about it? What could I do differently? What could I change? Am I still taking risks artistically or educationally?" [...] And [...] look at some of the current research in education and how you might apply that to theatre. Karen Kay Husted, Consultant

I think our theatre teachers really are [...] in a position in the [school] to [...] be [...] instructional [...] and [...] inspirational to their colleagues. When I see [...] integrated arts projects take off [...] in the schools [...] [what] I see is a commonality, a collaboration happen. [...] Those folks who have [...] artistic skills are able to bring [them] to their other colleagues in the school and take a leadership role. And together all of them find things that are not just exciting for the kids, but also exciting for all subject teachers also. I think arts teachers have a particular advantage to take that exciting leadership role in transforming the school. Kent Seidel, Arts Administrator

I am learning that teaching is really about students first and subject matter second. Preservice Teacher

I have a theme that we deal with called "Each one reach one. Each one teach one. Each one pull one into the sun." It's a Malcolm X quote. [I tell students] "You have a responsibility that once you have attained a gift, to pass it on to your community." [...] So they tour [to nearby elementary schools] and [...] they learn how to teach [...] or [...] we help them with their play. [...] "What is education for and about?" [...] I ask kids that all the time and try to get them to want to learn to be excited about learning, to be positive about themselves. Jan Mandell, Teacher

We were talking over lunch, and several of the kids said [one of our teaching artists] was their favorite teacher. I said "Why?" And they said "Because she's hard but she's fun, and it's clear she's a real actress herself." Abigail Adams, People's Light and Theatre Company

I am 100 percent here for the students. This isn't a fallback profession, or something I do during the day while I do theatre at night. I'm not here for my ego or to be in charge of a theatre company. I do not want or need the spotlight or praise from others. I have extremely high expectations, can work two years ahead in planning for the program, keep things extremely balanced in my personal life, have tremendous connections with the students, deliver what I talk about, and would give it all up if I thought I wasn't doing right by the students of my program. M. Scott Tatum, Teacher

Figure 7.1: A teacher shares her vision of theatre with the next generation.

Works Cited

Adams, Abigail. 2002. Interview with the author. Tape recording. 16 July.

Affolter, Tara. 2002. Telephone interview with the author. Tape recording. 28 June.

Alexander, Deb. 2012. Interview with the author. 5 February.

Alexander, Deb. 2002. Interview with the author. Tape recording. 13 February.

Alexander, Deb. 1999. "A Middle School Theatre Curriculum Model." Master's thesis, The University of Texas at Austin.

Albany Park Theater Project (APTP). 2011a. Accessed 1 July, 2011. http://www.aptpchicago.org/.

Albany Park Theater Project (APTP). 2011b. "Our Story." Albany Park Theater Project brochure.

American Alliance for Theatre and Education (AATE). 1992. "Standards for High School Education." Bethesda, MD: American Alliance for Theatre and Education

American Psychology Association (APA). 2007. *Sexualization of Girls: Executive Summary.* Washington, DC: American Psychology Association. Accessed 28 September, 2011. http://www.apa.org/pi/women/programs/girls/report.aspx.

Argyris, Chris, and Donald A. Schon. 1992. *Theory in Practice: Increasing Professional Effectiveness.* San Francisco: Jossey-Bass.

Barnes, Dave. 2002. Interview with the author. Tape recording. 2 August.

Barnes, Dave. 1999. *Oswego High School Theatre Handbook.* Oswego, IL: Oswego High School.

Barnes, Donna. 2002. Interview with the author. Tape recording. 2 August.

Barth, Roland. 2007. "The teacher leader." In *Uncovering Teacher Leadership: Essays and Voices from the Field*, edited by Richard M. Ackerman, and Sarah V. Mackenzie. Thousand Oaks CA: Corwin, 9–36.

Bartow, Arthur. 1988. *The Director's Voice.* New York: Theatre Communications Group, Inc.

Beijaard, Douwe, Paulien C. Meijer, and Nico Verloop. 2004. "Reconsidering research on teachers' professional identity." *Teaching and Teacher Education* 20 (2): 107–28.

Berghammer, Gretta. 2002. Telephone interview with the author. Tape recording. 6 May.

Bennett, William, J. 2011. *The Book of Man: Readings on the Path to Manhood.* Nashville, TN: Thomas Nelson.

Bishop, Nancy. 1992. "Are your classes gender fair?" *Teaching Theatre* 4 (1): 1–10.

Block, Peter. 2008. *Community: The Structure of Belonging.* San Francisco: Berrett-Koehler Publishers

Bloom, Michael. 2001. *Thinking Like a Director.* New York: Faber and Faber, Inc.

Boal, Augusto. 1994. *Games for Actors and Non-actors.* Translated by Adrian Jackson. London: Routledge.

Boal, Augusto. 1985. *Theatre of the Oppressed.* Translated by Charles A. and Maria-Odilia Leal McBride. New York: Theatre Communications Group.

Bogart, Anne. 2001. *A Director Prepares*. New York: Routledge.

Bogart, Steve. 2003. Telephone interview with the author. Tape recording. 3 July.

Bowe, L. 2007. "It isn't just a dream." In *Uncovering Teacher Leadership: Essays and Voices from the Field*, edited by Richard M. Ackerman, and Sarah V. Mackenzie. Thousand Oaks CA: Corwin, 321–23.

Brockett, Oscar G. 1985. "Drama: A Way of Knowing." *Theatre Education: Mandate for Tomorrow*. Louisville: Anchorage Press and the Children's Theatre Foundation.

Brophy, Jere E., and Carolyn M. Evertson. 1976. *Learning from teaching: A developmental perspective*. Needham Heights, MA: Allyn and Bacon.

Burtaine, Amy. 2003a. Interview with the author. 24 June.

Burtaine, Amy. 2003b. "Socially Responsible Theatre Practice." Pre-thesis Organizational Draft, The University of Texas at Austin. April.

Burtaine, Amy. 2003c. "Searching for 'Socially Responsible Theatre Practice (SRTP)': A Journey." Pre-thesis paper, The University of Texas at Austin. May.

Byrne-Jiménez, Monica. 1992. "Los Solos: The education and experience of Latino children." Master's thesis, University of Michigan.

Cain, Carol. 2003. Telephone interview with the author. Tape recording. 19 July.

Cameron, Ben. 2010. Keynote. Association of Arts Administration Educators. Washington, DC. 4 June. Accessed 28 October, 2011. http://www.artsadministration.org/cameron.

Cameron, Ben. 2008. Congress Keynote. International Society for the Performing Arts. New York. 8 January. Accessed 28 October, 2011. http://www.ispa.org/resources/ideasexchange/50-cameron.

Cameron, Ben. 2000. Interview with the author. Tape recording. 13 March.

Cameron, Ben. 2001. "Keynote Address." *TYA Today* 15 (2): 18–23.

Carroll, John, Michael Anderson, and David Cameron. 2006. *Real Players?: Drama, Technology, and Education*. Staffordshire, England: Trentham Books Limited.

Casey, Autumn Samsula. 2003. Interview with the author. Tape recording. 24 January.

Chapman, Jennifer. 2011. "Methods for Teaching Theatre: Preparation through Collaborative Partnerships." Unpublished essay submitted to the author. 20 July.

Chapman, Jennifer. 2002. Telephone interview with the author. Tape recording. 25 April.

Chapman, Jennifer. 2000. "Female Impersonations: Young Performers and the Crises of Adolescence." *Youth Theatre Journal* (14): 123–31.

Chapman, Jennifer, Heather Sykes, and Anne Swedberg. 2003. "Wearing the Secret Out: Performing Stories of Sexual Identities." *Youth Theatre Journal* (17): 27–37.

Chuter, Frank. 2011a. Researcher field notes. 18–19 April.

Chuter, Frank. 2011b. Interview with the author during site visit. Digital recording. 18–19 April.

Chuter, Frank. 2011c. Telephone interview with the author. Digital recording. 18 February.

Clunie, Gloria Bond. 2002. Interview with the author. Tape recording. 5 August.

Colby, Bob. 2002. Interview with the author. Tape recording. 29 July.

Conklin, Deborah. 2011. Interview with Jo Beth Gonzalez. 16 June.

Consortium of National Arts Education Associations. 2002. *Authentic Connections*. Reston, VA: Consortium of National Arts Education Associations.

Consortium of National Arts Education Associations. 1994. *National Standard for Arts Education*. Reston, VA: Consortium of National Arts Education Associations.

Cooper, C. Gary. 2011a. Researcher field notes. 20–21 April.

Cooper, C. Gary. 2011b. Interview with the author during site visit. Digital recording. 20–21 April, and 24 May.

Cooper, C. Gary. 2011c. Telephone interview with the author. Digital recording. 11 March.

Cooperrider, David L., and Diana Whitney. 1999. *Appreciative Inquiry*. San Francisco: Berrett-Koehler Communications.

Cooperrider, David. L., Peter F. Sorensen, Jr., Diana Whitney, and T. F. Yaeger, eds. 1999. *Appreciative Inquiry: Rethinking Human Organization Toward a Positive Theory of Change*. Champaign, IL: Stripes Publishing.

Cougle, Bryar. 2002. Telephone interview with the author. Tape recording. 30 May.

Cox, Barbara. 2002. Interview with the author. Tape recording. 29 July.

Crotwell, Eleshia. 2011a. Researcher field notes. 2–3 March.

Crotwell, Eleshia. 2011b. Interview with the author during site visit. Digital recording. 2–3 March.

Crotwell, Eleshia. 2011c. Instructional materials shared with the author. 2–3 March.

Crotwell, Eleshia. 2011d. Schedules and lesson plans e-mailed to the author. 1 March.

Crotwell, Eleshia. 2010a. Telephone interview with the author. Digital recording. 15 December.

Crotwell, Eleshia. 2010b. Survey response submitted to the author. 4 June.

Dawson, Katie, et al. 2011a. Drama for Schools. Accessed 1 May, 2011. http://www.finearts.utexas.edu/tad/special_programs/outreach_programs/drama_for_schools.cfm.

Dawson, Katie, et al. 2011b. E-mail to the author. 5 May.

Davidson, Cathy N. 2011. "Edu-Traitor! Confessions of a Prof Who Believes Higher Ed Shouldn't Be the Only Goal." *Now You See It Blog*. Accessed 6 August, 2011. http://hastac.org/blogs/cathy-davidson/2011/08/06/edu-traitor-confessions-prof-who-believes-higher-ed-isnt-only-goal.

Deasy, Richard J., and Lauren M. Stevenson. 2005. *Third Space: When Learning Matters*. Washington, DC: Arts Education Partnership.

DeLong, Steve. 1995–96. "Make It So." Accessed 2 July, 2011. http://www.sherryart.com/newstory/makeitso/index.html.

de Winter, Micha. 1997. *Children as Fellow Citizens: Participation and Commitment*. New York: Radcliff Medical Press, 38–39.

DiMartino, Sandra. 2003. Telephone interview with the author. Tape recording. 22 June.

diRende, Susan. 2002. Telephone interview with the author. Tape recording. 21 June.

diRende, Susan. 1996. Facsimile letter to the author. 30 October.

Dixon, Michael Bigelow, and Joel A. Smith, eds. 1995. *Anne Bogart Viewpoints*. Lyme, NH: Smith and Kraus.

Dramatic Publishing. 2011. Online catalogue. Accessed 18 July, 2011. http://www.dramaticpublishing.com/p2560/Sangre-de-un-Angel-(Blood-of-an-Angel)/product_info.html.

Dynak, Dave. 2002. Telephone interview with the author. Tape recording. 1 July.

Eaton, Gillian. 2001. Interview with the author. Tape recording. 23 February.

Ervi, Lindsey. 2011. Interview with the author during site visit. Digital recording. 17 May.

Ewing, Jason. 2002. Telephone interview with the author. Tape recording. May 22.

Feiner, David. 2011. "Post-show Question and Answer Session." Discussion with attendees at the American Alliance for Theatre and Education National Conference, Chicago, Illinois. 27 July.

Fenton, Traci. 2011. "Democratic Workplaces." Accessed 14 March, 2011. http://tedxtalks.ted.com/video/TEDxMadtown-Traci-Fenton-WorldB

Flint Community Schools. 1995. *Profile of Student Life, Research and Testing*. Flint, MI: Flint Community Schools. 52.

Flint Youth Theatre. 2001. *Fact Sheet: Flint Youth Theatre Animating Democracy Initiative*. Flint, MI: Flint Youth Theatre. 10 January.

Freire, Paolo. 1996. *Pedagogy of the Oppressed*. New York: The Continuum Publishing Company.

Garbarino, James. 1999. *Lost Boys*. New York: Free Press.

Garcia, Lorenzo. 1998. "Multiculturism, Diversity, and AATE?" *Stage of the Art* 9 (7): 3.

Garcia, Lorenzo. 1998. "Learning In and Through Dialogue." *Stage of the Art* 9 (6): 3–5.

Garcia, Lorenzo. 1997. "Drama, Theatre, and the Infusion of Multiethnic Content: An Exploratory Study." *Youth Theatre Journal* (11): 88–101.

Garcia, Rick. 2002. Interview with the author. Tape recording. 12 February.

Gee, James Paul. 2000/2001. "Identity as an analytic lens for research in education." In *Review of Research in Education*, edited by W. G. Secada. Washington, DC: American Educational Research Association, (25): 99–126.

Giffin, Holly. 1999. "Coda Essay." *Stage of the Art* 11 (1): 34.

Gonzalez, Jo Beth. 2011. "Recognizing Spirituality in a High School Theatre Program." Unpublished essay submitted to the author. 14 July.

Gonzalez, Jo Beth. 2003. E-mail to the author. 27 May.

Gonzalez, Jo Beth. 2002a. "From Page to Stage to Teenager: Problematizing 'Transformation' in Theatre for and with Adolescents." *Stage of the Art* 14 (3): 17–21.

Gonzalez, Jo Beth. 2002b. Interview with the author. Tape recording. 13 February.

Gonzalez, Jo Beth. 1999. "Beyond the Boundaries of Tradition: Cultural Treasures in a High School Theatre Arts Program." *Stage of the Art* 10 (3): 14–18.

Gonzalez, Jo Beth, and William O. Donnelly. 2008. "When It Matters Most: Organizing Post-Show Talk-Backs." *Teaching Theatre* 19 (3): 30–36.

Goodrich, Frances, and Albert Hackett. 1958. *The Diary of Anne Frank*. New York: Dramatist Play Service.

Goodrich, Frances, Albert Hackett, and Wendy Ann Kesselman. 2000. *The Diary of Anne Frank*. Rev. edn. New York: Dramatist Play Service.

Gotuaco, Fursey. 2002. Interview with the author. Tape recording. 20 February.

Grady, Sharon. 2000. *Drama and Diversity*. Portsmouth, NH: Heinemann.

Greene, Maxine. 2000. Interview with the author. Tape recording. 14 March.

Greene, Maxine. 1995. *Releasing the Imagination: Essays on Education, the Arts, and Social Change*. San Francisco: Jossey-Bass.

Gribbons, Tal. 2011a. Researcher field notes. 26–27 January.

Gribbons, Tal. 2011b. Interview with the author during site visit. Digital recording. 26–27 January.

Gribbons, Tal. 2011c. Instructional and production materials shared with the author. 26–27 January.

Gribbons, Tal. 2010. Telephone interview with the author. Digital recording. 15 December.

Griffith, Chris. 2002a. *News from the Playground*. Galumph Theatre Newsletter. 10 (Summer).

Griffith, Chris. 2002b. Telephone interview with the author. Tape recording. 28 July.

Hall, Brian. 2003a. E-mail to the author. 22 June.

Hall, Brian. 2003b. E-mail to the author. 21 June.

Hall, Brian. 2003c. E-mail to the author. 21 March.

Hall, Brian. 1999. Instructional materials shared with the author.

Hancock, Stephen D. 2010. "Awakening the Spirit: Teaching, Learning, and Living Holistically." In *Culture, Curriculum, and Identity in Education*, edited by H. Richard Milner IV. NY: Palgrave/ Macmillan.

Hanes, Stephanie. 2011a. "Pretty in Pink?" *The Christian Science Monitor*, 26 September: 26–31.

Hanes, Stephanie. 2011b. "Little girls of little women: The Disney princess effect." *The Christian Science Monitor*, 24 September: 1–7. Accessed 30 September, 2011. http://www.csmonitor.com/ USA/Society/2011/0924/Little-girls-or-little-women-The-Disney-princess-effect.

Hansen, Bill. 2003. "The Spot." E-mail to the author. 7 July.

Hansen, Bill. 2002. Interview with the author. Tape recording. 6 August.

Harvey, Billie. 2010. Interview with the author. Digital recording. 17 December.

Hartford, Dwayne. 2004. *Eric and Elliot*. Woodstock, IL: Dramatic Publishing

Heathcote, Dorothy, and Gavin Bolton. 1995. *Drama for Learning: Dorothy Heathcote's Mantle of the Expert*. Portsmouth, NH: Heinemann.

Heinemann, John. 2002. Telephone interview with the author. Tape recording. 11 June.

Henig, Robin, Marantz. 2010. "What Is It About 20-Somethings?" *New York Times*, 18 August. Accessed 30 May, 2011. http://www.nytimes.com/2010/08/22/magazine/22Adulthood.

Hock, Dee. 1999. *Birth of the Chaordic Age*. San Francisco: Berrett-Koehler Publishers, Inc.

Hodge, Francis. 1994. *Play Directing: Analysis, Communication, and Style*. 4th edn. Upper Saddle River, NJ: Prentice Hall.

Howard, Gary R. 2006. *We Can't Teach What We Don't Know: White Teachers, Multiracial Schools*. 2nd edn. New York: Teachers College Press.

Imagination Stage. 2011. Accessed 12 July, 2011. http://www.imaginationstage.org.

Imagination Stage. 2010. Accessed 12 August, 2011. http://www.imaginationstage.org/blog/2010/09/highlights-from-2009-2010/.

Interstate New Teacher Assessment and Support Consortium Arts Education Committee (InTASC). 2002. *Model Standards for Licensing Classroom Teachers and Specialist in the Arts*. Draft for Comments. Washington, DC: Council of Chief State School Officers.

Intrator, Sam. 2007. "The Heart of Teaching: Making the Connection Between Teaching, Leadership and Inner Life." In *Uncovering Teacher Leadership: Essays and Voices from the Field*, edited by Richard M. Ackerman, and Sarah V. Mackenzie. Thousand Oaks CA: Corwin, 325–31.

Jallings, Rebecca. 2002. Interview with the author. Tape recording. 6 August.

James, Stephen and David S. Thomas. 2009. *Wild Things: The Art of Nurturing Boys*. Carol Stream, IL: Tyndale House Publishers, Inc.

James, William. 1903/1985. *The Varieties of Religious Experience: A Study in Human Nature*. London: Penguin.

Jenkins, Henry. 2006. *Confronting the Challenges of Participatory Culture*. Chicago, IL: MacArthur Foundation.

Jensen, Amy. 2011. "Embracing Digital Media in a Learner-centered Program." Unpublished essay submitted to the author. 15 July.

Jensen, Eric. 2011. "Jensen Learning: Practical Teaching with the Brain in Mind." Accessed 18 May, 2011. http://www.jensenlearning.com.

Jensen, Eric. 2009. *Teaching with Poverty in Mind: What Being Poor Does to Kid's Brains and What Schools Can Do About It*. Alexandria, VA: Association for Supervision and Curriculum Development.

Jensen, Eric. 2001. *Arts with the Brain in Mind*. Alexandria, VA: Association for Supervision and Curriculum Development.

Johns, Patsy Koch. 2003. E-mail to the author. 25 October.

Johns, Patsy Koch. 2002. Telephone interview with the author. Tape recording. 19 June.

Johnson, Justine. 2003. E-mail to author. 15 July.

Katzenmeyer, Marilyn, and Gayle Moller. 2001. *Awakening the Sleeping Giant: Helping Teachers Develop as Leaders*. 2nd edn. Thousand Oaks, CA: Corwin Press.

Kelin, Daniel. 2001. Interview with the author. Tape recording. 4 August.

Kelley, Brendan. 2011. Questionnaire responses e-mailed to the author. 18 April.

Kent, Sarah. 2003. E-mail to the author. 31 August.

Kindlon, Daniel J., and Michael Thompson. 2000. *Raising Cain: Protecting the Emotional Life of Boys.* New York: Ballantine.

Knighton, Aline. 2003. E-mail to the author. 1 July.

Koern, Candace. 2011. Questionnaire responses e-mailed to the author. 7 May.

Koern, Candace. 2010. Texas Theatre Educators Forum Teacher Profile. E-mail to the author. 4 October.

Kornhauser, Barry. 2011a. Youtheatre One-Page Description. E-mail to the author. 2 August.

Kornhauser, Barry. 20011b. Youtheatre. Accessed 8 August, 2011. http://www.thefulton.org/index.php?pID=40.

Kornhauser, Barry. 2011c. Compilation of critical responses. E-mail to the author. 2 August.

Korza, Pam. 2001. Notes from welcome to the Flint study circles (unpublished). 22 February.

Korza, Pam. 2001. E-mail correspondence to the author. 9 February.

Labonski, Valerie Roberts. 2011a. Questionnaire responses e-mailed to the author. 28 April.

Labonski, Valerie Roberts. 2011b. Researcher field notes. 24–25 January.

Labonski, Valerie Roberts. 2011c. Interview with the author during site visit. Digital recording. 24–25 January.

Labonski, Valerie Roberts. 2002. Telephone interview with the author. Tape recording. 12 October.

Ladson-Billings, Gloria. 1994. *The Dreamkeepers: Successful Teachers of African American Children.* San Francisco: Jossey-Bass Inc.

Lamb, Gregory, M. 2003. "Some serious child's play." *The Christian Science Monitor.* 17 October: 13–20.

Lang, Linda, L. 2002. "'Whole play is it anyhow?' When Drama Teachers Journey into Collective Creation." *Youth Theatre Journal* (16): 48–62.

Larson, Jeanette. 2003. Review of *With Their Eyes; September 11th – View from a High School at Ground Zero,* edited by Annie Thoms. *Austin American Statesman.* 7 September.

Lazarus, Joan. 2011. "Profiles of Best Practice in Theatre Education: Phase II." Unpublished research findings.

Lazarus, Joan. 2004. *Signs of Change: New Directions in Secondary Theatre Education,* 1st edn. Portsmouth, NH: Heinemann.

Lazarus, Joan. 2002. "Rethinking Theatre Teacher Education: A National Think Tank for Change-Makers." *Stage of the Art* 14 (3): 5–6.

Lazarus, Joan. 2001. "Theatre as Civic Dialogue: Questions and Considerations Raised by Flint Youth Theatre's Animating Democracy through the Arts Project." *TYA Today* 15 (2): 24–27.

Lazarus, Joan. 2000. "On the Verge: Promise or Peril for Theatre Education in the Next One Hundred Years." *Arts Education Policy Review* Nov/Dec 101 (2): 37–38.

Lazarus, Joan. 1986. "Theatre Survey." *Southern Theatre* XXVII (3): 6–7.

Lazarus, Joan, and Amy Jensen. 2011. "Best Practices: Reflecting on Teachers' Embodied Practice." Unpublished paper. American Alliance for Theatre and Education National Conference. Chicago, IL. 30 July

Lemov, Doug. 2010. *Teach Like a Champion: 49 Techniques that Put Students on the Path to College.* San Francisco: Jossey-Bass.

Lerman, Liz, and John Borstel. 2003. *Liz Lerman's Critical Response Process.* Takoma Park, MD: Liz Lerman Dance Exchange, Inc.

Levine, David, Robert Lowe, Bob Peterson, and Rita Tenorio, eds. 1995. *Rethinking Schools: An Agenda for Change.* New York: The New Press.

Lindbloom, Angie. 2010. Telephone interview with the author. Digital Recording. 15 December

Lindahl, Brianna. 2002a. Instructional materials shared with the author. August.

Lindahl, Brianna. 2002b. Telephone interview with the author. Tape Recording. 22 July.

Lindsay, D. Michael. 2003. "Youth on the Edge." *The Christian Century* 120 (20): 26–29.

Lutringer, Jenny. 2002a. Interview with the author. Tape recording. 20 February.

Lutringer, Jenny. 2002b. Interview with the author. 22 July.

Lutringer, Jenny. 2003a. E-mail to the author. 5 April.

Lutringer, Jenny. 2003b. E-mail to the author 22 July.

Lutringer, Jenny. 2003c. The Open Theatre instructional materials shared with the author. 5 April, and 22 July.

MacDonald, George. 1969. *The Light Princess*. New York: Farrar, Straus and Giroux.

Malone, Bobby. 2011a. Researcher field notes. 9 February.

Malone, Bobby. 2011b. Interview with the author during site visit. Digital recording. 9 February.

Malone, Bobby. 2010. Survey response submitted to the author. 2 June.

Mandell, Jan. 2002. Interview with the author. Tape recording. 30 July.

Mardirosian, Gail Humphries, and Yvonne Pelletier Lewis. 2009. "How to Use Theatre to Teach At-Risk Students." Washington, DC: The Chronicle of Higher Education. Accessed 15 September, 2011. http://chronicle.com/article/How-toUse-Theaterer-toTeach/22799.

Markowitz, Elaine. 2003. "A teen improves with 'Crime and Punishment.'" *The Christian Science Monitor*. 18 June.

Marzano, Robert J., Jennifer S. Norford, Diane E. Paynter, Debra J. Pickering, and Barbara B. Gaddy. 2001. *A Handbook for Classroom Instruction that Works*. Alexandria, VA: Association for Supervision and Curriculum Development.

McCammon, Laura, A. 2011a. "Teacher Leaders." Unpublished essay submitted to the author. 4 July.

McCammon, Laura, A. 2011b. "The heart of a teacher." Unpublished essay submitted the author. 4 July.

McCammon, Laura, A. 2008. "Developing teacher leaders: Following the way of the heart." Paper presented at The National Arts and Learning Symposium, Kingston, ON, 29–31 October.

McCammon, Laura, A. 2002a. E-mail to the author. 27 August.

McCammon, Laura, A. 2002b. "Deconstructing Youthland." *Stage of the Art* 14 (3): 7–11.

McCammon, Laura, A. 2002c. Telephone interview with the author. Tape recording. 3 June.

McCammon, Laura A., and Johnny Saldaña, with Angela Hines and Matt Omasta. 2011. "Lifelong impact: Adult perceptions of their high school speech and/or theatre participation." Unpublished monograph.

McLauchlan, Debra. 2001. "Collaborative Creativity in a High School Drama Class." *Youth Theatre Journal* (15): 42–58.

McNally, Gillian. 2011. "Creative Spaces: Arts Integration with a Social Justice Focus." Unpublished essay submitted to the author. 20 July.

McNally, Gillian. 2002a. "Empowering Ophelia: Feminist Theater Principles in Devising and Directing Youth Theater." Master's thesis, The University of Texas at Austin.

McNally, Gillian. 2002b. E-mail to the author. 30 June.

Meek, Marissa. 2010. Questionnaire responses e-mailed to the author. 30 December.

Merton, Thomas. 1966. *Conjectures of a Guilty Bystander*. New York: Doubleday Religion.

Metz, Allison Manville. 2002. "Recognizing Relationships: Avant-Garde Theatre and Marginalized Youth." Master's thesis, The University of Texas at Austin.

Metz, Allison Manville, and Gillian McNally. 2001. "Reassuming Assumptions: Pedagogy for Gender Fair Classrooms Using Creative Drama." *Stage of the Art* 14 (1): 14–17.

Morse, Richard. 2009. *Theatre: Its Healing Role in Education*. New York: Vantage Press.

Muñoz, Luis. 2011. "Strangers in a Strange Land." Unpublished essay submitted to the author. 5 September.

National Center for Education Statistics. 2011. "A Snapshot of Arts Education in Public Elementary and Secondary Schools: 2009–10: First Look." Washington, DC: Institute of Education Sciences, U.S. Department of Education. May.

Neelands, Jonothan, and Tony Goode. 2000. *Structuring Drama Work*. New York: Cambridge University Press.

Nelson, Bethany. 2011. "I Made Myself: Playmaking as a Pedagogy of Change with Urban Youth." Final Draft.

Nelson, Bethany, Robert Colby, and Marisa McIlrath. 2001. "'Having Their Say': The Effects of Using Role with an Urban Middle School Class." *Youth Theatre Journal* (15): 59–69.

Newmann, Fred, and Gary Wehlage. 1995. *Successful School Restructuring: A Report to the Public and Educators by the Center on Organization and Restructuring of Schools*. Alexandria, VA: Association for Supervision and Curriculum Development.

Norris, Renee. 2011a. Researcher field notes. 7 March.

Norris, Renee. 2011b. Interview with the author during site visit. Digital recording. 7 March.

Norris, Renee. 2011c. Questionnaire responses e-mailed to the author. 4 January.

Oddleifson, Eric. 1992. "What Do We Do? Mainstreaming the Theatre Arts in the Public School Curriculum." Address given at Alliance for Wisconsin Theatre Education Fall Conference, LaCrosse, WI, 18 September.

O'Fallon, David. 2002. Telephone interview with the author. Tape recording. 28 May.

Olson, Kirsten. 2009. *Wounded by School: Recapturing the Joy in Learning and Standing Up to Old School Culture*. New York: Teachers College Press.

O'Neill, Cecily. 1995. *Drama Worlds: A Framework for Process Drama*. Portsmouth, NH: Heinemann.

Orenstein, Peggy. 1994. *School Girls: Young Women, Self-Esteem, and the Confidence Gap*. New York: Doubleday.

Overmyer, Eric. 1993. "On the Verge (or The Geography of Yearning)." *Eric Overmyer: Collected Plays*. Newbury, VT: Smith and Kraus.

Palmer, Parker J. 2007. *The Courage to Teach: Exploring the Inner Landscape of a Teacher's Life*. 10th edn. San Francisco: Jossey-Bass.

Partnership for the 21st Century. 2010. *Arts Skills Map*. Washington, DC: Partnership for 21st Century Skills. http://www.p21.org/documents/P21_arts_map_final.pdf.

Paulauskas, Lena. 2010. Survey response submitted to the author. 10 September.

People's Light and Theatre Company (PLT). 2011. Accessed 19 September, 2011. http://peopleslight.org/.

Perlowski, Julia. 2011a. Telephone interview with the author. Digital recording. 5 June.

Perlowski, Julia. 2011b.Questionnaire responses e-mailed to the author. 5 June.

Perlowski, Julia. 2011c. Materials shared with the author. 5 June.

Peterson, Tory. 2002. Interview with the author. Tape recording. 29 July.

Pierce, Abi. 2011. Questionnaire responses e-mailed to the author. 18 April.

Piper, Mary. 1994. *Reviving Ophelia: Saving the Selves of Adolescent Girls*. New York: Ballatine Books.

Pollack, William. 1998. *Real Boys: Rescuing Our Sons from the Myth of Boyhood*. New York: Random House.

Pollack, William. 2000. *Real Boys' Voices*. New York: Random House.

Postman, Neil. 1990. "The Re-enchantment of Learning." *Youth Theatre Journal* 5 (2): 3–6.

President's Committee on the Arts and the Humanities. 2011. *Reinvesting in Arts Education: Winning America's Future Through Creative Schools*. Washington, DC: President's Committee on the Arts and the Humanities.

President's Committee on the Arts and the Humanities. 1997. *Creative America* Washington, DC: President's Committee on the Arts and the Humanities.

Quinn, Betsy. 2011. "Theatre in the Middle: Big Enough for Everyone." Unpublished essay submitted to the author. 14 July.

Quinn, Betsy. 2009. Interview with the author. Digital recording. 15 May.

Remer, Jane. 1990. *Changing Schools Through the Arts: How to Build on the Power of an Idea*. New York: American Council for the Arts.

Richter, Hans Peter. 1987. *Friedrich*. New York: Holt, Reinhart, and Winston.

Rohd, Michael. 1998. *Theatre for Community, Conflict, & Dialogue*. Portsmouth, NH: Heinemann.

Rowling, J. K. 2000. *Harry Potter and the Goblet of Fire*. New York: Scholastic, Inc.

Ruppert, Sandra S. 2009. "Raising Student Achievement In and Through the Arts Can Help Put More Students on the Path to Success in High Schools and Beyond." *Arts at the Core*. New York: The College Board.

Ryan, Tammy. 2000. "The Music Lesson." Unpublished script. Available through Rosenstone/Wender Agency, New York.

Ryoo, Jean J., Jenifer Crawford, Dianna Moreno, and Peter McLaren. 2009. "Critical Spiritual Pedagogy: reclaiming humanity through a pedagogy of integrity, community, and love." *Power and Education* 1 (1): 132–46. Accessed 12 August, 2011. http://dx.doi.org/10.2304/power.2009.1.1.132.

Saldaña, Johnny. 1991. "Drama Theatre and Hispanic Youth: Interviews with Selected Teachers and Artists." *Youth Theatre Journal* 5 (4): 3–8.

Scarborough, Sue. 2003. Telephone interview with the author. Tape recording. 28 September.

Schlomann, Rebecca. 2004. "Theatre in the Peer Mentorship Classroom: A High School Arts Integration Model." Master's thesis, The University of Texas at Austin.

Schroeder-Arce, Roxanne. 2011. "Breaking the Cycle." Unpublished essay submitted to the author. 13 July.

Schroeder-Arce, Roxanne. 2010. *Sangre de un Ángel/Blood of an Angel*. Woodstock, IL: Dramatic Publishing.

Schroeder-Arce, Roxanne. 2009. "Tough choices, new voices: ¡Bocon! staging helps Boston-area school connect with its Latino community." *Teaching Theatre Journal*. Cincinnati, OH: International Thespian Society. Fall. 20 July, 2011. http://schooltheatre.org/publications/teaching-theatre/2009/fall/tough-choices-new-voices.

Schroeder-Arce, Roxanne. 2002a. "Walking on Ice." *Stage of the Art* 14 (3): 22–24.

Schroeder-Arce, Roxanne. 2002b. Interview with the author. Tape recording. 12 February.

Seidel, Kent. 2002. Telephone interview with the author. Tape recording. 7 June.

Seidel, Steve, Shari Tishman, Lois Hetland, Ellen Winner, and Patricia Palmer. 2009. "Deepening the Quality of Arts Education." *The Qualities of Quality: Excellence in Arts Education and How to Achieve It*. Project Zero Research Overview. Cambridge, MA: the President and Fellows of Harvard College.

Serleth, Laurel. 2011. Interview with the author. Digital recording. 25 May.

Serleth, Laurel. 2009. Interview with the author. Digital recording. 24 May.

Serleth, Laurel. 2002. Interview with the author. Tape recording. 2 August.

Shellard, Elizabeth, and Nancy Protheroe. 2000. "Effective teaching: How do we know it when we see it?" *The Informed Educator Series*. Arlington, VA: Educational Research Services.

Shippey, Kim. 1999. "Arguing on The Side of Good." *The Christian Science Sentinel*, 8 November, 18–20.

Silberg, Richard. 2012. E-mail to the author. 7 January.

Silberg, Richard. 2011a. Telephone interview with the author. Digital recording. 17 May.

Silberg, Richard. 2011b. E-mail to the author. 18 May.

Silberg, Richard. 2011c. Teacher journal and lesson outline shared with the author. 21 August.

Smith, Jerry. 2002. Telephone interview with the author. Tape recording. 1 June.

Smith, J. Lea, and J. Daniel Herring. 2001. *Dramatic Literacy: Using Drama and Literature to Teach Middle-Level Content*. Portsmouth, NH: Heinemann.

Spolin, Viola. 1983. *Improvisation for the Theatre*. Evanston, IL: Northwestern University Press.

Staley, Betty. 1988. *Between Form and Freedom: A practical guide for the teenage years*. Lansdown, Stroud, UK: Hawthorn Press.

Stanfield, Holly. 2009. Interview with the author. Digital recording. 12 May.

Stanfield, Holly. 2002. Interview with the author. Tape recording. 3 August.

Stewart, Diane. 2003. E-mail correspondence with the author. 5 September.

Stewart, Diane. 2002. Interview with the author. Tape recording. 22 July.

Stewart, Diane. 1999. Shakespeare Unit Plan by Dr. Dave Dynak, University of Utah. November.

Still, James. 2003. Conversation with the author and students in Issues and Practices in Youth Theatre class, The University of Texas at Austin. 7 March.

Stronge, James H., Pamela D. Tucker, and Jennifer L. Hindman. 2004. *Handbook for Qualities of Effective Teachers*. Alexandria, VA: Association for Supervision and Curriculum Development. http://www.ascd.org/publications/books/104135/chapters/Classroom-Management-and-Organization.aspx.

Sullivan, Dan. 2011. Researcher field notes. 10 February.

Sullivan, Dan. 2010. Telephone interview with the author. Digital recording. 15 December.

Sutterfield, April Gentry. 2011. Unpublished teaching philosophy shared with the author. 18 April.

Sutterfield, Spencer. 2007. Unpublished Master's thesis, The University of Texas at Austin. May.

Tarlington, Carole, and Wendy Michaels. 1995. *Buidling Plays*. Portsmouth, NH: Heinemann.

Tatum, M. Scott. 2011. Questionnaire e-mailed to the author. 6 February.

The College Board National Task Force on the Arts in Education. 2009. *Arts at the Core: Recommendations for Advancing the State of Arts Education in the 21st Century*. New York: The College Board.

The Geena Davis Institute on Gender in Media. 2011. Accessed 30 September, 2011. http://www.thegeenadavisinstitute.org.

The Knowledge Loom. 2011. *Meeting the Literacy Needs of English Language Learners (ELLs)*. The Education Alliance at Brown University. Accessed 10 November, 2011. http://knowledgeloom.org/elemlit/ells_meetnds.jsp.

Thomas, Bridgid. 2011. "Reaching the 'Unreachable.'" *Bringing a little drama into the classroom... Blog*. 6 July. Accessed 15 July, 2011 http://icanteachdramatoo.blogspot.com/.

Thompson, Michael, and Teresa Barker. 2009. *It's a Boy!: Your Son's Development from Birth to Age 18*. New York: Ballatine Books.

Travers, Kathleen A. 2000. "Preservice Teacher Identity Made Visible: A Self Study Approach." Paper presented at the Annual Meeting of the American Educational Research Association, New Orleans, LA, 28 April.

Underwood, Tammy. 2004. Conversation with the author. 10 December.

University of Northern Colorado. 2011. Theatre Educator Intensive. Accessed 10 November, 2011. http://arts.unco.edu/tei/.

Valenta, Misty. 2002. Lesson plan created for Creative Drama I class. The University of Texas at Austin. Summer session.

Vera, Eric. 2011. Questionnaire e-mailed to the author. 8 March.

Vine, Chris. 2000. Interview with the author. Tape recording. 14 March.

Ward, William. 2001a. Interview with the author. Tape recording. 23 February.

Ward, William. 2001b. ... *My Soul to Take*. Unpublished play.

Wax, Seth. 2005. "Spirituality at Work." *Good Works Project Series 41*. Cambridge, MA: Harvard University. http://www.goodworkproject.org/wp-content/uploads/2010/10/41-Spirituality-at-Work.pdf.

Weeks, Jeffrey. 2000. *Making Sexual History*. Cambridge: Polity Press, 98–99.

Wheatley, Margaret. 1994. *Leadership and the New Science: Learning about Organization from an Orderly Universe*. San Francisco: Berrett-Koehler Publishers, Inc.

Wheetley, Kim. 2009. "Arts Integration." *Arts at the Core*. New York: The College Board.

Wheetley, Kim. 2002. Telephone interview with the author. Tape recording. 4 May.

Wheetley, Kim, and the Southeast Center for Education in the Arts (SCEA). 1996. *Discipline-Based Theatre Education: A Conceptual Framework for Teaching and Learning Theatre*. Chattanooga, TN: Southeast Center for Education in the Arts, University of Tennessee at Chattanooga.

Wheetley, Kim, and the Southeast Center for Education in the Arts (SCEA). 2003. "Transforming Education Through The Arts Challenge." http://www.utc.edu/SCEA/Intro_TETAC_Report.pdf.

Wiley, Laura. 2011. Albany Park Theater Project. Accessed 18 August, 2011. http://www.aptpchicago.org/.

White, Helen, and Chris Vine. 2001. "From the Streets To Academia... And Back Again: Youth Theatre, Arts Training and the Building of Community." *Stage of the Art* 12 (2): 5–11.

White, Helen. 2000. Interview with the author. Tape recording. 14 March.

Whitlock, Mandy. 2011a. Researcher field notes. 2–3 February.

Whitlock, Mandy. 2011b. Interview with the author during site visit. Digital recording. 2–3 February.

Whitlock, Mandy. 2011c. Instructional materials shared with the author. 2–3 February.

Whitlock, Mandy. 2011d. Web announcement. Accessed 16 March, 2011. https://nisd.schoolnet.com/outreach/bh/departments/fine_arts/whitlock/.

Whitlock, Mandy. 2010. Questionnaire responses e-mailed to the author. 23 December.

Wood, Sue. 2001. Interview with the author. Tape recording. 24 February.

Woodson, Stephani Etheridge. 2004. "Creating an educational theatre program for the 21st century." *Arts Education Policy Review* 104 (4): 24–29.

WorldBlu. 2011. Accessed 14 March, 2011. http://www.worldblu.com/.

Young, Abe Louise, and youth contributors. 2001. *How to Respect and Protect Your Lesbian, Gay, Bisexual, and Transgender Students*. Providence, RI: Next Generation Press.

Zemelman, Steven, Harvey Daniels, and Arthur Hyde. 2005. *Best Practice: Today's Standards for Teaching and Learning in America's Schools*. Portsmouth, NH: Heinemann.

Zemelman, Steven, Harvey Daniels, and Arthur Hyde. 1998. *Best Practice: New Standards for Teaching and Learning in America's Schools*. Portsmouth, NH: Heinemann.

Zielinski, Sandy. 2002. Interview with the author. Tape recording. 5 August.

Index

CPSIA information can be obtained
at www.ICGtesting.com
Printed in the USA
FSHW011539191019
63107FS